A SUFI SAINT OF THE TWENTIETH CENTURY

Published under the auspices of the
NEAR EASTERN CENTER
University of California, Los Angeles

The Shaikh Al-'Alawī in about 1930

A SUFI SAINT OF THE TWENTIETH CENTURY

Shaikh Aḥmad al-ʿAlawī

HIS SPIRITUAL HERITAGE AND LEGACY

BY

MARTIN LINGS

SECOND EDITION
REVISED AND ENLARGED

UNIVERSITY OF CALIFORNIA PRESS
Berkeley and Los Angeles

UNIVERSITY OF CALIFORNIA PRESS
Berkeley and Los Angeles, California

FIRST EDITION PUBLISHED IN 1961
as *A Moslem Saint of the Twentieth Century*
SECOND EDITION 1971
FIRST CALIFORNIA PAPERBACK EDITION 1973

ISBN: 0–520–02486–9

PRINTED IN THE UNITED STATES OF AMERICA

He whose soul melteth not away like
snow in the hand of religion, in his
hand religion like snow away doth melt.

Sufi saying

To the

SHAIKH ʿĪSA NŪR AD-DĪN AḤMAD AL-ʿALAWĪ

but for whom this book

could never have been written

CONTENTS

ILLUSTRATIONS

PREFACE TO THE FIRST EDITION

The Shaikh Al-'Alawī is almost entirely unknown outside the precincts of Islamic mysticism. It is true that between 1910 and 1930 he published more than ten works, several of which went to a second edition, the places of publication varying between Algiers, Tunis, Cairo, Damascus, and Mostaganem where he lived; but these have eluded the academic world to an extent that is quite abnormal, including even those specialists who, like Brockelmann, make a point of registering every Arabic book or treatise that is known to exist. Moreover there is no copy of any of the Shaikh's writings in the Bibliothèque Nationale and until very recently there was none in the British Museum, which still has not succeeded in obtaining either his major work or his collected poems, two of the main sources of quotation throughout this book.

It may be that his disciples, who by the end of his life were to be numbered by thousands, bought up between them each edition almost as soon as it came out, thus acting, despite themselves, as a barrier between their Master and the general public. Nor would he himself have minded this, for he knew that most of what he wrote was not for everybody. His fame has none the less reached Dermenghem, who refers to him in passing as 'one of the most celebrated mystic Shaikhs of our time' (*Vies des Saints Musulmans*, p. 30); and Massignon also very occasionally mentions him, though here again it is never more than a passing reference.

The translations from Arabic and most else of what this volume contains formed the main part of a thesis which was approved by the University of London for a Ph.D. degree. But the interest of this material goes far beyond academic orientalism, and I have now revised it and rearranged it, with some omissions and many additions, so as to make it into a self-sufficient book which can be read without any special knowledge of the subject, and even without any general knowledge of Islam. It only presupposes one quality in the reader, and that is—for want of a better expression—a sincere interest in 'the things of the Spirit'.

Before I conclude this preface I wish to thank Dr Marcel Carret for giving me full liberty of quoting from his wonderfully vivid account of the Shaikh. I have taken him at his word and give here a translation of almost the whole of that precious document, fearing lest it should be forgotten.

MARTIN LINGS
London, 1959

PREFACE TO THE SECOND EDITION

After the publication of the first edition of this book I was asked to write an article on the Shaikh Al-ʿAlawī for the new *Encyclopaedia of Islam*. This article has now been published; it had to be under *Ibn ʿAlīwah*, because the first two volumes, comprising the letters A–G, were already in print. But this heading was not a mere subterfuge, for the Shaikh opened one of his last treatises with the words: 'The slave of his Lord, Ibn ʿAlīwah, says:', referring to himself by no other name.

As to the differences between the two editions of this book, the second edition may claim precedence over the first, not only by reason of minor changes here and there, but also and above all in virtue of two new chapters. The longer of these, which is based on the Shaikh's aphorisms, reveals an important aspect of his teaching and guidance which in his treatises remains scarcely more than implicit. This chapter has been placed next to his poems to which the dry and elliptical aphorisms form a striking complement.

MARTIN LINGS
London, 1970

PART ONE

THE PATH AND THE ORDER

CHAPTER I

SEEN FROM OUTSIDE

The narrative which follows is by Dr Marcel Carret. It speaks for itself and needs no introduction; and having read it, the reader will no doubt understand why I have chosen to begin with it rather than with anything else, although at its outset the Shaikh is already fifty years old.

'I met the Shaikh Al-'Alawī for the first time in the spring of 1920. It was not a chance meeting, for I had been called in to him in my capacity as doctor. It was then only a few months since I had started a practice at Mostaganem.

'What could have prompted the Shaikh to consult a doctor, seeing that he attached so little importance to the petty misfortunes of the flesh. And why had he chosen me, a newcomer, from among so many others?

'It was from him himself that I eventually learned the answers to these questions: not long after my arrival at Mostaganem, I had set up a clinic in the Arab town of Tigitt[1] exclusively for the use of Moslems, and three times a week I gave consultations there for a minimum fee. Moslems have an instinctive repugnance for State-organized dispensaries, and my clinic which was set up in their very midst and arranged to suit their tastes and customs, was a success. Echoes of this came to the ears of the Shaikh.

[1] Mostaganem is one of the few places in Algeria where the European and Arab towns are quite separate one from the other. Such a separation is the rule in Morocco where Lyautey was able to profit from the mistakes made in Algeria. In the case of Mostaganem, it was the lie of the land which had made it what it now is. The two quarters are separated by a deep ravine, and each retains its own particular characteristics. The Moslem town alone has from twelve to fifteen thousand inhabitants, and is called Tigitt. It was there that the Shaikh Al-'Alawī lived, and it was there, overlooking the sea, that they built the Zāwiyah* which he made so famous, and where he now lies buried. (This is Dr Carret's note. The other notes are mine.)

* This word, literally 'corner' or 'nook', is used of the regular meeting place of a Sufic order. It may denote a single room or, as in the case of the 'Alawī Zāwiyah, a mosque with various outbuildings. To translate *zāwiyah* by 'monastery' would no doubt lead to misunderstanding; none the less the monastic orders are the nearest equivalent in Christianity to the Sufic brotherhoods in Islam, although the Sufis are not celibates.

'His attention was attracted by this initiative on the part of a newly arrived French doctor who, unlike most Europeans, apparently did not look down on Moslems from the heights of a disdainful pride. Without my knowing it, and without the least attempt at investigation on his part, he was benevolently informed by his disciples as to how I looked, what I did, my movements, my way of treating the sick and my sympathetic attitude towards Moslems. As a result, the Shaikh Al-ʿAlawī already knew me quite well when I was still ignorant of his very existence. A rather serious attack of influenza which he had during the Spring of 1920 made him decide to send for me.

'From my first contact with him I had the impression of being in the presence of no ordinary personality. The room I was shown into, like all rooms in Moslem houses, was without furniture. There were simply two chests which, as I found out later, were full of books and manuscripts. But the floor was covered from end to end with carpets and rush mats. In one corner was a rug-covered mattress, and here, with some cushions at his back, sitting straight upright, cross-legged, with his hands on his knees, was the Shaikh, in a motionless hieratic attitude which seemed at the same time perfectly natural.

'The first thing that struck me was his likeness to the usual representations of Christ. His clothes, so nearly if not exactly the same as those which Jesus must have worn, the fine lawn head-cloth which framed his face, his whole attitude—everything conspired to reinforce the likeness. It occurred to me that such must have been the appearance of Christ when he received his disciples at the time when he was staying with Martha and Mary.

'My surprise stopped me for a moment on the threshold. He too fixed his eyes on *my* face, but with a far-away look, and then broke the silence by asking me to come in, with the usual words of welcome. His nephew, Sidi Muḥammad, acted as his interpreter, for although the Shaikh understood French well he had some difficulty in speaking it, and in the presence of a stranger he made as if he did not know it at all.

'I asked for some sandals to cover my shoes, so as not to defile the carpets and the mats, but he said that this was quite unnecessary. A chair was brought for me, but it seemed so ridiculous in such surroundings that I declined it, saying I would rather sit on a cushion. The Shaikh smiled almost imperceptibly, and I felt that by this simple gesture I had already gained his sympathy.

'His voice was gentle, somewhat subdued. He spoke little, in short sentences, and those about him obeyed in silence, waiting on his least word or gesture. One felt that he was surrounded by the deepest reverence.

'I already knew something of Moslem ways, and realizing that I had to do with someone who was not just "anyone", I was careful not to broach too abruptly the subject for which I had been called in. I let the Shaikh question me, through Sidi Muḥammad, about my stay in Mostaganem, what had brought me there, the difficulties I had met with, and how far I was satisfied.

'During this conversation a young disciple had brought in a large brass tray with some mint-flavoured tea and some cakes. The Shaikh took nothing, but invited me to drink when the tea had been served, and himself pronounced the "Bismillah" (in the Name of God) for me as I raised the cup to my lips.

'It was only after all this usual ceremonial was over that the Shaikh decided to talk to me about his health. He said that he had not sent for me to prescribe medicines for him; certainly, he would take medicine, if I thought it absolutely necessary and even if I thought it would help him, but he had no desire to do so. He simply wanted to know if the illness he had contracted a few days previously was a serious one. He relied on me to tell him quite frankly, and without keeping anything back, what I thought of his condition. The rest was of little or no importance.

'I felt more and more interested and intrigued: a sick man who has not the cult of medicines is rare enough as it is, but a sick man who has no particular desire to get better and who simply wants to know where he stands is a still greater rarity.

'I proceeded to make a most thorough medical examination, to which the patient docilely submitted. The more circumspect I showed myself during this examination, the more confidently he put himself into my hands. He was amazingly thin, so much so that one had the impression of an organism in which life was only working at a reduced speed. But he had nothing seriously wrong with him. The only other person present at this examination was Sidi Muḥammad who, with his back towards us and eyes cast down, stood sadly and respectfully in the middle of the room, translating the questions and answers in a low voice, but seeing nothing of what took place.

'When I had finished, the Shaikh resumed his hieratic attitude on the cushions, Sidi Muhammad clapped his hands, and the young man brought in some more tea.

'I then explained to the Shaikh that he had a fairly bad attack of influenza, but that there was nothing seriously wrong with him, that his chief organs were working quite normally and that probably all his troubles would disappear of their own accord after a few days. But although it was unlikely there would be any complications, there was always a certain risk of them in such cases, so that his illness must be closely watched, and I would have to come and see him again by way of precaution. I added that I found his thinness somewhat alarming, and that he ought to eat a little more. I had in fact learnt, in answer to my questions, that his daily diet consisted of no more than one litre of milk, a few dried dates, one or two bananas, and some tea.

'The Shaikh seemed very satisfied with the result of my examination. He thanked me with dignity, apologized for having troubled me, and told me I could come to see him again whenever I thought it necessary. As to the question of food, his point of view was somewhat different from mine: for him eating was an obligation, but he was in the habit of reducing his diet to a minimum.[1]

'I pointed out that if he did not have enough to eat he would grow weaker and weaker and would have less resistance against future illnesses. I understood very well that he attached no importance to this, but on the other hand if he felt at all bound to prolong his life or simply to keep himself alive, it was indispensable for him to bow to the demands of nature, however annoying they might be.

'This argument evidently impressed him, for he remained

[1] Ibn 'Abd al-Bārī', one of the Shaikh's disciples, once asked him why he ate so very little. He replied: 'It is because I find that I have so little inclination to eat. This is not asceticism on my part as some of the *fuqarā'** think, though it is true that I do not like my disciples to be either gluttons or epicures' (*Shahā'id*, p. 116).

* Plural of *faqīr* (whence the English 'fakir'), 'poor', which is used in Islam in the sense of spiritual poverty to denote the members of a Sufic order.

silent for quite a time. Then, with an evasive waive of the hand and a slight smile he said gently: "God will provide."

'He was now sitting just as he had been at my entry, and there was a far-away look in his eyes. I retired discreetly, carrying with me an impression which, after more than 20 years, remains as clearly engraved on my memory as if it was barely yesterday since all this took place.

'I have described this first visit to the Shaikh Al-'Alawī in all its detail because I thought that the best way to bring out his personality was to start by transmitting the impression he made on me at our first meeting. This impression is all the more reliable for my having known nothing about him before I set eyes on him.

'I tried to find out something about this unusual person, but no one seemed able to tell me anything in particular. North African Europeans live as a rule in such ignorance of the inner workings of Islam, that for them a Shaikh or a Marabout is a kind of wizard, without any importance except for what political influence he may have; and as this Shaikh had no such influence, they knew nothing about him.

'Moreover, on second thoughts, I began to wonder whether I had not been rather the victim of my imagination. That Christ-like face, that gentle voice, so full of peace, those courteous manners, might have influenced me into supposing a spirituality which was in fact non-existent. His attitude might have been a calculated "pose", and beneath this promising surface there might be nothing at all.

'None the less he had seemed so simple and natural that my first impression persisted, and it was duly confirmed by what followed.

'The next day I went to see him again, and also for several days after that, until he had quite recovered. Each time I found him just the same, motionless, in the same position, in the same place, with the far-away look in his eyes and the faint smile on his lips, as if he had not moved an inch since the day before, like a statue for which time does not count.

'At each visit he was more cordial and more confiding. Although our conversations were fairly limited and altogether general in topic, apart from medical questions, my impression grew stronger and stronger that the man in front of me was no impostor. We were soon on friendly terms, and when I told him that I considered my visits as doctor no longer necessary, he said that he had been very pleased to make my acquaintance and that he would be glad if I would come to see him now and then, whenever I had time.

'This was the beginning of a friendship which was to last until the death of the Shaikh in 1934. During these fourteen years I was able to see him at least once a week. Sometimes I went for the pleasure of talking to him when I had a few spare moments, sometimes it was because he had had me sent for on account of some member of his family, and often also because his own precarious health needed my attention.

'Little by little my wife and I became intimates of the house. After a certain time they made us feel altogether at home there, and eventually they came to consider us almost as members of the family. But this took place gradually and imperceptibly.

'When I first met the Shaikh the present zāwiyah had not yet been built. A group of fuqarā had bought the ground and made a present of it to the Shaikh, and the foundations had already been laid, but the troubles of 1914 had interrupted the work, which was not resumed until 1920.

'The way in which this zāwiyah was built is both eloquent and typical: there was neither architect—at least, not in the ordinary sense—nor master-builder, and all the workmen were volunteers. The architect was the Shaikh himself—not that he ever drew up a plan or manipulated a set-square. He simply said what he wanted, and his conception was understood by the builders. They were by no means all from that part of the country. Many had come from Morocco, especially from the Riff, and some from Tunis, all without any kind of enlistment. The news had gone round that work on the zāwiyah could be started once more, and that was all that was needed. Among the Shaikh's North African disciples there began an exodus in relays: masons some, carpenters others, stone-cutters, workers on the roads, or even ordinary manual labourers, they knotted a few meagre provisions in a handkerchief and set out for the far-off town where the Master lived to put at his disposal the work of their hands. They received no wages. They were fed, that was all; and they camped out in tents. But every evening, an hour before the prayer, the Shaikh brought them together and gave them spiritual instruction. That was their reward.

'They worked in this way for two months, sometimes three, and then went away once more, glad to have contributed to the work, and satisfied in spirit. Others took their place and after a certain time went off in their turn, to be immediately replaced by new arrivals, eager to start work. More always came, and there was never any lack of hands. This went on for two years, by the end of which the building was finished. This manifestation of simple and outspoken devotion gave me a deep sense of inward happiness. The world evidently still contained some individuals disinterested enough to put themselves, without any recompense, at the service of an ideal. Here, in mid-twentieth century, was the same fervour that had built the cathedrals in the Middle Ages, and no doubt the actual building itself had taken place along somewhat the same lines. I was happy to have been an astonished eye-witness.

'As soon as the zāwiyah was finished, the fuqarā said that they would like to have a big festival to celebrate its inauguration, and the Shaikh gave his consent, feeling that he could scarcely do otherwise.

'By that time I had known him long enough to be able to tell him exactly what I thought, and I expressed my surprise that he should consent to a manifestation which accorded so ill with his habits and which was so contrary to his taste for solitude and self-effacement.

'He had already given up using his nephew as interpreter during our conversations. None the less, Sidi Muḥammad was nearly always present at our meetings. We spoke as a rule in French, and he only intervened when the Shaikh felt himself unable to give exact expression in our language to some particular thought.

'At my expression of surprise he gave an almost imperceptible shrug of the shoulders, and said more or less—I cannot remember his exact words: "You are right. Such things are superfluous. But one must take men as they are. Not all can find complete satisfaction in pure intelligence and contemplation. They have a need now and then to gather together and to feel that their own ideas are shared by a great many others. That is all they are asking for now. Besides, there is no question of the sort of festivity that you must have seen at some of the Moslem places of pilgrimage, with pistol shots, displays of riding, various games and far too much food. For my disciples a festival means spiritual rejoicing. It is simply a reunion for the exchange of ideas and for communal prayer."

'When looked at in this light, the idea of a festival no longer jarred on me. To judge by the number of disciples who came, it was a success. They came from all directions and from all classes of society. According to what the Shaikh had told me, I had expected that this reunion would be no more than a sort of congress where the academically minded hope to shine in discussing knotty questions of doctrine and displaying their talent for pin-point hair-splitting quibbles.

'As far as I could gather from certain passages of inaugural speeches which Sidi Muhammad roughly translated for me, it was in fact something of the sort, especially among the younger disciples. It was not there, however, that the interest lay, but with the older disciples who did not talk and who were rapt in deep meditation. I was specially struck by the most humble of them all, the Riff mountaineers, who had been travelling for a whole month, going on foot from hamlet to hamlet, with their spirits kept up by the inward fire that burned in their simple souls.

'They had set out full of enthusiasm, like the pioneers of the gold-rush, but it was no temporal riches that they had come in search of. Their quest was purely spiritual, and they knew that they would not be deceived. I watched them, motionless, silent, drinking in the atmosphere as if plunged in a kind of beatitude through the very fact of being there, penetrated by the holiness of the place, with their chief aspiration realized. They were happy, in complete accord with themselves, in the Presence of God. . . .

'At other times, after remaining motionless and silent for hours at a time, the disciples would softly start up a lingering chant. Then they would divide up into circular groups, and holding hands would begin to sway forwards and then backwards, slowly and rhythmically, pronouncing clearly, in time to each movement, the Name "Allah". This began to a fairly slow rhythm which was given by a sort of choir leader at the centre of each circle, whose voice could be heard above the others. Meantime some of them went on with the chant, which grew progressively louder and more vigorous. Little by little the speed of the rhythm increased. The slow swaying to and fro gave place to an up-and-down movement with knees bent and then suddenly straightened. Soon, in each circle of rhythmic movement (the feet remained stationary), they began to gasp[1] and the voices became hoarse. But the time went on growing quicker and quicker; the up-and-down movements became more and more violent, jerky and almost convulsive. The Name of God was now no more than a breath, and so it went on, always quicker and quicker, until the breathing itself was no longer heard. Some of them would fall to the ground in a state of exhaustion.

'This exercise, which is analogous to those of the whirling dervishes, is evidently intended to produce a particular state of soul. But I wondered what could be the spiritual link between such rough and crude practices as these and the nobility and refinement of the Shaikh.

'And how had the Shaikh's fame spread so far? There was never any organized propaganda. The disciples made not the slightest attempt to proselytize. In any town or village that happened to contain some of their number they had, and they still have today, their own little secluded zāwiyahs, each under the guidance of a muqaddam, that is, one who is invested with the confidence and authority of the Shaikh. These little brotherhoods refrain on principle from all outward action, as if they were jealously bent on letting no one share their secrets. None the less, the influence spreads, and would-be novices are always coming forward to ask for initiation. They come from all walks of life.

'One day I voiced my surprise to the Shaikh. He said:

' "All those come here who feel haunted by the thought of God."

'And he added these words, worthy of the Gospels:

"They come to seek inward Peace."

'That day I did not dare to question him any further for fear

[1] This 'gasping' is a means of integrating the body into the rhythm.

of seeming too inquisitive. But I realized that there was a connection between what he had said and the incantations which I had sometimes heard and which had intrigued me. Fairly often, in fact, while I was talking quietly with the Shaikh, the Name "Allāh" had come to us from some remote corner of the zāwiyah, uttered on one long drawn out, vibrant note:

' "A . . . l . . . lā . . . h!"

'It was like a cry of despair, a distraught supplication, and it came from some solitary cell-bound disciple, bent on meditation. The cry was usually repeated several times, and then all was silence once more.

' "Out of the depths have I cried unto Thee, O Lord"[1]

' "From the end of the earth will I cry unto Thee, when my heart is overwhelmed: lead me to the rock that is higher than I."[2]

'These verses from the Psalms came to my mind. The supplication was really just the same, the supreme cry to God of a soul in distress.

'I was not wrong, for later, when I asked the Shaikh what was the meaning of the cry which we had just heard, he answered:

' "It is a disciple asking God to help him in his meditation."

' "May I ask what is the purpose of his meditation?"

' "To achieve self-realization in God."

' "Do all the disciples succeed in doing this?"

' "No, it is seldom that anyone does. It is only possible for a very few."

' "Then what happens to those who do not? Are they not desperate?"

' "No: they always rise high enough to have at least inward Peace."

'Inward Peace. That was the point he came back to most often, and there lay, no doubt, the reason for his great influence. For what man does not aspire, in some way or other, to inward Peace? . . .

'When he was relatively well, the Shaikh always received me, except in winter, on a sort of verandah at the bottom of a little garden surrounded by high walls, reminiscent of certain paint-

[1] Psalm CXXX, 1.

[2] Psalm LXI, 2.

ings in Persian manuscripts. It was in these peaceful surroundings, far from the noise of the world, amid the rustling of leaves and the song of birds that we exchanged remarks sometimes interspersed with long silences.

'As happens with those who understand each other and have reached a certain degree of intimacy, we did not mind being silent; and silence was sometimes imposed on us by a remark that called for reflection. Moreover the Shaikh never wasted words, and we felt no need to talk except when we really had something to say.

'He had been surprised at first to find that I knew a little about the Moslem religion, at least as regards its essence and principles, that I knew something about the life of the Prophet, in its outlines at any rate, and the history of the first Caliphs, and that I was not altogether uninformed about the Kaaba and the Well of Zamzam and the flight of Ishmael in the desert with his mother Hagar. All this was very little, but the average European is generally so ignorant about these things that the Shaikh could not hide his surprise.

'For my part, I was surprised by his broad-mindedness and tolerance. I had always heard that every Moslem is a fanatic and could never have anything but the greatest contempt for non-Moslem foreigners.

'The Shaikh said that God had inspired three[1] Prophets, first Moses, then Jesus, then Muḥammad. He concluded that Islam was the best in that it was based on the most recent message of God, but said that Judaism and Christianity were none the less divinely revealed religions.

'His conception of Islam was equally broad. He only insisted on the essential. He used to say:

' "To be an orthodox Moslem it is enough to observe five points: to believe in God and to recognize Muḥammad as His last Prophet, to pray the five daily prayers, to give the prescribed alms to the poor, to keep the fast, and to make the pilgrimage to Mecca."

[1] He did not mean three in a limitative sense, since the Qoran mentions twenty-eight. Moreover, in one of his treatises for novices (*Al-Qaul al-Maqbūl*, p. 7), he draws attention to the words of the Qoran (addressed to Muḥammad): *Verily We have sent Messengers before thee: about some of them have We told thee, and about some have We not told thee* (Qoran, XL, 78), and he warns his disciples against limiting either the number of God's Messengers and Prophets, or the number of His Revealed Scriptures.

'What I appreciated especially in him was his complete lack of proselytism. He expressed his views when I questioned him, but seemed to care very little whether they did me any good. Not only did he never make the least attempt to convert me, but for a long time he seemed totally indifferent to what my religious beliefs might be. That was, moreover, altogether characteristic of him. He used to say:

' "Those who have need of me come to me. Why seek to attract the others? They care little for the only things that matter, and they go their own way."

'Our conversations were thus not unlike what might take place between two neighbours on good terms with each other who exchange remarks from time to time over the hedge that separates their gardens.

'But one day my own ideas happened to come up for discussion and this led him to sound me a little. Perhaps he had already thought of doing so, without knowing how to broach this delicate question, and was simply waiting for the opportunity.

'It came in connexion with those Negro Moslems who have brought some Sudanese practices into Islam. They go through the streets at certain times leading a bull garlanded with flowers and ribbons, to the sound of drums and tambourines accompanied by dances, shouts, songs and the clapping of metal castanets. It was now one of these occasions, and beneath the verandah, at the end of the peaceful garden, the distant and muffled sounds of one of these processions came to our ears. I do not know why, but I gave vent to a comparison between these manifestations and certain Catholic processions, which, I added, seemed to me pure idolatry, just as the Eucharist was nothing more or less than sorcery, unless one considered it symbolically.

' "It is none the less your religion," he said.

' "In a sense", I replied. "I was baptized when I was still at my mother's breast. Apart from that there is nothing that binds me to it."

' "What is your religion then?"

' "I have none."

There was a silence. Then the Shaikh said:

' "That is strange."

' "Why strange?"

' "Because usually those who, like yourself, have no religion are hostile to religions. And you do not seem to be so."

'What you say is true, but the people you refer to have kept the intolerant religious mentality. They have remained restive. They have not found, in the loss of their beliefs, the inward Peace that you speak of. On the contrary.'

' "And you? Have you found it?"

' "Yes. Because I have followed things to their furthest conclusions and I look at everything according to its true value and in its proper place."

'He thought for some time, and then he said:

' "That also is strange."

' "What?"

' "That you should have arrived at this conception by means other than those of the doctrine."

' "What doctrine?"

'He made a vague gesture and sank into a state of meditation. I understood that he was unwilling to say any more about it, and I withdrew.

'From this day I had the impression that I interested him more. Until then our relationship, always very cordial, with every appearance of intimacy, had not gone beyond the limits of a casual friendship. He had found me a pleasant enough acquaintance and he liked me, but none the less I was a foreigner and somewhat remote. Several years had passed during which I had been for him no more than a fleeting distraction, probably of very little importance in his eyes, the passer-by that one meets on life's journey, a momentary companion that one accepts for part of the road because he is polite and not tedious, and then forgets.

'After this, whenever we were alone together, the conversation took an abstract turn . . . I regret with all my heart that I did not write down then and there those wonderful conversations which implied far more even than was actually said, and which I now realize would have made a document that was precious not only for me but also for others. But at that time I did not attach the importance to them that they have acquired in my memory with the lapse of the years.

'I can only therefore give a general glimpse of these meetings, simply noting down one or two striking points which have remained fixed in my mind. Sometimes the dialogue was limited to a few remarks interspersed between long silences; sometimes it consisted of an exposition of my point of view, asked for by him. For now it was he who was the questioner. We never argued, that is we never had anything in the nature of those controversies in which each party tries to convince the other that he is right. It was just an exchange of ideas, no more.

'That was how I came to explain to him my attitude towards religion. I said that since everyone is troubled by the enigma of his existence and his future, we each seek some explanation that will satisfy us and set our minds at rest. The religions provide an answer which satisfies most people. What right have I to trouble those who have found spiritual tranquility in religion? Besides, whatever means are used, whatever path is chosen, anyone who is bent on gaining peace of mind is always obliged to take some belief as his starting point. Even the path of science, which is the one I have followed, is based on a certain number of assumptions, that is, affirmations which are considered as self-evident truths but which none the less cannot be proved. Along whatever line one looks, there is always some element of belief, whether it be great or small. The only truth is what one believes to be true. Everyone follows the course which suits him best. If he finds what he is looking for, then for him this course is the right one. They are all equal.

'Here he stopped me, saying:

' "No, they are not all equal."

'I said nothing, waiting for an explanation, which came.

' "They are all equal if you only consider the question of being set at rest. But there are different degrees. Some people are set at rest by very little; others find their satisfaction in religion; some require more; it is not only peace of mind that they must have, but the Great Peace, which brings with it the plenitude of the Spirit."

' "What about religion?"

' "For these last religion is only a starting point."

' "Then is there anything above religion?"

' "Above the religion there is the doctrine."

'I had already heard him use this word: the doctrine. But

when I had asked what he meant by it he had been unwilling to answer. Timidly I tried again:

' "What doctrine?"

'This time he answered:

' "The means of attaining to God Himself."

' "And what are these means?"

'He gave me a smile tinged with pity.

' "Why should I tell you, since you are not disposed to make use of them. If you came to me as my disciple I could give you an answer. But what would be the good of satisfying an idle curiosity?"

'On another occasion it so happened that we were talking about prayer, which I considered as a piece of inconsequence on the part of those who believe in the Sovereign Wisdom of the Divinity.

' "What is the point of prayer?" I had asked.

' "I see what you have in mind", he said. "In principle you are right. Prayer is superfluous when one is in direct communication with God. For then one has direct knowledge. But it helps those who aspire to this communication and have not yet reached it. None the less, even in this case, prayer is not indispensable. There are other means of reaching God."

' "What means?"

' "The study of the doctrine and meditation or intellectual contemplation are among the best and most effective means. But they are not within the scope of everyone."

'What surprised him the most was that I should be able to go on living quite serenely in the conviction that I was destined to total annihilation, for he saw beyond doubt that I was deeply sincere. Little by little, when, at various intervals, he came back to this question, I brought him to understand that my serenity was due to humility rather than to pride. Man's anxieties spring from his wanting at all costs to survive his own death. Calm is obtained when one has altogether rid oneself of this desire for immortality. The world existed before me and would continue to exist without me . . . It was no more than an entertainment to which I had been invited without knowing why or how, and the meaning of which I could not grasp, if indeed it had one. But this entertainment was none the less not without its interest. That is why I turned my eyes towards nature rather than towards abstract ideas. When I had to leave the entertainment I would do so regretfully, because I found it interesting. But in time it would no doubt end by boring me. Besides, in any case, I had no choice. And what did it matter? When one crushes an ant the world goes on just the same.

' "What you say is true of the body no doubt", he said. "But what of the Spirit?"

' "True, there is also the spirit. The consciousness we have of ourselves. But we did not have it at birth. It was developed slowly together with our bodily sensations. We only acquired it progressively, little by little, as our knowledge increased. It developed alongside of the body, grew up with it, came to full strength with it, like a sum total of acquired ideas, and I fail to convince myself that it could survive this body to which it really owes its existence."

'There was a long silence. Then, coming out of his meditation, the Shaikh said:

' "Do you want to know what is lacking in you?"

' "Yes, what?"

' "To be one of us and to see the Truth, you lack the desire to raise your Spirit above yourself.[1] And that is irremediable."

'One day he asked me point-blank:

' "Do you believe in God?"

'I replied:

' "Yes, if you mean by that an indefinable principle on which all depends and which no doubt gives a meaning to the Universe."

'He seemed satisfied by my reply. I added:

' "But I consider this principle as being beyond our reach and our understanding. What surprises me, however, is to see that so many people who claim to be religious and even believe that they are so, and who are convinced of their immortality in God, should be able to go on attaching importance to their earthly existence. They are neither logical, nor honest with themselves. . . . It seems to me that if I were certain of life after

[1] In one of his poems the Shaikh wrote:

'Thou seest us amongst men, but we are not as thou seest,
For our Spirits shine clear above the highest heights'

(*Dīwān*, p. 5. All references to the *Dīwān* are to the second edition.)

death, the scene of this earthly life would become devoid of all interest for me and I should be utterly indifferent to it. I would live entirely in expectation of the true life yonder, and like your fuqarā I would devote myself altogether to meditation."

'He looked at me for a while as if he were reading my thoughts. Then his eyes met mine with a piercing glance which went far beyond them, and he said slowly:

' "It is a pity that you will not let your Spirit rise above yourself. But whatever you may say and whatever you may imagine, you are nearer to God than you think."

' "You are nearer to God than you think."

'When he spoke these words, the Shaikh Al-'Alawī had not much longer to live. The pilgrimage to Mecca which he had been bent on making before his death and to which he had added a journey to Syria and Palestine had exhausted him. He was extremely weak, but his mind was still alert.

'Meantime Sidi Muhammad[1], his nephew, who had fulfilled the function of muqaddam, had died, and his place had been taken by another of the Shaikh's nephews of whom he was particularly fond, Sidi Addah Bin-Tūnis.[2]

'Sidi Addah did not hide his anxiety from me. Through him I learnt that the Shaikh was becoming more and more given to deep meditation, from which he seemed to emerge only against his will. He ate practically nothing, and although I both scolded and entreated him, he simply gave me the shadow of a smile and said gently:

' "What is the use? The hour is drawing near."

'There was nothing I could answer.

[1] One of the Shaikh's sisters had two children, Sidi Muhammad and a daughter named Khairah, both of whom he adopted. I wrote to one of his oldest living disciples, Sidi Muhammad al-Hāshimī who emigrated from Tlemcen to Syria many years before the Shaikh's death, and is now head of the 'Alawī Zāwiyah in Damascus, and I asked him if the Shaikh had had any children of his own. He answered: 'I know he had none by his first or second wife. Then when he came to visit us in Damascus on his way from the Pilgrimage I said to him: "Have you had any children in all this time?" and he answered "No". Then he said: "Yes, *you* are my children", at which all the brethren who were present rejoiced.' (The Shaikh Al-Hāshimī died in 1961.)

[2] Sidi Adda (or rather 'Udda) Bin-Tūnis, the Shaikh's nephew by marriage (he married Sidi Muhammad's sister), died in 1952.

'The fuqarā began to look at me in a special way. I realized that they were trying to make out what I thought of the Shaikh's health. Usually I saw little of them. They knew who I was, and the friendship that the Shaikh showed me was enough to make them well disposed towards me. But none the less, they generally remained somewhat aloof. The feeling that their Master was in danger brought them nearer to me. I reassured them with a smile. I was in fact convinced that the Shaikh would go on living to the very last flicker of his strength—not that he would fight to live, but that he had accustomed his body to do with so little that his organism went on working at a reduced speed. I knew that he would continue like this, with a minimum of strength which would have long since proved insufficient for anyone else. He would use up the very last drop of oil in the lamp of life, which he had turned so low that it was now no more than a night-light. And he knew this as well as I did.

The Shaikh scarcely ever introduced me to any of the fuqarā except those who were of Western origin. Westerners did in fact come to him now and then. But my relationship with them was always rather limited. Not being an initiate, I did not speak their language, and I felt it would have been inquisitive to question them as to what had brought them to this path.

'Some of them were real personalities—for example, a well-known artist,[1] whose acquaintance I would never have expected to make in this way. On joining the tradition this artist had taken to wearing Moslem dress, which suited him so well that he might himself have passed for a Shaikh. He spent eight days in the zāwiyah, and was accompanied by a member of the Tribunal of Tunis and by a lady, both initiates, as he was, and extremely likeable.

'There was also an American, more or less without means, who had arrived no one knew how, but who fell ill after a few days, and had to be sent to hospital, and eventually repatriated. . . .

'Despite his increasing weakness, the Shaikh continued to talk to his disciples, but was obliged to make his sessions with them shorter. His heart was growing feeble, and its beat became irregular, and I had much trouble to make him take the stimulants which were necessary to restore its defective rhythm. Fortunately, infinitesimal doses were enough to act on an

[1] 'Abd al-Karīm Jossot.

organism that had never been contaminated by the action of medicines.

'In 1932 we were badly shaken by his having a partial heart attack. I was summoned in all haste, and when I arrived his pulse was imperceptible and he seemed to have lost all consciousness. An intra-veinous injection brought him round. He opened his eyes, and looked at me reproachfully.

' "Why did you do that?' he said. "You should have let me go. There is no point in keeping me back. What is the good?"

' "If I am at your side", I answered, "it is because God willed it so. And if He willed it so, it was in order that I might do my duty by you as your doctor."

' "Very well", he said. '*In shā'Allāh*"[1]

'I stayed with him for some time so as to watch his pulse, fearing that he might have a relapse, and I only left him when he seemed to me to be out of immediate danger.

'After this warning there were others. None the less the Shaikh lived on, with ups and downs, for nearly another two years. When he was relatively well he resumed his normal life as if nothing had happened. He seemed however to be waiting, eagerly but patiently, for the end. His intense inward life only showed itself in his expression. His body seemed no more than a worn-out prop which at any moment was going to crumble to powder.

'One morning he sent for me. His condition, to all appearances, was no more serious than it had been the day before or the day before that, but he said:

' "It will be today. Promise me to do nothing, and to let things take their course."

'I said that he seemed to be no worse, but he insisted.

' "I know it will be today. And I must be allowed to return to God."

'I left him, impressed by what he had said, but none the less a little sceptical. I had seen him so often with his life hanging by a thread without the thread having broken, and so, I thought, it would be again that day.

'But when I came back in the afternoon, the picture had changed. He was scarcely breathing, and I could not count his pulse. He opened his eyes when he felt my fingers on his wrist, and recognized me. His lips murmured:

[1] If God wishes.

' "I am going at last to take my rest in the Presence of God."

'He clasped my hand feebly and closed his eyes. It was a last farewell. My place was no longer there. He belonged from then on to his fuqarā, who were waiting in the background. I withdrew, telling Sidi Addah that I had seen the Shaikh for the last time.

'I learnt that evening that two hours after I had left he had gently passed away, almost imperceptibly, reverently surrounded by all those disciples who lived at the zāwiyah or were staying there.

'The last drop of oil had been used up.

'I have tried to give here an idea of what the Shaikh Al-ʿAlawī was like. I am well aware that this account leaves much to be desired, but I was bent on relating nothing except what I was absolutely sure of. Some of the remarks I have quoted are exactly, word for word, those that were used by the Shaikh himself. As regards others, I cannot be sure that he used exactly the same expressions that I have ascribed to him, but I can guarantee the general sense as being his.

'It would have been easy to embroider such a theme, but I preferred to keep to the dry sobriety of the memories of which I was certain, and I feel that the Shaikh stands out all the clearer and truer to life. My portrayal of him has moreover the special characteristic of having been made impartially and objectively, without needless panegyrics and without the halo that a disciple would no doubt have been tempted to put in. It is enough in itself, and perhaps gains for having been sketched by one of "the profane".

'I have avoided any personal appreciation of the Shaikh's doctrine. My opinion about such questions would have been in any case irrelevant, because my intention was simply to give an impression of the Shaikh as I had known him, and not to discuss his ideas. I know that the doctrine in question was an esoteric one, and since I am not an initiate my ideas are inevitably very vague about it.

'Perhaps the initiates will smile when they read some of my impressions, but they will thank me for my sincerity and for having been as simple and straightforward as I could. They will notice also that never in any place have I used the word "faith" . . . I remember once having said to him that what prevented me from trying to "raise my spirit above myself" was no doubt lack of faith.

'He answered:

' "Faith is necessary for religions, but it ceases to be so for those who go further and who achieve self-realization in God. Then one no longer believes because one sees. There is no longer any need to believe, when one *sees* the Truth." '

In addition to Dr Carret's 'Souvenirs', we are fortunate in having the Shaikh's own account of the earlier part of his life. But before going on to this, and to avoid interrupting it unduly once we start, there are one or two points which need explaining.

CHAPTER II

THE ORIGINS OF SUFISM

As a translation of *ṣūfī* the word 'mystic' is only adequate if used in its original sense to denote one who has access, or seeks access, to 'the Mysteries of the Kingdom of Heaven', for Sufism is the Islamic way of transcending one's own soul, that is, of 'letting one's Spirit rise above oneself,' and it is where the human self ends that the Heavenly Mysteries begin.

Although the name Sufism only came to be used after two or three generations of Islam, its reality[1] is rooted in the first generation; and one of its roots may be said to reach back across the threshold of Islam to Muḥammad's pre-Islamic practice of spiritual retreat which was a practice of the scattered hermits of Arabia known as the Ḥunafā', and in virtue of which he was already, before his mission, a representative of all that was left of the mysticism of his ancestors Abraham and Ishmael. It was in one of his retreats in a cave on Mount Hira at the outskirts of Mecca, when he was about forty years old,[2] that he received the first Qoranic Revelation.

In order to understand what is meant by the doctrine that the Qoran is the Eternal, Uncreated Word of God, it is necessary to make a distinction—one that is familiar to Hindus and Jews as well as to Moslems though it is not immediately so to Christians—between inspiration and revelation. If a work of the highest inspiration may be likened to a spark that is struck

[1] Hujwīrī, an eleventh century Sufi of Lahore, quotes the tenth century Fushanjī as having said: 'Today Sufism is a name without a reality, but formerly it was a reality without a name', and Hujwīrī himself adds: 'In the time of the Companions (of the Prophet) and their successors this name did not exist, but the reality thereof was in everyone; now the name existeth, but not the reality'. (Kashf al-Maḥjūb, ch. iii; in Nicholson's translation, p. 44.)

Hujwīrī is bent here on emphasizing the degeneracy of his times, and is not weighing his words. To have his exact opinion we should no doubt substitute some much less absolute term for the word 'everyone'. He would also certainly have admitted that the reality of Sufism still existed in his day, although confined to a small minority, for whom in fact he is writing his book. With these reservations his statement may be said to express the unanimous opinion of the mystics of Islam.

[2] *c.* 610. All dates are A.D. unless otherwise stated.

from a flint, the flint being man and the striker God, then a Revelation is as a spark struck by God from Himself.[1]

It is an essential point of Islamic orthodoxy that the Qoran is revealed. In reference to its own 'naked' potentialities, which are providentially veiled from man, the Holy Book says of itself, speaking with the voice of God: *If We caused this Qoran to descend upon a mountain, thou wouldst see the mountain lying prostrate with humility, rent asunder through fear of God*[2]; and since Revelation confronts time with Eternity, thus eluding the normal conditions of time, it says that the *Lailat al-Qadr*, the night on which the Archangel Gabriel placed the Qoran in the heart of the Prophet, *is better than a thousand months*.[3]

The first word to be revealed was the imperative *iqra'*, 'recite'; and *qur'ān* itself means 'recitation'. The revealing of a text to be recited necessarily amounts, at the summit of the community which receives it, to the inauguration of a form of mysticism, since to recite such a text is to undergo a Divine 'interference', a mysterious penetration of the soul by the Spirit, of this world by the next, and the practice of taking advantage of this possibility becomes, after a certain point, no less than following a mystic path. The Sufis have always sought to take full advantage of the Presence of the Infinite in the finite by 'drowning' themselves in the verses (*āyāt*, literally 'miraculous signs') of the Revelation. In one of his poems the Shaikh Al-'Alawī says of the Qoran:

'It hath taken up its dwelling in our hearts and on our tongues and is mingled with our blood and our flesh and our bones and all that is in us.'[4]

Elsewhere[5] he tells of the exceptional case of a saintly woman who made a vow never to waste another breath with the utterance of anything except the Qoran[6], a vow which she

[1] In Christianity the 'Revelation' is, not the Gospels, but Christ.

[2] LIX, 21.

[3] XCVII, 3. The other 'great night' of the Islamic year, in a sense complementary to the *Lailat al-Qadr*, is the *Lailat al-Mi'rāj*, the Night of the Ascension, on which, about eleven years before his death, the Prophet was taken by the Archangel from Mecca to Jerusalem and thence up through the seven Heavens to the Divine Presence.

[4] *Dīwān*, p. 64.

[5] *Al-Mawādd al-Ghaithiyyah*, pp. 44-6.

[6] There is a certain analogy between this and the abstinence of some Christian Saints, for given periods, from any food and drink other than the Sacred Host.

kept until her death, for a period of over forty years.

In certain passages where the impact of the Qoranic 'substance' is given a particular direction by the impact of the meaning there lies, virtually, the entire path of the mystics. Such verses as *God leadeth to His Light whom He will*[1] and *Lead us along the straight path*[2] and *He it is Who hath sent down the Spirit of Peace into the hearts of the faithful that they may increase in faith upon faith*[3] are only limited in so far as the intelligence of one who recites them is limited.[4] They can be, if interpreted in their highest sense, as openings through which the immortal in man may pour itself out in escape from the mortal limitations of the soul. But anything that can be said of this two-fold transcendence of words which are metaphysical in content as well as in 'fabric' applies pre-eminently to the Divine Names and above all to the Supreme Name *Allāh* ('God' in the absolute sense of the word). One of the first injunctions revealed to the Prophet was: *Invoke in remembrance the Name of thy Lord, and devote thyself to Him with an utter devotion.*[5] This verse inaugurated for the new religion a practice which has been ever since the Moslem mystic's chief means of approach to God.

The Qoran is the Book of *Allāh* in every sense of the word 'of'. It comes from Him, it is 'of one substance' with Him, and He is its basic theme; and if what might seem to be digressions

[1] XXIV, 35.

[2] I, 6.

[3] XLVIII, 4.

[4] The Qoran was revealed as a means of Grace for the whole Islamic community, not only for an elect, nor yet only for the generality of Moslems, and it abounds in verses which, like those just quoted, may be applied to every level of spirituality, treasuries from which everyone is free to carry off as much as he has strength to bear. Massignon was probably not thinking of verses like these, and almost certainly not of the revelationary and therefore mystical 'fabric' of the Qoran as a whole, when he wrote: 'Contrary to the Pharasaical opinion of many *fuqahā'* (canonists), an opinion which has been accepted for the last sixty years by many Arabists, I have had to admit, with Margoliouth, that the Qoran contains real seeds of mysticism, seeds capable of an autonomous development without being impregnated from any foreign source' (*La Passion d' Al-Hallāj*, p. 480.) But even from the point of view in question, that is, simply considering the Qoran as an exposition of doctrine and practice, Massignon's verdict, though relatively refreshing, is an understatement as we shall see.

[5] LXXIII, 8. When the Shaikh Al-'Alawī spoke to Dr Carret about 'meditation', he almost certainly had in mind the word *dhikr* (remembrance, mention, invocation). The first three letters of this word are pronounced like the first three of the English 'this'. For pronunciation in general, see p. 217, note.

from this theme do not soon lead up to it, they are abruptly snatched up to it again, as if the Qoran was bent on demonstrating its own continuously repeated words: *Do not all things return to Allāh*? The Name *Allāh* occurs so often that it may be considered as the warp on which the Qoranic text is woven.

The verse: *Verily ye have a fair pattern in the Messenger of God*[1] is full of meaning at every level of Islam, but its highest significance must be understood in the light of an earlier Revelation, another of the very first injunctions received by the Prophet at Mecca: *Prostrate thyself and draw nigh* (to God)[2]. The ritual act of prostration, which is an extremity of self-effacement, is implicit in one of Muḥammad's secondary names, *'Abd Allāh*, the Slave of God. Without the complete self-effacement of slavehood it is impossible to *draw nigh* or, in other words, without first being empty of other than God it is impossible to be filled with the ever-present Reality of His Nearness, of which the Qoran says: *We* (*God*) *are nearer to him* (*man*) *than his jugular vein*[3]. The realization of this Nearness is implicit in another of the Prophet's names, *Ḥabīb Allāh*, the Beloved of God, for the following Tradition,[4] though it is of universal import, refers to him first and foremost:

'My slave ceaseth not to draw nigh unto Me with devotions of his free will[5] until I love him; and when I love him, I am the Hearing wherewith he heareth, and the Sight wherewith he seeth, and the Hand wherewith he smiteth, and the Foot whereon he walketh.'[6]

The full range of Sufism, as it has shown itself to be throughout the centuries, lies summed up in this Tradition.

In speaking to his closest followers Christ said: 'It is given

[1] XXXIII, 21

[2] XCVI, 19

[3] L, 16.

[4] I have used this word throughout with a capital to denote a saying of the Prophet. Such sayings are of two kinds, 'Holy Traditions' where, as in the present instance, God speaks in the first person on the tongue of the Prophet, and 'Noble Traditions' which were uttered by the Prophet in his own capacity, as for example: 'The slave is nearest his Lord when he prostrateth himself' (Ibn Ḥanbal, II, 421).

[5] Devotions in addition to the obligatory legal minimum.

[6] Bukhārī, *Riqāq*, 37

unto you to know the mysteries of the Kingdom of Heaven, but to them it is not given.'[1] In speaking to the whole community of Moslems the Qoran generalizes the same idea in the words: *We exalt in degree whom We will; and above each one that hath knowledge is one that knoweth more.*[2] But none the less, subtly and unobtrusively, the Qoran is elsewhere more explicit. Three times in the earliest Revelations the faithful are divided into two groups. In one chapter the lower group is called *the Companions of the Right* and these are no doubt the generality of believers, since they are said to be *many among the earlier generations and many among the later generations,*[3] and they are contrasted with *the Companions of the Left*, who are the damned. Above *the Companions of the Right* are *the Foremost*, and these are said to be *many among the earlier generations and few among the later generations.*[4] The superlative implicit in their title is confirmed by their definition as *Near* (literally 'brought near' by God to Himself), this being the word that is used to distinguish the Archangels from the other Angels. In another chapter *the Near* are represented as drinking at a fountain named *Tasnīm*. Below them are *the Righteous*[5] who have not direct access to this fountain but who are given to drink a draught that has been flavoured at it with the perfume of musk. The same imagery is used in a third chapter where *the Righteous* are represented as drinking a draught which has been flavoured

[1] St Matthew, XIII, 11.

[2] XII, 76.

[3] LVI, 27-40

[4] LVI, 13-4. In a commentary usually attributed to 'Abd ar-Razzāq al-Kāshānī (died c. 1330) but sometimes to Muḥyi'd-Dīn Ibn 'Arabī (d. 1240)—whence the title of the only two printed editions, *Tafsīr ash-Shaikh al-Akbar* (Bulaq, 1867; Cawnpore, 1883)—these words are glossed: 'There were many among the earliest members of this community, that is, those who saw the Prophet and were born in time to benefit from the spiritual vigour of the Revelation during his life, and those of the second generation who were born shortly after his death and who saw his Companions, whereas the later generations are those between whom and the Revelation *much time had elapsed, so that their hearts were hardened.*' (These last words are quoted by the commentator from the Qoran, LVII, 16.).

The Prophet himself is said to have applied the above commented verse not only to the history of Islam, as here, but also, according to Ṭabarī, to the history of mankind as a whole, in the sense that there were many of the *Foremost* among the earlier generations of man but that there would be few among the later generations.

[5] LXXXIII, 22-8.

with camphor from a fountain named *Kāfūr*, to which only *the Slaves of God*[1] have direct access. According to the commentary, 'slavehood' and 'nearness' are two aspects of the one highest spiritual degree, representing respectively extinction in God and Eternal Life in God. The Saints drink at *Kāfūr* inasmuch as they are *Slaves* and at *Tasnīm* inasmuch as they are *Near*.

It must be remembered that what is significant in itself, however unobtrusively it may be set in its context, will lose nothing of its significance for those who are spiritually sensitive and who devote themselves to constant recitation of the Qoran. This point is relevant not only to the passages just mentioned but also to some of the Qoranic formulations of doctrine; for just as Christ spoke to the multitude in parables, the Qoran expresses great mysteries by means of aphorisms which are too elliptic to 'cause offence', but which have at the same time an overwhelming directness, as for example the already quoted words *We are nearer to him than his jugular vein*. There can be no question of any divergence of interpretation as regards such statements: the difference here between exoterism and esoterism, between piety which saves and mysticism which sanctifies, is like the difference between two and three dimensions respectively, esoterism's extra dimension being that of 'depth' or 'height'. The same is true as regards the understanding of the Divine Names, and certain Traditions such as the Holy Tradition in which it is said, 'I am the Hearing wherewith he heareth and the Sight wherewith he seeth'. The difference is as between one who takes such statements as a manner of speaking, allowing them to pass over his head, and one in whom they awaken a 'vertical' consciousness which is what the Sufis call *dhauq*, literally 'taste'. This word is used in view of the directness of such perception, to show that it transcends indirect mental knowledge, being no less than some degree of 'Heart-knowledge'.

QORAN

[1] LXXVI, 5-6. The Qoran is a synthesis of many points of view, and cannot be reduced to any system as regards terminology. From one point of view all creatures, including Satan, are the slaves of God. The 'slavehood', like the 'nearness', is already there in every case. But since only the supreme Saints realize this truth with full realization, the term 'slaves of God' is sometimes used to refer to them exclusively, as here and, for example, in XVII, 65, and LXXXIX, 29.

In connection with one of the Prophet's mystical visions, the Qoran says that it was his *Heart* which *saw*,[1] and Baidāwī[2] comments that 'other-worldly realities are perceived first by the Heart'.[3] What is meant by Heart here, and what the ancients of both East and West mean by saying that the Heart is the throne of the Intellect may be understood with the help of Kāshānī's already quoted commentary, which bases some of its interpretations on the correspondence between outward phenomena and inward faculties. The night corresponds to the soul, the moon to the Heart (which is to the soul what the corporeal heart is to the body) and the sun to the Spirit. Just as the moon is the last outpost of daylight in the darkness of night, so the Heart is the last outpost of Divine Light, that is, direct Knowledge (Gnosis)[4] in the darkness of the soul's knowledge, which even in its highest form, that is, as theoretic understanding of the doctrine, is only mental and therefore indirect. The 'Eye of the Heart', which corresponds to the ray of light that connects the moon with the sun, is the Intellect in its true sense—the sense in which *Intellectus* was used throughout the Middle Ages—the organ of transcendent vision.

The aspiration 'to let one's Spirit (that is, as here meant, one's centre of consciousness) rise above oneself' presupposes at the very least some remote awareness of the existence of the Heart, which is the point where the human self ends and the Transcendent Self begins. If the clouds in the night of the soul are so thick as to prevent the moon of the Heart from showing the slightest sign of its presence, there can be no such aspiration.

Most of the Qoranic verses quoted so far are among the earliest to be revealed, which is enough to show that a strong mystical element was present from the outset. But coming when it did,

[1] LIII, 11.

[2] d. 1286 The author of the most widely read of all Qoranic commentaries.

[3] The Prophet said of Abu Bakr, who later became the first Caliph of Islam: 'He is not your superior by reason of much fasting and prayer, but because of something which hath been fixed in his heart.' (Kalābādhī *The Doctrine of the Sufis*, in Arberry's translation, p. 66.)

[4] This word is used throughout as a translation of the Arabic *ma'rifah* in the sense of Intellectual Knowledge. Similarly 'Gnostic' (*'ārif*) is used here exclusively to indicate one who attains to this knowledge. It bears no reference to any sect.

as the last religion of this cycle of time, Islam could not be an effective vehicle of the Divine Mercy if it did not take into account the conditions of a world which was long since past its best (the Prophet said: 'Naught is left of this world but trial and affliction'[2] and 'No time cometh upon you but is followed by a worse'[3]), a world in which *the Foremost* would be in an increasingly small minority. These conditions are implicit in the following passage which was revealed towards the end of the Prophet's life,[4] many years after he and his followers had been forced to emigrate from Mecca to Medina, and after they had returned in triumph to Mecca and had become masters of all Arabia, with an inevitable sacrifice of quality to quantity as regards converts to Islam:

The Arabs of the desert say: 'We believe'. Say thou (Muḥammad): *'Ye believe not, but say rather: 'We submit',*[5] *for faith hath not yet entered your hearts. Yet if ye obey God and His messenger, He will not withhold from you any reward that your deeds deserve. Verily God is Forgiving, Merciful.'*[6] We see here as it were the net of Divine Mercy stretched out to find a place in the new religion for some of those who would not have been worthy of the first small Meccan community of Moslems. Yet the growth of Islam throughout the time of the Prophet's mission is not only in this one direction but in all. The Qoran undertakes to answer any questions which might arise during the period of its revelation, and in responding to the needs of the increasingly complex community of Islam as a whole it does not neglect those who follow the path of approach to God; for while it is more and more concerned, in the Medina period, with outward questions—legal, administrative and political—its verses are at the same time more markedly charged with peace and serenity. The much loved and often repeated verse which the Qoran recommends especially for recitation in times of adversity: *Verily we are for God, and verily unto Him are we returning*[7] has a distinctly

[1] XXXVIII, 29.

[2] Ibn Mājah, *Fitan* 23.

[3] Bukhārī, *Fitan*, 6.

[4] He died in 632.

[5] This might also be translated: *We have become Moslems*. The word *islām* means 'submission' (to God).

[6] XLIX, 14.

[7] II, 156.

Medinan flavour. It is significant also that some of those passages which form as it were the crown of the Sufic doctrine of Gnosis[1] were revealed at Medina.

As regards rites, the first Revelations prescribed, both for day worship and for night vigil,[2] litanies of glorification, prostrations, recitations of what had already been revealed of the Qoran, and invocations of the Divine Name. These devotions became voluntary after the obligatory ritual purification and prayer[3] had been established; and other voluntary litanies were revealed at Medina such as the invocation of Divine Blessings upon the Prophet, an orison which is analogous in more than one respect to the Christian *Ave.* Voluntary fasts were also recommended in addition to the obligatory fast of the month of Ramadan. All these devotions, both the obligatory and the voluntary, reinforced by the spiritual retreat, were undoubtedly the practices of Muḣammad's greatest Companions; and they are still and have always been the chief devotions of the mystics of Islam, all other practices being purely subsidiary.

It is therefore scarcely possible to speak of any development, after the death of the Prophet, as regards the essentials of Sufism; but during the first six or seven centuries of Islam the tension between the general downstream drifting of the community as a whole and the upstream movement of the mystic path produced a kind of secondary development in Sufism which is neither upward nor downward,[4] and which did not alter the essentials in themselves, but was concerned rather with such questions as varying formulations and disciplines to suit varying needs.

[1] For example the Verse of Light, (XXIV), 35), and also LVII, 3, both of which are quoted later (pp. 174, note 2 and 130, note 1).

[2] *Keep vigil all the night save a little* (LXXIII,2); *Glorify Him the livelong night* (LXXVI, 26).

[3] The prostration was included in the ritual prayer, the movements of which are described in a later chapter.

[4] Many Orientalist misunderstandings have sprung from failure to perceive the 'horizontal' and entirely secondary nature of this development. For not a few of those who write on the subject, Sufism consists of a heroic asceticism punctuated by mystical poems, treatises and paradoxical ejaculations, none of which one finds in the first two generations of Islam, and none of which can be considered as an essential feature of Sufism.

Kalābādhī, a tenth century Sufi of Bukhara, says 'Then (after the second generation of Islam) desire diminished and purpose flagged: and with this came the spate of questions and answers, books and treatises.'[1]

The inevitable movement from concentrated synthesis to differentiated analysis, which brought about the formation of the four different schools of canon law and, on another plane, the organization of the Sufi brotherhoods, was largely the result of an analogous change that was taking place in human souls. Nicholson is referring to this change—which he clearly did not understand—when he says: 'Neither he (the Prophet) nor his hearers perceived, as later Moslems did, that the language of the Qoran is often contradictory.'[2]

It would have been less equivocal to say that later Moslems were in general not so well able to make, of two outwardly conflicting statements (as for example the Qoranic affirmations that man is responsible for his actions and that his actions are predestined), a synthesis through which they might perceive the spiritual truth in question. In other words, intellectual activity was giving way to mental activity, and it was to meet the needs of the general rationalistic ferment, and also to counteract certain heresies that had sprung from it, that scholastic theology was developed in Islam; and since those who aspired to follow the mystic path could not help being more mentally dilated than their seventh and eighth century counterparts had been, it was necessary that the Sufi Shaikhs also should make more ample formulations of doctrine in their own domain. But the Sufis have never set too great a store by these attempts to express what is universally admitted to be inexpressible. 'Take knowledge from the breasts of men, not from words' and 'Whoso knoweth God, his tongue flaggeth' are among the most often repeated of Sufic maxims.

In order to understand how secondary development fits into the structure of Islam, it is necessary to know that after the Qoran and the Prophet the third highest authority is *Ijmā'*, that is, the unanimous opinion of those who are thoroughly

[1] *The Doctrine of the Sufis*, in Arberry's translation, p. 3.
[2] *A Literary History of the Arabs*, p. 223.

versed in the Qoran and the Traditions and who are therefore qualified to establish, by inference and on analogy, precedents about points not definitely and explicitly laid down by the two higher authorities. The deductive process by which they reach their conclusions is called *ijtihād*, (literally 'striving'). Below *Ijmā'* there is a certain relative authority in the *ijtihād* of a group of qualified persons or even of a single qualified individual. The differences between the four great schools of Islamic law, for example, are due to the differing *ijtihād* of four eminent canonists. But each school admits the right of the other schools to hold their own opinions, and it is often said: 'In the canonists' differences there lieth a mercy.'

The law is not the only plane of the religion, however, as is made clear in the following Tradition which was reported by 'Umar, the second Caliph:

'One day when we were with the Messenger of God there came unto us a man whose clothes were of exceeding whiteness and whose hair was of exceeding blackness, nor were there any signs of travel upon him, although none of us had seen him before. He sat down knee unto knee opposite the Prophet, upon whose thighs he placed the palms of his hands, saying: 'O Muḥammad, tell me what is the surrender unto God (*al-islām*)'. The Prophet answered: "The surrender is that thou shouldst testify that there is no god but God and that Muḥammad is God's Apostle, that thou shouldst perform the prayer, bestow the alms, fast Ramadan and make, if thou canst, the pilgrimage to the Holy House". He said: "Thou hast spoken truly" and we were amazed that having questioned him he should corroborate him. Then he said: "Tell me what is faith (*īmān*)", and the Prophet answered: "It is that thou shouldst believe in God and His Angels and His Books and His Apostles and the Last Day, and that thou shouldst believe that no good or evil cometh but by His Providence."[1] "Thou hast spoken truly", he said, and then: "Tell me what is excellence (*iḥsān*)" The Prophet answered: "It is that thou shouldst worship God as if thou sawest Him, for if thou seest Him not, verily He seeth thee." . . . Then the stranger went away, and I stayed there

[1] It is the objective content of faith which is here defined, not its subjective quality.

long after he had gone, until the Prophet said to me: "O Umar, knowest thou the questioner, who he was?" I said: "God and His Prophet know best, but I know not at all." "It was Gabriel" said the Prophet. "He came to teach you your religion".[1]

Thus Islam in its fullest sense consists of three planes—surrender or submission (*islām* in the narrower sense of the word), faith (*īmān*) and excellence (*iḥsān*), and the Shaikh Al-ʿAlawī points out that there is scope on all three for the exercise of *ijtihād*: just as the plane of *islām* crystallized into the different schools of law and the plane of *īman* into scholastic theology, so also, beneath the *ijtihād* of Junaid[2] and other Sufis, the plane of *iḥsān* became a definitely organized branch of the religion.

In the Prophet's definition of *iḥsān* the word for 'worship' (*ʿabada*) means literally 'to serve as a slave', and indicates not merely a series of acts but a perpetual state. Thus to worship God 'as if thou sawest Him' implies perpetual remembrance of God, and to achieve this some form of spiritual guidance and method is, practically speaking, indispensable. Here in fact lies the origin of the Sufic brotherhoods, without which the plane of *iḥsān*, which in the first generations of Islam was relatively spontaneous and unorganized, could never have been prolonged throughout the centuries.

The Qoran insists without respite on remembrance of God, *dhikr Allāh*, and this insistence holds the place in Islam that is held in Christianity by the first of Christ's two commandments. It is the Qoranic use of the cognitive term 'remembrance' rather than 'love' which has, perhaps more than anything else, imposed on Islamic mysticism its special terminology.

The predominances, in Christian mysticism of 'Love' and in Sufism of 'Knowledge', that is, Gnosis, are so strong that many of the terms currently used in these two mystical forms are apt to be quite misleading outside their own particular sphere. For example, in the light of Hinduism, where both perspectives

[1] Muslim, *Imān*, I.
[2] A great Sufi of Baghdad, d. 910.

are to be found side by side,[1] it can be seen at once that the 'contemplative' orders of monasticism in the Roman Catholic Church are closer to the path of Love than to that of Gnosis. On the other hand what has been termed 'the Sufi path of Love' is far more akin to *jnâna* than to *bhakti*,[2] for it is Love within the general framework of Knowledge.

Very typical of Sufism is Ḥasan al-Baṣri's[3] saying: 'He that knoweth God loveth Him, and he that knoweth the world abstaineth from it', and the saying of another early Sufi: 'Intimacy (*uns*) with God is finer and sweeter than longing.'[4]

Whereas one aspect of this path of Knowledge reflects the symbolism of light in which the Qoran abounds and also the joyous and often dazzling imagery through which it allows its reader to 'taste' the Mysteries of the next world,[5] another aspect reflects not only the stark simplicity of some of the Qoranic formulations but also certain sayings of the Prophet which have an unmistakable 'dry' flavour about them, a sober objectivity which puts everything in its proper place, as for example: 'Be in this world as a stranger or as a passer-by'[6], and :'What have I to do with this world? Verily I and this world are as a rider and a tree beneath which he taketh shelter. Then he goeth on his way and leaveth it behind him.'[7]

These two aspects of Moslem spirituality make themselves

[1] The comprehensiveness of Hinduism makes it something of a norm by which to measure other mysticisms, for after thousands of years it has crystallized into two main currents, which evidently correspond to two main mystic possibilities, the path of Gnosis (*jnâna-marga*) and the path of Love (*bhakti-marga*).

[2] The Egyptian Sufi 'Umar ibn al-Fāriḍ, (1181-1235) who is often called 'the Sultan of the Lovers', would rank in Hinduism as a pure Gnostic (jnâni).

[3] d. 728.

[4] Quoted by Abū Sa'īd al-Kharrāz (d. *c.* 900) in his *Kitāb aṣ-Ṣidq* ('The Book of Truthfulness'), Arabic Text, p. 56, Arberry's translation, p. 46. The author of the remark is not specified.

[5] Men tend to judge others by themselves, and it has become almost a habit in the West to comment on the 'unexalted materialism' of the Qoranic descriptions of Paradise. The following remark puts the whole question in a truer light: 'To speak of the Gardens and Fountains of Paradise, as also of Its Rivers, Fruits and Consorts, is to speak the truth, whereas to speak of such blessings in this world is only a manner of speaking, for the Realities are in Firdaus (the Supreme Paradise), and what we see in this world are only the remote shadows of Reality.' (Abū Bakr Sirāj Ad-Dīn, *The Book of Certainty*, p. 18, note 2—Samuel Weiser, New York, 1970.)

[6] Bukhārī, *Riqāq*, 3.

[7] Ibn Mājah, *Zuhd*, 3.

felt in varying modes throughout the whole Islamic civilization, and they are especially pronounced in its art, as might be expected, for sacred art is an expression of the Mysteries and therefore springs directly from the deepest layer of its religion. The following passage brings this out very clearly:

'Islamic art is abstract, but also poetical and gracious; it is woven of soberness and splendour . . . uniting the joyous profusion of vegetation with the abstract and pure vigour of crystals: a prayer niche adorned with arabesques holds something of a garden and something of a snowflake. This admixture of qualities is already to be met with in the Qoran where the geometry of the ideas is as it were hidden under the blaze of the forms. Being, if one can so put it, haunted by Unity, Islam has also an aspect of the simplicity of the desert, of whiteness and of austerity which, in its art, alternates with the crystalline joy of ornamentation.'[1]

The Shaikh Al-'Alawī, to whose life and teaching this chapter serves as introduction, in no sense belies the roots of the tree on which his spirituality flowered, and his presence, as we feel it from his writings and from the accounts of those who knew him, is fraught now with one, now with the other of these two complementary and alternating aspects of Islam which have their origin at the Fountains of Kāfūr and Tasnīm, in the 'slavehood' and the 'nearness' of the first representative of the reality of Sufism.

[1] Frithjof Schuon, *Spiritual Perspectives and Human Facts*, pp. 38–9 Perennial Books, 1969.

CHAPTER III

SEEN FROM WITHIN

The Shaikh was born at Mostaganem in 1869. His name, as given on the title-pages of most of his books, was Abu 'l-'Abbās Aḥmad ibn Muṣṭafa 'l-'Alawī, and he was an only son, with two sisters. A little less than a year before his birth his mother Fāṭimah 'saw in her sleep the Prophet with a jonquil in his hand. He looked her full in the face and smiled at her and threw the flower to her, whereupon she took it up with humble modesty. When she woke, she told her husband of the vision, and he interpreted it as meaning that they would be blessed with a pious son, and he had in fact been importuning God not to leave him without an heir . . . and after a few weeks God confirmed her dream, and she conceived her son.'[1]

After the Shaikh's death in 1934, the following autobiographical extract[2] was found among his papers. He had evidently dictated it some years previously[3] to one of his disciples:

'As to learning how to write, I never made much effort in that direction, and I never went to school, not even for a single day. My only schooling was what I learned from my father at home during the Qoran lessons which he used to give me, and my handwriting is still quite unproficient. My learning by heart the Book of God went as far as the Sūrat ar-Raḥmān,[4] and there I came to a standstill owing to the various occupations which I was forced to turn to through sheer necessity. The family had not enough to live on—although you would never have thought it, for my father was proud and reserved to

[1] *Ar-Raudat as-Saniyyah*, p. 9. This work was compiled by Sidi 'Uddah and published two years after the Shaikh's death. It contains information of various kinds about his life and spiritual activity.

[2] *Ar-Raudat as-Saniyyah*, pp. 9-27. Except for abridgements here and there to avoid repetition, I have quoted it in full, interspersed with other quotations which help to complete it.

[3] The references to Turkey at the end show that it was dictated after 1923 at the earliest.

[4] That is, he had learned by heart just over a tenth of the Qoran.

The Shaikh Al-'Alawī in about 1905

the point of never showing on his face what was in his mind, so that nobody could have concluded from outward signs that he was in need of anything.[1] I hesitated between several different crafts, and finally took to cobbling and became quite good at it, and our situation improved in consequence. I remained a cobbler for a few years, and then went into trade, and I lost my father when I was just sixteen. Although I was so young I had been doing all sorts of things for him and I was bent on nothing so much as giving him pleasure. He was exceedingly fond of me, and I do not remember him ever blaming me for anything or beating me, except when he was giving me lessons, and then it was because I was lazy in learning the Qoran. As to my mother, she was even more lavish in her affection, and she worried more about me than he had done. In fact after his death she did all she could in the way of harsh words and blows and locking the door and so on to prevent me from going out at night. I wanted very much to humour her, but I could not bring myself to give up attending lessons at night and gatherings for *dhikr*. What made her so anxious was that our house was outside the town on a road which one might well fear to go along alone at night; and she continued in her attempts to stop me, and I for my part continued to attend those gatherings, until by the Grace of God she gave her full consent, and there was nothing to mar our love for each other, which remained unclouded until the day of her death in 1332,[2] when I was 46.

'As to my attendance at lessons, it did not amount to much, as it was only possible now and then, in between work, and if I had not had a certain natural aptitude and understanding I should not have gained anything worth speaking of. But I was very much addicted to learning, and would sometimes steep myself in books the whole night long; and I was helped in these nocturnal studies by a Shaikh whom I used to bring back to our house. After this had been going on for several months, my wife took offence and claimed divorce from me on the grounds of my not giving her her rights, and she had in fact some cause

[1] The Shaikh is clearly echoing Qoran II, 273. His family had no doubt been in somewhat better circumstances previously.
At any rate the Shaikh's great-grandfather Aḥmad is referred to in an early nineteenth century poem as one of the 'notables' of Mostaganem, eminent for his piety and his knowledge of Islamic law.

[2] 1914.

to complain. My attendance at lessons, such as it was, did not go on for as much as two years; it none the less enabled me to grasp some points of doctrine in addition to what I gained in the way of mental discipline. But it was not until I had busied myself with the doctrine of the Folk,[1] and had come to know its Masters, that my mind opened and I began to have a certain breadth of knowledge and understanding.'

(At this point the scribe to whom this was dictated asked him about how he first came into contact with those who follow the path of the mystics.)

'My first leaning in that direction was marked by my attachment to one of the Masters of the 'Īsāwī Ṭarīqah[2] who impressed me by his unworldliness and evident piety. I made every effort to comply with the requisites of that order, and this came quite easily to me on account of my youth and the instinctive attraction for wonders and marvels[3] which is part of human nature. I became proficient in these practices, and was well thought of by the men of the order, and I believed in my ignorance that what we did was purely and simply a means of

[1] The Sufis are known as 'the Folk' (*al-qaum*) in virtue of the following Tradition and others like it:

'Verily God hath Angels, a noble company of travellers, who seek out the circles of remembrance on earth, and when they find one they throng together above it, wing against wing, so that the highest of them are in Heaven. God saith unto them: 'Whence come ye?', and they say: 'We come from Thy slaves who are glorifying Thee and magnifying Thee and testifying that there is no god but Thee and praying unto Thee and seeking Thy Protection.' . . . Then He saith: 'Bear ye witness that I have forgiven them, and that I have granted them that for which they pray unto Me, and I have vouchsafed them My Protection against that wherefrom they sought it.' Then they say: 'Lord, amongst them, sitting with them, is a sinner.', and He saith: 'Him also have I forgiven, for he is among a folk (qaum) whose fellow, that sitteth with them, shall not be confounded.' (Muslim, *Dhikr*, 8).

[2] The word *ṭarīqah* (way) is used especially of the path of the mystics, and by extension has come to denote, as here, an order or brotherhood of those who follow this path.

[3] In the 'Īsāwī Ṭarīqah, at any rate in certain branches of it, fire-eating, snake-charming and other such practices are prevalent. Their origin in this order is traced back to its founder, Muḥammad ibn 'Īsā (d. 1523). Having incurred the jealousy of the Sultan of Meknes, he was ordered to leave the town with his disciples. They had no provisions for this exodus and were soon extremely hungry, so they begged their Master, who was famed for miracles, to give them some food. He told them they could eat anything they found on the road, and since there was nothing there but pebbles, scorpions and snakes, they ate these, which fully satisfied their hunger without any ill-effects. (See L. Rinn, *Marabouts et Khouan*, p. 305.)

drawing near to God. On the day when God willed that I should be inspired with the truth we were at one of our gatherings and I looked up and saw a paper that was on one of the walls of the house we were in, and my eye lit on a saying that was traced back to the Prophet. What I learned from it caused me to give up what I had been doing in the way of working wonders, and I determined to limit myself in that order to the litanies and invocations and recitations of the Qoran. From that time I began to extricate myself and to make excuses to my brethern until I finally gave up those other practices altogether. I wanted to drag the entire brotherhood away from them also, but that was not easy. As for myself, I broke away as I had intended, and only retained from that contact the practice of snake-charming. I continued to charm snakes by myself or with some of my friends until I met Shaikh Sidi Muḥammad Al-Būzīdī.

'As to my meeting with this Shaikh, whichever way I look at it, it seems to me to have been a pure Grace from God; for although we—that is, I and my friend Sidi al-Ḥājj Bin-'Awdah who shared my business with me—were longing to find someone who could take us by the hand and guide us, we did not go to the Shaikh Al-Būzīdī and seek him out where he was, but it was he who came to us, quite unexpectedly. My friend had already told me about him. He said: "I used to know a Shaikh called Sidi Ḥamū[1] of the family of the Prophet. He left his home and went for several years to Morocco, and when he returned many people attached themselves to him. He used to speak with authority about the path of the mystics, but to try him God sent against him a man who did him much harm so that he found himself faced with all sorts of opposition, and now he is as subdued as any disciple, without a trace of his former spiritual activity. However, I think that he is one who could be relied on for guidance upon the path. No true spiritual guide has ever appeared whom God did not try with someone who wronged him either openly or behind his back."

'This was the gist of what he said, and immediately I determined to go to this Shaikh on my friend's recommendation. I myself knew nothing about him except that once, when a boy, I had heard his name in connection with an illness which I had.

[1] The Shaikh Al-Būzīdī was generally known by this name, which is short for Muḥammad.

They brought me an amulet and said: "This is from Sidi Ḥamū Shaikh Būzīdī", and I used it and was cured.

'My friend and I were at work together some days after this conversation, when suddenly he said: "Look, there is that Shaikh going down the road." Then he went up to him and asked him to come in, which he did. They talked for a while, but I was too busy with my work to be able to notice what they were talking about. When the Shaikh got up to go, my friend begged him not to stop visiting us. He said good-bye and went, and I asked my friend what impression he had had, and he said: "His talk is far above what one finds in books." He came to see us from time to time, and it was my friend who talked to him and plied him copiously with questions, whereas I was more or less tongue-tied, partly out of reverence for him and partly because my work left me no time to talk.

'One day, when he was with us in our shop, the Shaikh said to me: "I have heard that you can charm snakes, and that you are not afraid of being bitten." I admitted this. Then he said: "Can you bring me one now and charm it here in front of us?" I said that I could, and going outside the town, I searched for half the day, but only found a small one, about half an arm's length. This I brought back with me and putting it in front of him, I began to handle it according to my custom, while he sat and watched me. "Could you charm a bigger snake than this?" he asked. I replied that the size made no difference to me. Then he said: "I will show you one that is bigger than this and far more venomous, and if you can take hold of it you are a real sage." I asked him to show me where it was, and he said: "I mean your soul which is between the two sides of your body. Its poison is more deadly than a snake's, and if you can take hold of it and do what you please with it, you are, as I have said, a sage indeed." Then he said: "Go and do with that little snake whatever you usually do with them, and never go back to such practices again", and I went out, wondering about the soul and how its poison could be more deadly than a snake's.

'Another day, during this period when the Shaikh used to call on us, he fixed his eyes on me and then said to my friend. "The lad is qualified to receive instruction" or "He would be receptive to instruction", or some such remark; and on another occasion he found a paper in my hand on which was written something in praise of Shaikh Sidi Muhammad ibn ʿĪsā,[1] and after looking at it he said to me: "If you live long enough you will be, God willing, like Shaikh Sidi Muhammad ibn ʿĪsā", or "You will attain to his spiritual rank"—I forget his exact words. This seemed to me a very remote possibility but I said: "God willing"; and it was not long before I was attached to his order and took him as a guiding light in the path of God. My friend had already been received into the order about two months previously, though he had kept this from me, and only told me after I myself had been received. I did not understand at that time the reason for this secrecy.

'After the Shaikh had transmitted to me the litanies for morning and evening recitation, he told me not to speak about them to anyone—"until I tell you", he said. Then in less than a week he called me to him and began to talk to me about the Supreme Name (Allāh) and the method of invoking it. He told me to devote myself to *dhikr Allāh* in the way generally practised in our order at that time; and since he had no special cell of retreat for *dhikr*, I was unable to find a place where I could be alone undisturbed. When I complained of this to him, he said: 'There is no place better for being alone than the cemetery." So I went there alone at nights, but it was not easy for me. I was so overcome with fear that I could not concentrate on the *dhikr*, although for many nights I tried to do so.

'I complained again to the Shaikh, and he said: "I did not give you a binding order. I merely said there was no place better for being alone than the cemetery." Then he told me to limit my *dhikr* to the last third of the night, and so I invoked at night and made contact with him during the day. Either he would come to me, or else I would go to him, although his house was not always a good place for meeting on account of the children and for other reasons. In addition to this, at midday, I went on attending the lessons in theology which I had attended previously. One day he asked me: "What lessons are those that I see you attending?" I said: 'They are on the Doctrine of Unity (*at-tawḥīd*) and I am now at "the realization of proofs".'

[1] The already mentioned founder of the ʿĪsāwī Ṭarīqah.

He said: "Sidi So-and-so used to call it 'the doctrine of turbidity' (*at-tawḥīl*)". Then he added: "You had better busy yourself now with purifying your innermost soul until the Lights of your Lord dawn in it and you come to know the real meaning of Unity. But as for scholastic theology, it will only serve to increase your doubts and pile up illusion upon illusion." Finally he said: "You had better leave the rest of those lessons until you are through with your present task, for it is an obligation to put what is more important before what is of lesser importance."

'No order that he ever gave me was so hard to obey as this. I had grown very fond of those lessons and had come to rely on them so much for my understanding of the doctrine that I was on the point of disobeying him. But God put into my Heart this question: How do you know that what you are receiving from the Shaikh Al-Būzīdī is not the kind of knowledge that you are really seeking, or something even higher than it? Secondly, I comforted myself with the thought that the prohibition was not a permanent one; thirdly, I remembered that I had taken an oath of allegiance to obey him; and fourthly I told myself that perhaps he wanted to put me to trial, as is the way of Shaikhs. But all these arguments did not stop the ache of sorrow that I felt within me. What sent that away was my spending in solitary invocation the hours which I had previously devoted to reading, especially after I had begun to feel the results of this invocation.

'As to his way of guiding his disciples, stage by stage, it varied. He would talk to some about the form in which Adam was created and to others about the cardinal virtues and to others about the Divine Actions, each instruction being specially suited to the disciple in question. But the course which he most often followed, and which I also followed after him, was to enjoin upon the disciple the invocation of the single Name with distinct visualization of its letters until they were written in his imagination. Then he would tell him to spread them out and enlarge them until they filled all the horizon. The *dhikr* would continue in this form until the letters became like light. Then the Shaikh would show the way out of this standpoint—it is impossible to express in words how he did so—and by means of this indication the Spirit of the disciple would quickly reach beyond the created universe provided that he had sufficient preparation and aptitude—otherwise there would be need for purification and other spiritual training. At the abovementioned indication the disciple would find himself able to distinguish between the Absolute and the relative, and he would see the universe as a ball or a lamp suspended in a beginningless, endless void. Then it would grow dimmer in his sight as he persevered in the invocation to the accompaniment of meditation, until it seemed no longer a definite object but a mere trace. Then it would become not even a trace, until at length the disciple was submerged in the World of the Absolute and his certainty was strengthened by Its Pure Light. In all this the Shaikh would watch over him and ask him about his states and strengthen him in the *dhikr* degree by degree until he finally reached a point of being conscious of what he perceived through his own power. The Shaikh would not be satisfied until this point was reached, and he used to quote the words of God which refer to: *One whom his Lord hath made certain, and whose certainty He hath then followed up with direct evidence.*[1]

'When the disciple had reached this degree of independent perception, which was strong or weak according to his capability, the Shaikh would bring him back again to the world of outward forms after he had left it, and it would seem to him the inverse of what it had been before, simply because the light of his inward eye had dawned. He would see it as *Light upon Light,* and so it had been before in reality.[2]

'In this degree the disciple may mistake the bowstring for the arrow as has happened to many of those who are journeying

[1] Qoran, XI, 17. This verse is open to several different interpretations, one of which only can be kept in translation, to the exclusion of the others. The Shaikh Al-Būzīdī clearly understood the word *shāhid* in the sense of 'direct evidence' or 'concrete illustration'.

[2] It is not irrelevant to quote here the following Far Eastern Buddhist formulation: 'As one of the Zen Masters has put it, at first the disciple, his mind still entangled in the cosmic mirage, beholds around him objects such as mountains and trees and houses; then with the gaining of partial knowledge, mountains and trees and houses fade from sight; but lastly having arrived at complete understanding, the man, no longer a disciple, again beholds mountains and trees and houses, but this time without the superimpositions of illusion.' (Marco Pallis, *The Way and the Mountain*, p. 108. Peter Owen, 1960.)

to God, and he may say as more than one has said: "I am He whom I love, and He whom I love is I",[1] and the like—enough to make anyone who has no knowledge of the attainments of the mystics and is unfamiliar with their ejaculations throw at him the first thing that he can lay hands on. But the master of this degree comes before long to distinguish between the spiritual points of view, and to give to each of the different degrees of existence its due and to each of the spiritual stations what rightly belongs to it. This station took hold of me, and it has been my home for many years, and I have become as it were expert in it, and made known its obligations, and my followers have had what I wrote about it when I was first in its grip, and some of them now have knowledge of its obligations, and some of them fall short of this knowledge. The acuteness of this state still comes back to me sometimes, but it does not compel me to write about it. True, it prompts me to speak about it, but it is easier to live with than it was, something that I feel rather than something that I am submerged in.

'This path which I have just described as being that of my Master is the one that I have followed in my own spiritual guidance, leading my own followers along it, for I have found it the nearest of the paths which lead to God.'

The Shaikh is speaking here with the voice of unmitigated 'slavehood', and it is consistent with the general tone of this passage that even with regard to the very Summit of all spiritual attainment he should single out for mention its aspect of 'obligation', to which the Qoran refers in the words: *We offered the trust* (of being Our representative) *unto the heavens and the earth and the mountains, but they shrank from bearing it, and were afraid of it. And man took it upon himself. Verily*

[1] Al-Ḥallāj. *See Le Dîwân d'al-Hallâj*, edit. Massignon, 1955, p. 93. The verse continues: 'We are two spirits in one body,' and is largely the basis of Massignon's theory, so undiscriminatingly followed by other Orientalists, that Al-Ḥallaj was not a 'monist', that is, that he did not believe in *waḥdat al-wujūd*, Oneness of Being. This question is considered in more detail later, but it may be noted here that Ghazālī, in his *Mishkāt al-Anwār* (*see Jawāhir al-Ghawālī*, Cairo, 1343, p. 115), quotes these verses in much the same context as the above, and like the Shaikh Al-'Alawī he takes them as springing from a state of spiritual drunkenness which is as yet unbalanced by a complementary spiritual sobriety, and which therefore does not represent Al-Ḥallāj's ultimate conviction.

he hath proved an ignorant tyrant.[1] Reaching the end of the spiritual path, which is none other than the state in which man was originally created, means, amongst other things, reassuming the tremendous responsibilities from which mankind in general has fallen away.

This ultimate station, that is, the state of Supreme Sainthood, which he referred to in speaking to Dr Carret as the 'Great Peace', is defined elsewhere in his writings as being one of inward intoxication and outward soberness, in virtue of which the mind fulfils its analytical function with perfect clarity, although, as he has just indicated, there is nothing in the nature of an absolute barrier between it and the Heart's rapture. But in the case of the mystic who, though far advanced upon the path, has not yet reached the end, other-worldly drunkenness is liable to invade the mind and make it supernaturally and unbearably active, or produce some other abnormality in it, thus throwing the soul off its balance. It is even possible, as is shown by the reference to al-Ḥallāj and as we shall see more clearly in a later chapter, for a mystic to reach in a sense the end of the path and to attain to a plenitude of drunkenness which is as yet unstabilized by the complementary perfection of sobriety. For although the Divine Nature of the Saint is Eternal and does not develop, his human nature is subject to time and may not be able to adapt itself in one day to the Supreme Presence, especially in cases where the spiritual journey has been completed with phenomenal speed as it almost certainly was in the case of the Shaikh Al-'Alawī.

More than once in his writings he quotes Abu 'l-Ḥasan ash-Shādhilī[2] as having said: 'Vision of the Truth came upon me and would not leave me, and it was stronger than I could bear, so I asked God to set a screen between me and It. Then a voice called out to me, saying: "If thou besoughtest Him as only His Prophets and Saints and Muḥammad His beloved know how to beseech Him, yet would He not screen thee from It. But ask Him to strengthen thee for It."

[1] XXXIII, 72.

[2] d. 1258. As the founder of the great Shādhilī Ṭarīqah he was doubly the Shaikh Al-'Alawī's spiritual ancester, since both the Darqāwīs (to whom the Shaikh Al-Būzīdī belonged) and also the 'Īsāwīs are branches of the Shādhilīs.

So I asked for strength and He strengthened me—praise be to God!'

The dictation continues: 'When I had reaped the fruit of the *dhikr*—and its fruit is no less than knowledge of God by way of contemplation—I saw clearly the meagreness of all that I had learned about the doctrine of Divine Unity, and I sensed the meaning of what my Master had said about it. Then he told me to attend once more those lessons which I had attended previously, and when I did so I found myself quite different from what I had been before as regards understanding. I now understood things in advance before the Shaikh who was teaching us had finished expounding them. Another result of the invocation was that I understood more than the literal sense of the text. In a word, there was no comparison between the understanding which I now had and that which I had before, and its scope went on increasing, until when anyone recited a passage from the Book of God, my wits would jump to solve the riddle of its meaning with amazing speed at the very moment of recitation. But when this took hold of me and became almost second nature, I was afraid that I should come altogether under the sway of its imperious and persistent impulsion, so I took to writing down what my inward thoughts dictated to me by way of interpretation of the Book of God, and I was so much under its sway that I brought them out in a strange and abstruse form. This is what led me to begin my commentary on *Al-Murshid al-Muʿīn*,[1] in an attempt to stop myself from falling into a still more abstruse manner of expression. God be praised that this did in fact help to stem the onslaughts of that surge of thoughts which I had tried by every means to stop and could not, and my mind came near to being at rest. It was much the same kind of predicament which had previously led to my putting together my book on astronomy called *Miftāḥ ash-Shuhūd* (*The Key of Perception*). I was absorbedly pre-occupied for certain reasons with the movements of the heavenly bodies, and the arrow of my thoughts had gone awry. To make a long story short—and I

[1] *Guide to the Essentials of Religious Knowledge*, by Ibn ʿĀshir (d. 1631). The Shaikh's commentary on this, *Al-Minaḥ al-Quddūsiyyah*, which he revised several years later, is one of his most important works, and one of the most difficult to come by.

have already referred to this question in the book itself[1]—when I found that I was unable to resist this surge of thoughts, I complained to my Master about it, and he said: "Take them out of your brain and put them in a book, and then they will let you rest", and it was as he had said. But I have still not been able to bring myself to allow the book to be published, and God alone knows whether it ever will be.[2]

'To revert to what I was saying, when after many long days I was freed from the obligation of devoting myself exclusively to the Divine Name, my Master said to me: "Now you must speak and guide men to this path inasmuch as you are now certain where you stand." I said: "Do you think they will listen to me?", and he said: "You will be like a lion: whatever you put your hand on you will take hold of it." It was as he had said: whenever I spoke with anyone in the intention of leading him to the path he was guided by my words, and went the way I pointed out to him; and so, praise God, this brotherhood increased.'

Elsewhere he says:

'Our Master, Sidi Muḥammad al-Būzīdī, was always urging us to visit the tomb of Shaikh Shuʿaib Abū Madyan[3] at Tlemcen. He spoke of him with great reverence and said that prayers made at his tomb were answered; and he used to tell us: "It was through his blessing and with his permission that I went to Morocco. I spent a night at his shrine, and after I had recited some of the Qoran I went to sleep, and he came to me with one of my ancestors. They greeted me, and then he said: "Go to

[1] In his introduction to *Miftāḥ ash-Shuhūd* he says: 'The cause of my writing it was a state of inward absorption which would sweep over my heart and prevent my thoughts from roaming in any domain lower than that of the heavenly bodies; and sometimes this state would seize me, Heart and all, and take me even to the Holy Essence Itself. But whatever degree I was in, inspirations and flashes of direct knowledge beyond the scope of my understanding would come over me one after another without respite. At first I tried to turn away from them, refusing to trust as authentic the demands they made upon me, but finally they overcame me and set the seal of their authority upon my innermost convictions. Knowing therefore that I was powerless to resist them, and believing myself to be a prisoner in this station, I inclined to it in acceptance, and submitted to the Will of God, having taken refuge in the counsel of my Master, who told me to write this book. He told me moreover not to make it, through what I put into it, the marvel of all marvels, and he quoted the Tradition: 'Speak to men according to the capacity of their intelligences.'

[2] It was published in 1941, that is, seven years after his death. The manuscript was dated AH 1322 (AD 1904)

[3] d.1197. His tomb is a place of pilgrimage from all over the Moslem world.

Morocco. I have smoothed out the way for thee." I said: "But Morocco is full of poisonous snakes. I cannot live there." Then he passed his blessed hand over my body and said: "Go and fear not. I will protect thee from any mishap that might befall thee." I woke trembling with awe, and immediately on leaving his shrine I turned my face westwards, and it was in Morocco that I met Shaikh Sidi Muḥammad ibn Qaddūr."[1]

The Shaikh Al-'Alawī's own narrative continues:

'I asked my Master why he had ordered me to speak after first having imposed silence on me. He said: "When I returned from Morocco I taught our doctrine as I had taught it there. Then when I found myself faced with opposition I saw the Prophet of God in my sleep and he ordered me to remain silent. From that time I kept such a hold of silence upon myself that sometimes I felt I would burst into flames. Then, just before my meeting you, I had another vision in which I saw a gathering of fuqarā, and every single one of them had my rosary round his neck. When I woke I took what I had seen as a good sign of activity in the future. That is why I am willing that you should propagate the doctrines of our order. Otherwise I should not have dared to allow you to make them known. Moreover, I saw very lately one who said to me: "Speak to people; there is no harm in it." By "one who said" he no doubt meant the Prophet, though God knows best.

'Such was my beginning; and I remained at his side for fifteen years, doing all that I could for our order. Many others helped me in this, though of the old ones there are now only about ten left—may God lengthen their lives and show increasing solicitude for them!

'As for myself, I was so taken up during all that time with the service of the Shaikh and with furthering the increase of our order, that I neglected the demands of my own livelihood, and but for the friendship of Sidi al-Ḥājj Bin-'Awdah[3] who took care of my finances and kept my affairs in order, my business would

[1] By becoming the disciple of this Darqāwī-Shādhili Shaikh in Morocco, the Shaikh Al-Būzīdī became the descendant of Abū Madyan who was the spiritual great-grandfather of Abu 'l-Ḥasan ash-Shādhilī (see Appendix B).

[2] Al-Mawādd al-Ghaithiyyah, p. 13.

[3] He also, like the Shaikh Al-'Alawī, was by this time a representative (*muqaddam*) of the Shaikh Al-Būzīdī, with power to receive novices into the ṭarīqah in his name and instruct them.

have been altogether ruined. I was so busy in the service of the order that our shop was more like a zāwiyah than anything else, what with teaching there at night and *dhikr* during the day—all this, God be praised, without any loss of money or lessening of trade.

'Then, not long before the death of my Master, God put into my heart the desire to emigrate. I was so struck with the moral corruption in my own country that I began to make all possible arrangements for moving further East, and some of my friends had the same intention; and although I knew very well that my Master would not allow me to leave the country unless he came with us, I was driven on by all sorts of plausible motives. However, after I had actually started on the removal—this was some days before his death—freed myself from all trade obligations, sold my possessions and mortgaged what was difficult to sell in the way of immovables with the intention of having them sold by someone else when I had gone, and after my cousins had already started off ahead of me, and just when I myself was on the point of leaving, my Master who was already ill suddenly grew much worse, and one could see on him the signs of approaching death. I could not bring myself to leave him in that state, nor would my friends have allowed me to do so. His tongue was paralysed so that he could not speak, but he understood everything.

What was especially painful to me myself was that I felt pulled in different directions to do things which were scarcely reconcilable one with another: on the one hand there was my Master's illness which obliged me to stay with him, and on the other hand I had a permit to travel for myself and my family which was due to expire on a certain date, after which it was no longer valid, and what made matters worse was that at that time it was difficult to obtain a permit. In addition I was also burdened with winding up my business and selling my furniture; and I had sent my wife to her family in Tlemcen so that she could say good-bye to them. In fact it was as if I were no longer in my own country. None the less I decided that I could not possibly leave my Master just as he was dying, and go off after I had spent fifteen years with him, doing all I could to serve him and never having once crossed him even about the smallest point.

'It was not many days before he was taken to the Mercy of God. He only left one son, Sidi Muṣṭafā, who had something of the holy simpleton about him; he also left a wife and two brothers, of whom one, Sidi al-Ḥājj Aḥmad is now dead, whereas the other, Sidi 'Abd al-Qādir, is still in the bonds of life. The Shaikh was exceedingly fond of his family and especially of his son, Sidi Muṣṭafā. Just before his death I saw him give a long look at him, and it was clear that he was thinking of his simpleness, and that he was afraid he would be neglected after his death, and when I realized this I said to him: "Sidi, act on our behalf and take care of our interests in the next world before God, and I will act on your behalf in this world and take care of Sidi Muṣṭafā." His face shone with joy, and I kept my promise and did everything I could for his son until the day of his death, and was never in the least troubled by his state of mind which others found so irksome. I took care of the Shaikh's daughter also—he only had one—until she married.

'After we had said a last farewell to our Master,[1] some of us prepared him for burial, and he was buried in his zāwiyah after I had prayed over him the funeral prayers—may God shower Mercy and Blessings upon him! A few days later news came to me from my parents-in-law in Tlemcen: "Your wife is very seriously ill." So I went to Tlemcen, and when I arrived I found that my wife, who was so deeply religious and so full of kindness and so pleasant to live with, was almost at her last breath. I stayed with her for three days, and then she died and went full of grace to the Mercy of God; and I returned to Mostaganem, having lost my Master and my wife, homeless, without means of livelihood, and even without my permit to travel, which had expired. I went to the Ministry to have it renewed, and they put me off for several days. Then they promised to give me a permit for myself alone.

'Meantime, while I was waiting for it to be issued, the men of our order were conferring together about who should take charge of the fuqarā. I myself was not present at their discussion, being prepared to accept their choice. Moreover I was quite unreconciled to the idea of remaining in the country, so I said: "It is for you to appoint whom you wish for this function and I

[1] The Shaikh Al-Būzīdī died on Shawwāl 12, A.H. 1327 (October 27, 1909).

will support you." for I knew that there was one amongst them who would be capable of it (apart from myself, and I assumed that they would appoint him)[1]. But since this meeting of the fuqarā proved somewhat argumentative, because (although they would all have agreed to choose me) they knew that I was determined to go away, so that each one proposed the solution that seemed best to him and there was much difference of opinion, the Muqaddam Sidi al-Ḣājj Bin-ʿAwdah said: "We had better leave this question for the moment, and meet again next week. Meantime if any of the fuqarā has a vision, let him tell us about it." They all approved of this suggestion, and before the appointed day many visions had been seen—they were all written down at the time—and every one of them was a clear indication that the matter in question devolved upon me. So the fuqarā were strengthened in their determination to make me stay with them and act as their remembrancer.'

While trying to find some details of the visions, I came upon the following passage by Sidi ʿUddah:

'The Shaikh Al-Būzīdī died without ever having told anyone who was to succeed him. The question had in fact been broached to him by one of his more prominent disciples who thought well of himself and fancied that he was qualified to fulfil in our order the functions of upbringing and remembrancing; but the Shaikh Al-Būzīdī answered him as follows:

'I am like a man who has been living in a house by permission of the Landlord, and who when he wishes to leave that house gives the keys back to the Landlord. He it is, the Landlord, that sees who best deserves to have the house placed at his disposition; I have no say in the matter. God *createth what He will, according to His Choice*'[2]. . . and after his death his followers were left in a state of great upheaval, although most of them showed quite plainly their leanings towards Sidi Aḣmad Bin-ʿAlīwah[3] on

[1] The Shaikh's manner of expression becomes very elliptical here. I have tried to expand it.

[2] Qoran, XXVIII, 68.

[3] The Shaikh Al-ʿAlawī's great-great-great-grandfather Al-Ḣājj ʿAlī (ḣājj being the title of one who has made the Pilgrimage) was known in Mostaganem as Al-Ḣājj ʿAlīwah (a dialectal diminutive), whence the name Bin-ʿAlīwah was given to his descendants.

account of his having, as was known, already exercised the function of his Shaikh, even to the point of guiding disciples to the end of their journey, although his Shaikh was still alive. This was the strongest indication of how well he was thought of by him, and how qualified he was to succeed him.

'Now since visions are to be relied on for ascertaining the truth about things which lie hidden from our normal perceptions,[1] just as they are to be counted as glad tidings[2] for him who sees them, or for him on behalf of whom they are seen, I wish to set down here some of those visions that were seen on behalf of our Master, Shaikh Sidi Aḥmad Bin-ʿAlīwah.[3]

He then gives an account[4] of some of the many visions which were seen after the Shaikh Al-Būzīdī's death, and of which here are a few:

'In my sleep I saw Shaikh Sidi Muḥammad al-Būzīdī, and not forgetting that he was dead I asked him of his state, and he said: "I am in the Mercy of God". Then I said to him: "Sidi, to whom have you left the fuqarā?", and he answered: "It was I who planted the shoot, but it is Sidi Aḥmad Bin-ʿAlīwah who will tend it, and it will come, God willing, to all fullness of fruition at his hands." ' (ʿAbd al-Qādir ibn ʿAbd ar-Raḥmān of Mostaganem).

'In my sleep I saw myself go to visit Shaikh Sidi Muḥammad al-Būzīdī, and Shaikh Sidi Aḥmad Bin-ʿAlīwah was sitting beside the tomb which was open. I saw the body of the dead rise up until it was on a level with the surface of the earth. Then Shaikh Sidi Aḥmad went and took the shroud from off his face, and there, unsurpassably beautiful, was the Shaikh. He asked Shaikh Sidi Aḥmad to bring him some water, and when he had drunk he gave what was left to me, whereupon I

[1] The Prophet said: 'The believer's vision is a forty-sixth part of prophecy' (Bukhārī, *Kitāb al-Ḥiyal, Bāb at-Taʿbīr*, 4 and most of the other canonical books), and: 'Visions are from God, and dreams are from Satan' (Bukhārī, ibid., 3).

[2] The Prophet said: 'Naught is now left of prophecy but the bearers of good tidings'. They said: 'What are the bearers of good tidings?' and he said: 'They are the visions of the pious' (*ibid.*, 5). He also said: 'If any of you seeth a vision that he loveth, it is from none other than God' (*ibid.*, 3).

[3] *Ar-Rauḍat as-Saniyyah*, pp. 129-31 (abridged).

[4] *Ibid.*, pp. 131-49.

started saying to the fuqarā: "In this water which is left over from the Shaikh there is a cure for all sickness". Then he began to talk to Shaikh Sidi Aḥmad, and the first thing he said to him was: "I shall be with you wherever you may be, so have no fear, and I give you tidings that you have attained to the best of this world and the next. Be very sure that in whatever place you are, there shall I be also." Then Shaikh Sidi Aḥmad turned to us and said: "The Shaikh is not dead. He is as you see him to be now and the death that we witnessed was just a rite which he had to perform." ' (Al-Munawwar Bin-Tūnis of Mostaganem).

'I saw Shaikh Sidi Muḥammad al-Būzīdī stop and knock at the door of my house, and when I rose to let him in I found that the door was already open. He came in, and with him was a companion, tall and very thin, and I said to myself: "This is Sidi Aḥmad Bin-'Alīwah." After they had sat with us for a while, Shaikh Sidi Muḥammad al-Būzīdī rose to his feet, and said he wanted to go. Then someone said to him: "If you go, who will you leave to look after us?", and he said: "I have left you *this* man—*this* man", and he pointed to Shaikh Sidi Aḥmad Bin-'Alīwah'. (A member of the family of Al-Ḥājj Muḥammad as-Sūsī of Ghalīzān).

'I saw the Imam 'Alī[1]—and he said to me: "Know that I am 'Alī and your Ṭarīqah is 'Alawiyyah." ' (Al-Ḥājj Ṣāliḥ ibn Murād of Tlemcen).

'After the death of Shaikh Sidi Muḥammad I had a vision that I was on the shore of the sea, and near at hand was a huge boat in the centre of which was a minaret, and there, on the topmost turret, was Shaikh Sidi Aḥmad Bin-'Alīwah. Then a crier called out: "O you people, come on board the boat", and they came on board from all sides until it was full, and each one of them was well aware that this was Shaikh Sidi Aḥmad's boat; and when it teemed with passengers, I went to the Shaikh and said: "The boat is full. Are you able to take charge of it?", and he said: "Yes, I shall take charge of it by God's Leave." ' (Al-Kīlānī ibn al-'Arabī).

[1] The Prophet's cousin and son-in-law, the fourth Caliph, sometimes described as 'the St John of Islam'. In most of the spiritual chains of succession by which the Sufic orders trace their descent from the Prophet, he is the connecting link with the Prophet himself.

Sidi ʿUddah also quotes the following from the Shaikh Al-ʿAlawī himself:

'In my sleep, a few days before the death of our Master, Sidi Muḥammad al-Būzīdī, I saw someone come in to where I was sitting, and I rose out of reverence for him, overcome with awe at his presence. Then, when I had begged him to be seated and had sat down facing him, it became clear to me that he was the Prophet. I turned on myself reproachfully for not having honoured him as I should have, for it had not occurred to me who he was, and I sat there huddled up, with my head bowed, until he spoke to me, saying: "Knowest thou not why I have come to thee?", and I said: "I cannot see why, O Messenger of God". He said: "The Sultan of the East is dead, and thou, God willing, shalt be Sultan in his stead. What sayest thou?" I said: "If I were invested with this high dignity, who would help me, and who would follow me?" He answered: "I shall be with thee, and I will help thee." Then he was silent, and after a moment he left me, and I woke up on the heels of his departure, and it was as if I saw the last of him, as he went, with my eyes open and awake"[1].

The dictation continues:

'Since the fuqarā knew well that there was no turning me away from my intention to go, they compelled me to take charge of them if only while I was waiting for the permit to travel, although their aim was to make me give up my journey by every possible means. One of those who were most bent on my staying was my dear friend Sidi Aḥmad Bin-Thuraiyā, and he spared no possible effort to that end, all for purely spiritual motives. One of his devices was to marry me to his daughter without imposing any conditions on me, despite his knowledge that I was determined to go away. I accepted his offer very gladly, and gave her what little I could in the way of marriage portion.

[1] One of the Shaikh's disciples, the only one of them with whom I have had any direct contact, once remarked to me that a vision shows its spiritual origin even in its 'texture', having a freshness and clarity which the ordinary dream-projections of the subconscious entirely lack. He added that one of the secondary characteristics of the vision is that it is often followed immediately by a state of entire vigilance without any intermediary process of waking up.

'Unfortunately she did not succeed in living on good terms with my mother. As time went on my dilemma grew worse and worse. I felt bound to do all I could for my mother, and I had already taken her part in more than one situation of this kind; but a separation which had been relatively easy for me in the case of other wives seemed very hard in the case of this last one. As for any possibility of reconciliation between the two, it was clearly very remote indeed; and when my father-in-law saw the dilemma I was in, he suggested divorce and even demanded it with some insistence, saying: "It is your duty to look after the rights of your mother.[1] As to the rights of your wife, they are guaranteed by the words: *If the two separate, God will enrich both out of His Abundance;*[2] and all that, God willing, shall not affect our friendship in the least." He went on and on repeating this suggestion, and I knew that he was sincere, although my own feelings were all against it; and when God brought it to pass, against the will of both parties, I was full of regrets, and so, no less, was my father-in-law. But there was nothing for it but to resign ourselves to what seemed clearly God's will. Our friendship however remained undiminished and that saintly man continued to be as devoted to me as ever until the very end of his life, thanks to the fineness of his feeling which was so well integrated into the spiritual path.

'Much the same took place between me and Sidi Ḥammādī Bin-Qāri' Muṣṭafā: I had to divorce a wife who was a member of his family and whose guardian he was; but God is Witness that both to my face and behind my back—to judge by what I heard of him—his attitude was very like that of Sidi Aḥmad Bin-Thurayyā, and we are still the best of friends. As to the cause of this divorce, it was my being pre-occupied at that time, almost to the point of intoxication, first of all with learning and then with the *dhikr*. Meanwhile the rights of my wife were neglected, as were, very nearly, the rights of my whole family. So, in one way or another, it has been my fate to divorce four wives. But this was not because of any ill treatment on my part,

[1] 'A man came unto the Prophet and said: 'O Apostle of God, who hath most claim upon my kindness of companionship?' The Prophet answered: 'Thy mother'. The man said: 'Then who?' He answered: 'Thy mother.' He said: 'Then who?' He answered: 'Thy mother.' He said: 'Then who?' He answered: 'Then thy father'. (Bukhārī, *Adab*, 2.)

[2] Qoran, IV, 130.

and therefore my fathers-in-law did not take it badly. In fact they are still fathers-in-law to me; and what is more surprising, some of my wives forewent the remainder of their marriage portion after we parted. In a word, any short-comings that there were were on my side, but they were not deliberate.

'When the fuqarā had made up their minds, with the circumstances all in their favour, not to let me go away, they decided to have a general meeting in our Master's zāwiyah, . . . and they took the oath cf allegiance to me by word of mouth, and it continued to be taken in this way by the older fuqarā, whereas all subsequent newcomers took it through the clasping of hands[1]. As to those members of the order who were outside Mostaganem, I did not write to any of them, nor did I put them under any obligation to come to me. But it was not long before groups of fuqarā started coming to me of their own free will to acknowledge me, testifying as to their own convictions and telling what they had heard about me from our Master or what had come to them by way of intuition or inspiration. So it went on, until all the members of the order were united except two or three. This union of the fuqarā was counted by us as a miraculous Grace from God, for I had no outward means of bringing within my scope individuals from so many different places. It was their unalloyed certainty, nothing else, as to how I had stood with our Master in this respect. Moreover the training that they had had from him was firmly ingrafted in them as regards recognizing the truth and acknowledging it whatever it might be, for he had gone on giving them the means of doing this until, thank God, it had become second nature to them.

'I received their oaths of allegiance and gave them advice, and I spent on those who visited me at that time part of what I had in hand for my journey, and I took nothing from them, for I never felt easy about taking money from people.

'As a result of all this I was left in a quandary, not knowing what to do or where the Will of God lay. Ought I to go away, according to what I felt to be an imperative need, or ought I to give up all idea of going and devote myself to acting as remembrancer to the fuqarā, according to what seemed to be already

[1] The older fuqarā did not repeat this rite of handclasping as they had already been formerly initiated into the order, once and for all, by the Shaikh Al-Būzīdī. Some of them did however repeat it five years later as a gesture when the Shaikh had decided to make himself independent of the Darqāwīs.

my fate? I was still hesitating when the time came at which God had ordained that I should visit the seat of the Caliphate.[1] One day He put into my soul a feeling of constriction which was so persistent that I began to look about for a means of relief, and it occurred to me to visit some of the fuqarā outside the town. So I took with me one of the disciples who was staying with us, Shaikh Muḥammad ibn Qāsim al-Bādisī, and off we went with God's Blessing. Then when we had reached our destination it occurred to us that we might as well visit some of the fuqarā in Ghalizan, which we did; and after we had stayed with them for about two days, my companion said to me: "If only we could go as far as Algiers! I have a friend there, and what is more, we could go to some of the publishers, and this contact might bring *Al-Minaḥ al-Quddūsiyyah* nearer to being printed." We had the manuscript of this book with us at the time, so I let him have his way. We had none of our fuqarā in Algiers, and when we arrived, my companion set about trying to find his friend, although he was not particularly anxious to do so. In this connection he said to me: "Places in which there are no fuqarā are empty"—such was his experience of their kindness and cordiality.

'After we had made contact with a publisher, we had the impression that for various reasons no Algerian firm would be likely to accept my book, so my companion said: "If only we could go as far as Tunis, the whole thing would be quite simple." I myself was busy revising my book (which I could do equally well elsewhere) in between visits to the publisher and other outings, so I let him have his way once more, and we travelled from town to town until we reached Tunis. The only practicer of remembrance (*dhākir*) that I knew there was a blind man who knew by heart the Book of God. He used to call on us at Mostaganem on his way to visit his Master in Morocco . . . But as to my numerous fellow countrymen who had settled in Tunis, there was none of them that I wanted to meet, so we entered the town at an hour of siesta, and found lodgings, and I constrained myself not to go out until there should come to us some *dhākir* whom we could go out with. This was on account of a vision I had had in which men who were members of Sufic brotherhoods came and entered the house where I was and took

[1] Istanbul.

me out with them to their place of gathering. When I told my companion this, my idea was too much for him, and he said: "I did not come here to stay shut in by these four walls." So he would go out on various errands and walk round parts of the town and then come back; and after we had spent four days in that house, there came to us the company of people I had seen in my vision. They were from among the followers of Shaikh Sidi Aṡ-Ṡādiq aṡ-Ṡaḣrāwī who had died only a few months previously. This holy man traced back his spiritual ancestry in the path of God through Sidi Muḣammad Żāfir and his father Sidi Muḣammad al-Madanī to Shaikh Sidi Mawlāy Al-ʿArabī ad-Darqāwī[1].'

Some twenty-five years previously Aṡ-Ṡādiq aṡ-Ṡaḣrāwī's Master, Muḣammad Żāfir al-Madanī, had written:

'My honoured guide and father, Shaikh Muḣammad Ḣasan Żāfir al-Madanī, left Medina about AH 1222 (AD 1807) and went as far as Morocco in search of a way by which he might attain to God, and he took guidance from many Shaikhs . . . Then God brought him together with his Master, the Standard-Bearer of the Shādhilī Ṫarīqah in his day, Sidi Mawlāy Al-ʿArabī ibn Aḣmad ad-Darqāwī. His meeting with him was on Ṡafar 23rd, A.H. 1224, in the Darqāwī Zāwiyah at Bu-Barih in Bani Zarwal, two days' journey from Fez. He took the path from him, and his heart was opened under his guidance, and if it be asked who was my father's Shaikh, it was Mawlāy Al-ʿArabī ad-Darqāwī.

'For about nine years he was his companion . . . . Then Mawlāy Al-ʿArabī said to him one day, in great earnestness: "Go to thy home, Madanī. Thou hast no longer any need of me"; and on another occasion he indicated that he had reached the end of all perfection, and said to him: "Thou hast attained unto that which is attained to by the perfect among men," and he told him to go to his native town, the House of the Perfumed Shrine, and when he bade farewell to him, he wept and said: "I have made thee the instrument of my credit with God[2] and a link between me and His Prophet".

'He went to Medina, and stayed there with his family for three years . . . and every year he joined the Pilgrims on Mt

[1] The founder of the ṫarīqah to which the Shaikh Al-Būzīdī belonged.
[2] Because he was going within easy reach of Mecca.

Arafat[1] and then returned to Medina where he visited continually the Shrine of the Prophet, spending his time turned towards God, steeped in contemplation, in utter detachment. . . . And he said: "During that time I met with the perfect Shaikh, the Gnostic, Sidi Aḥmad ibn Idrīs. I found him on a most exalted footing as regards following the Wont[2] of the Prophet, and I so marvelled at his state that I took initiation from him for the blessing of it."

'During his stay in Medina he was asked for spiritual guidance by some who were seeking a Master but he made no response to them out of pious courtesy to his Shaikh[3] until he heard a voice from the Pure Shrine which said to him: "*Be a remembrancer, for verily remembrancing profiteth the believers*[4]. He said: " I quivered and shook at the sweetness of that utterance, and I understood it to be an authorization from the Apostle of the All-Bountiful King". So he obeyed God's command and transmitted initiation to various persons in the city of the Prophet . . . and returned to his Master Mawlāy Al-ʿArabī ad-Darqāwī . . . and remained in his presence for some months. Then Mawlāy Al-ʿArabī died, and my father set out once more for Medina . . . and when he reached Tripoli the eyes of some of its people were opened to the excellence of his virtues and the fullness of his spiritual realization, so they took initiation from him. Then the number of his disciples increased and the brotherhood became famous and men associated it with him, and on this account it was named *Aṭ-Ṭarīqat al-Madaniyyah* and it is a branch of the Shādhilī Ṭarīqah.'[5]

[1] The culminating point of the Pilgrimage is when the Pilgrims stand on Mount Arafat, a few hours journey East of Mecca, on the day before the Great Feast.

[2] This word is used throughout to translate *sunnah* which comprises in its meaning all the customary practices of the Prophet, who said: 'I enjoin my Wont upon you.'

[3] Although anyone who has received initiation is capable of bestowing it, the Shaikh Ad-Darqāwī had not given him any formal instructions in this respect, perhaps because he felt that he could scarcely make a Muqaddam of one who had become his own spiritual equal.

It would seem that we have here, on both sides, a subtle example of that pious courtesy (*adab*) which tends to preside over human relationships in all theocratic civilizations, and in none more than in Islam, being especially stressed in the Sufic brotherhoods, where it takes on almost a methodic aspect as a means of purification.

[4] Qoran, LI, 55.

[5] *Al-Anwār al-Qudsiyyah fī Ṭarīq ash-Shādhiliyyah*, pp. 38-40 (Istanbul, 1884).

This last passage calls for some general remarks about initiation. The practise of grafting a new scion on to an old stock is alien to the modern world except on a material plane. But throughout the ancient world this was practised also and above all on higher planes; and since estrangement from the Mysteries had become 'second nature' to man, it was considered indispensable, before he could enter upon the path which leads to them, that a scion of primordial human nature should be grafted on to his 'fallen' stock, which by definition is dominated by the purely mental and therefore unmystical 'knowledge of good and evil'.[1]

At the outset of a religion the question of initiation is not so urgent, for the first believers are in the grip of a Divine Intervention, at a cyclic moment which is *better than a thousand months* and in which *the Angels and the Spirit descend*.[2] Since they stand at one of the mainsprings of spirituality, the dormant seeds within them (to use a different simile) can become impregnated as easily as those who stand near a fountain or a cascade can be splashed with water. But as the caravan moves away from this oasis across the desert of the centuries, men soon realise that the precious water is no longer in the air, and that it is only to be found stored in certain vessels.

Strictly speaking, the rite of transmission from one vessel to another cannot be confined to any particular set of forms. Its form may depend, in exceptional cases, on the inspiration of the moment. For example, in addition to the Shādhilī initiation which the Shaikh ad-Darqāwī received from his Master Shaikh 'Alī al-Jamal, he also received one from an aged Saint at the point of death who made him his spiritual heir by the ritually unprecedented yet highly significant act of placing his tongue in the Shaikh ad-Darqāwīs mouth, and telling him to suck. But normally transmission takes a form consecrated by apostolic

[1] By extension initiation was also considered necessary for the fulfilment of any function, sacerdotal, royal, chivalric etc., which presupposes that its holder is truly human, that is, that he is a mediator between Heaven and earth, or for the practise of an art or craft, such as masonry for example, which in virtue of its symbolism is capable of being integrated into the path of the Mysteries. Through initiation the novice acquires a new spiritual heredity. But this virtual restoration of the original human norm of sainthood does not exempt the initiate from the tremendous task of actualizing it, that is, of seeing that the new scion comes to full growth and flower, and that the old stock does not reassert itself.

[2] Qoran, XCVII, 4.

precedent. We have seen that the initiation into the Shādhilī—Darqāwī Ṭarīqah is an oath of fealty, and this rite is patterned on the Beatific Allegiance,[1] an outstanding occasion of spiritual overflow at the fountain-head of Islam, when the Prophet seated himself under a tree and called on all those of his Companions who were present to renew their oaths to him.

Apart from this occasion there was a continual spiritual overflow in the form of Divine Names for invocation or litanies for recitation which the Prophet transmitted to his Companions either singly or collectively, and initiation into some brotherhoods takes the form of some such transmission. Moreover such invocational transmissions are in any case indispensable, in all brotherhoods, as secondary or confirmatory initiations,[2] for anyone who seeks to benefit from the full spiritual resources of Sufism. On the title-pages of most of the Shaikh Al-'Alawī's books he is described as 'renowned for the transmission of the Supreme Name'. No Sufi would consider himself qualified to practice methodically an invocation unless he had been formally initiated into it.[3]

A transmission can be passed on by anyone who has received it, even if he has not brought it to fruition himself, though no

[1] Its name is taken from the Qoranic affirmation (XLVIII, 18) that the allegiance brought down, upon those who made it, God's *Riḍwān*. This word, which is often too weakly translated, is of tremendous significance when used of the Divinity. Many Traditions (e.g. Tirmidhī, *Jannah*, 18; Bukhārī, *Riqāq*, 151) declare that the beatitude in question is more excellent than Paradise, and 'the Companions of the Tree', as those who received it on this occasion came to be called, were especially venerated to the end of their lives, and afterwards.

[2] From the Shaikh Al-'Alawī's own account of his entry into the Darqāwī Ṭarīqah we can gather that he first made the initiatory pact of allegiance, then received, by transmission, the litanies of the order, and finally was initiated into the invocation of the Name.

[3] This may be said to apply to all methods in all mysticisms, from the Japanese Buddhists of the Far East to the Red Indian 'Medicine Men' of the far West. To take an example of a path which, being based on invocation (the Hindu Japa-Yoga), is akin to the various paths of Sufism, readers of that most inspiring autobiography of a nineteenth century Russian mystic which is translated into English under the title *The Way of a Pilgrim* (Published by the SPCK, in many editions) will remember how important it was for the Pilgrim to receive directly from a qualified *starets* the transmission of that particular form of the *Kyrie Eleison* which was to be his perpetual prayer. In the exceptional case of a great younger contemporary of the Shaikh Al-'Alawī, the Capuchin Sister Consolata Betrone, who also followed an invocational path, the invocation was transmitted by Christ himself. (See L. Sales, *Jesus Appeals to the World*, St Paul's Publications).

one can give expert guidance who is not an adept. This does not exclude the possibility that by strictly conforming to the traditional methods of the order a gifted initiate, even without a real Master, might avoid remaining stationary upon the path in virtue of the great weight of the spiritual heredity behind him. But the presence of a Master means direct contact with the Divine Source itself, while at the same time that presence transmits, as no other can, the full force of the spiritual heredity. In addition, most of the great Masters of Sufism could claim, like the Shaikh Al-ʿAlawī and the Shaikh Al-Madanī, to have received a special investiture directly from the Prophet.

The tree at the end of this book gives the main lines[1] of the ʿAlawīs' spiritual heredity, the unbroken chains of transmission, whatever form it may have taken, through which they trace their descent back to the Prophet. Apart from the normal initiation which marks the entry upon the spiritual path, it is possible to become attached to a chain 'for the blessing of it', as the Shaikh Al-Madanī did after his return to Medina; and though this particular case is an exceptional one, the 'initiation of blessing' is very frequently sought by those who are not capable of following a spiritual path or even of conceiving what a spiritual path is, but who have an indefinable urge to benefit from a sacred presence. By the end of his life the Shaikh Al-ʿAlawī had great numbers of such followers attached to him.

With regard to his meeting the Madanī fuqarā at Tunis he continues:

'The whole gathering sat down and we talked together for a long time, and I saw the lights of their love of God shining on their foreheads. They asked me to go out with them to a place they had in mind, and they did not stop insisting until they had taken me out and lodged me at the house of one of their friends. Then one after another the fuqarā came to visit us, full of ardour. Such was their hospitality to me,

[1] The Shaikh al-ʿAlawī's descent from Abu 'l-Ḥasan ash-Shādhilī through the chain of the ʿĪsāwī Ṭarīqah is not included. Moreover the ramifications of all the different branches, even if they were known, would be far too complex to be reproduced in one tree. The economy of this tree may be measured by the case of Ḥasan al-Baṣrī (AD 640-727) who in his long life must have received various transmissions from many different Companions of the Prophet, whereas here he is set down as the spiritual heir of one Companion only.

and the honour they showed me[1]—may God reward them!

'During my stay in Tunis I was continually visited by theologians and canonists and other eminent men . . . and with them came a number of their students. Some of them were already initiates and others were not, and of these last several entered upon the path. One of the students had suggested that I should give them a lesson in *Al-Murshid al-Muʿīn*. What I said found favour with my hearers, and this was the cause of some of the students becoming initiated into the order. That is how we spent our time, both as rememberers and remembrancers, and some derived benefit. God be praised for that visit!

'As to the question of printing *Al-Minaḥ al-Quddūsiyyah*, we made a contract with the owner of a press through the mediation of a fellow traveller. We liked them both very much indeed, and this was what prompted us to make the contract, although we knew that this particular press was not well equipped. As a result the book did not come out at the promised time, and I had to go and leave it behind me for somebody else to look after.

'I had decided to go on to Tripoli to visit my cousins, who had left Mostaganem, as I have already mentioned, to settle there. Since I had a permit to travel, I thought that I had better take this opportunity. I was also prompted by thoughts of visiting the Holy House of God and the tomb of the Prophet, but unfortunately a letter came to me from Mostaganem telling me that the Pilgrimage was forbidden[2] that year, and cautioning me against standing on Arafat[3] for fear of incurring the penalty.

'At all events I embarked for Tripoli—by myself—and suffered some hardship through travelling at that season, for it was cold winter weather. In fact I only had one day of relief: I was meditating on the crowd of people—men of Jerba[4] and others—who thronged the boat and I was wondering whether there was a *dhākir* amongst them, when one of the travellers stopped beside me and looked hard at me as if he were trying to read my face. Then he said: "Are you not Shaikh Aḥmad Bin-ʿAlīwah?"

[1] Two years later, in 1911, he sent to them from Mostaganem, and they all became his disciples (*Shahā'id*, p. 145).

[2] By the French authorities, owing to an epidemic that year in Saudi Arabia.

[3] See p. 71, note 1. The 'Day of Arafat' in question was December 22, 1909.

[4] An island off the coast between Tunis and Tripoli.

"Who told you?", I said. "I have always been hearing about you", he said, "and just now while I was looking at you, as I have been for some time, I suddenly realized that you must be that very man"; so I said that I was. Then I went with him to another part of the boat and having asked his name, was told that he was Al-Ḥājj Maʿtūq; when we began to talk together I realized that he was a Gnostic. I asked him if he found any spiritual support among his fellow countrymen, and he said: "I am the only man of this art in all Jerba." From my meeting with him the time passed as happily as I could have wished until he and those who were travelling with him landed at Jerba, and I was once more in the grip of loneliness and the inevitable hardships of travelling in winter until I myself landed at Tripoli.

'My cousins were waiting for me at the harbour. We were longing to catch sight of each other, all the more impatiently on account of our enforced separation. No sooner had we reached their house and sat down than we discussed the question of emigration and all that was connected with it, and they told me that materially speaking they were well off, thanks to God's safe care. As to the country, it seemed to me as far as I could tell a good place to emigrate to, since its people were as like as possible to those of our country both in speech and in ways.

'Towards sunset I asked my cousins if they knew any *dhākir* there, or any Shaikhs who were Gnostics, and they said that they only knew a Turkish Shaikh, who was the head of some government department, a man of the most evident piety. I asked if it would be possible for us to meet him the next day, and just as we were considering this there was a knock at the door and one of them went out and came back saying: "Here is the Shaikh himself at the door, asking if he can come in." He had never visited them at their home. I told them to bring him in, and in he came, a tall man with a long beard dressed from head to foot in Turkish fashion.

'We greeted each other, and when he had sat down he said: "A man from the West—he meant Shustarī[1]—says of the Divine Manifestation: 'My Beloved embraceth all existence, and appeareth in both black and white.' I said: 'Leave Western talk to Western folk and let us hear something from the East."

[1] An Andalusian mystic and poet. d. 1269. The poem is given by Massignon in *Receuil de textes inédits relatifs à la mystique musulmane*, p. 136.

He said: 'The poet said "embraceth all existence", and did not specify either West or East', whereupon I knew that he was well versed in the lore of the mystics. He sat with us for an hour or two that night, all eagerness, listening with all his faculties rapt in attention, as I noticed. Then he took leave of us, but not before he had made us promise to visit him at his office the next day. We went the next morning to where he worked—the department of maritime revenues, of which he was the director. He received us most joyfully and gave orders for work to be stopped and gave his staff a holiday, although there was much work to be done. Then we went off with him alone, and it would take too long to tell of all that we spoke of in the way of mystic doctrine, but I may mention that he said to me: "If you wish to stay in our country, this zāwiyah here is yours, and all the outbuildings that go with it, and I will be your servant." I knew that all he said was spoken in perfect sincerity, and I told him that I would leave my home and settle there. I went for a short walk round the district and found myself very attracted by that neighbourhood as if it corresponded to something in my nature . . .[1]

'On my third day in Tripoli I heard a town crier calling out: "Whoever wants to go to Istanbul can have a ticket for very little", and he added that the boat was due to leave at once. Immediately I had an urge to visit the capital of the Caliphate, and I thought that very likely I might find there the learning I felt the need for. So I asked one of my cousins to go with me. and he said he would, but the sight of the fury of the sea and the crash of the waves stopped him. It was certainly no weather for a crossing. Suffice it that we reached the other side!

'Don't ask me for any details about our embarkation! Once I had found a place on the deck I began to wonder where I should turn for help and refuge upon the journey, and I found no comfort in anything but reliance upon God.

'By the time we reached Istanbul I had almost died of sea-sickness, and what made my plight worse was that at that time I had not a single friend in Istanbul to take me by the hand, and I was so ignorant of Turkish that I was hard put to it to say the simplest thing.

'One day after my arrival I was walking at the outskirts of the

[1] There is no further mention of the Turkish Shaikh.

town, and suddenly a man took my hand and greeted me in clear Arabic, and asked me my name and where I came from. I told him who I was; and who should *he* be but an authority on Islamic law from Algiers, a man of the family of the Prophet. By that time I was very eager to see the sights of the capital, so I put myself in his hands, and he was a great help in showing me what I wanted to see. But I was unable to satisfy my thirst to the full owing to the upheavals in which the Caliphate[1] was involved and the troubles which were soon to break out between the Turkish people and their so-called "Renaissance Youth' or "Reformist Youth". This movement was headed by numerous individuals whom the Government had banished and who had consequently become scattered throughout various countries of Europe where they had started newspapers and periodicals in the sole purpose of criticising the Government and exposing its weaknesses in the eyes of foreign states; and self-seekers found in this subversive movement loopholes and doors through which they pushed their way and gained their ends. Thus was the Caliphate doomed to have its ruler arrested and thrown into prison, while the "Renaissance Youth" went about its work with utterly unbounded ruthlessness until in the end they succeeded in achieving their aim, and the meaning of their "Renaissance" and "Patriotism" and "Reform" became as clear as day to anyone who had eyes to see. But I will say no more: what the Kemalists have done makes it unnecessary for me to trace this degradation step by step.

'I was convinced that the stay which I had hoped to make in those parts was not feasable for various reasons, of which the chief was that I sensed the impending change from kingdom to republic, and from republic to unprincipled tyranny. So I went back to Algeria, feeling that my return was sufficient as fruit of my travels, even if I had gained nothing else; and truly I had no peace of soul until the day when I set foot on Algerian soil, and I praised God for the ways of my people and their remaining in the faith of their fathers and grandfathers and following in the footsteps of the pious.'[2]

[1] The Shaikh's visit to Istanbul was in the Winter of 1909-10. The Sultan 'Abd al-Ḥamīd had been deposed on April 28, 1909, and been suceeded by his brother, Muḥammad V, who was more or less a tool in the hands of the 'Committee of Union and Progress'.

[2] The Shaikh's autobiography ends here.

CHAPTER IV

THE SPIRITUAL MASTER

Many legends grew up around those few months during which the Shaikh visited Tunis, Tripoli and Istanbul. Consequently an article published in *Revue Africaine*[1] two years after his death tells us: 'He spent ten years of his life in the East, travelling in Egypt, Syria, Persia and India.[2] This remains the most mysterious and least known part of his life.' But although these ten years in the East were no more real than a dream, I think there can be little doubt that this dream corresponds to what the Shaikh would have chosen for himself if his destiny had allowed it. The urgency with which he sought to escape from his function shows at any rate that he would not have chosen to spend the rest of his life beneath the weight of the responsibility that was to be his, and one of his motives, possibly the chief, is no doubt to be understood in the light of what he says about the learning which he 'felt the need for'.

Berque writes: 'I knew Shaikh Bin-ʿAlīwah from 1921 until 1934. I saw him slowly grow old. His intellectual enquiringness seemed to become sharper each day, and to the very end he remained a lover of metaphysical investigation. There are few problems which he had not broached, scarcely any philosophies whose essence he had not extracted'.[3]

From his writings, as also from the testimony of those who knew him, one has the impression of a vast and penetratingly active intelligence of which the higher or central part was utterly and eternally satisfied—he speaks of 'remaining inwardly

[1] 1936, pp. 691-776, *Un Mystique Moderniste* by A. Berque. The title is a strange one, for Berque's quotations are in themselves enough, as we shall see, to show that the Shaikh was essentially very conservative. His so-called 'modernism' appears to have been nothing other than the great breadth of his spiritual interests.

[2] Sidi Muḥammad al-Hāshimī writes to me that the Shaikh certainly never went to India, and that apart from what he describes in his autobiography his only visit to the Near East was shortly before his death when he made the Pilgrimage and went on from Mecca and Medina to Jerusalem and Damascus and from there back again to Mostaganem.

[3] *Ibid.*, p. 693.

forever steeped in drunkenness'[1]—and of which the circumference, that is, the earthly or mental part, in so far as it had any respite from the demands made on him by his thousands of disciples, found ample sustenance in meditating on the Qoran and the Traditions and in exploring some of the Sufic treatises,[2] in particular those of Ibn 'Arabī and Jīlī. Moreover he was a great lover of poetry, especially of the odes of 'Umar ibn al-Fāriḍ, long passages of which he seems to have known by heart. But although it does not appear directly in his writings, and although it is relatively most unimportant, it is evident from what Berque says of the Shaikh's thirst for information about other religions that at the extreme edge of this circumference there was a certain 'nostalgia' for something which he would never have found unless he could have come into some kind of contact with representatives of other religions who were on a spiritual level with himself,. such as, for example, his slightly younger Hindu contemporary, Sri Ramana Maharshi of Tiruvannamalai, whose teaching was essentially the same as his own. But he seems to have had no knowledge of Hinduism, and none of Taoism or Buddhism, nor had he any intellectual exchanges with the Qabbalists of Judaism, and as regards Christianity, with which he always maintained a certain contact, it is extremely doubtful whether he ever met any representative of it who was even remotely comparable to himself.

Here, however, he would in any case have needed an exception, for generally speaking Christianity scarcely admits of mutual understanding with other religions. Even the Christian mystic, though he may not reject other religions as false[3], is indifferent to them, legitimately so, for the method of 'the

[1] Al-Minaḥ al-Quddūsiyyah, p. 22.

[2] He says: 'I do not think I am exaggerating if I say that there are amongst the Sufis men whose intelligences, each taken separately, would almost outweigh the combined intelligences of all the writers of this present age.' (*Risālat an-Nāṣir Ma'rūf*, p. 20).

[3] Unless one is content to imply that God is a monstrosity of injustice, caprice and ineffectuality, the words 'None cometh to the Father but by Me' must be considered to have been spoken by Christ as the Logos, the Divine Word, of which not only Jesus but also, for example, the Hindu Avataras, including the Buddha, are manifestations; and just as these are 'the Word made flesh', so the Vedas, the Torah and the Qoran are 'the Word made book'. But since so many people, especially Europeans and Semites, are incapable of following seriously a religion unless they believe it to be the only one or to be

straight and narrow path' of love scarcely admits of looking either to the right or to the left.[1]

But although all mystic paths are 'straight and narrow' in a certain sense, this description is not immediately apt as regards Islamic mysticism, for *wheresoe'er ye turn, there is the Face of God.*[2] In Islam, as we have seen, it is the vista of knowledge which predominates over that of love, and the Sufi is essentially a Gnostic. Sufism is not so much a path hedged by temptations and distractions on both sides as a passage across a wilderness, each stone of which is liable to be transformed in an instant from barren poverty to Infinite Riches. In one of the Shaikh's poems, the Creator is represented as saying:

'The veil of creation I have made
As a screen for the Truth, and in creation there lie
Secrets which suddenly like springs gush forth'.[3]

He also continually quotes the saying of the Prophet: 'Lord, increase me in marvelling at Thee.' The alchemy of Gnosis does not leave things at their face-value, but reduces them to nothingness or reveals them as aspects of the Face of God.

The full Islamic perspective, that is, the Qoranic perspective, is far too vast for the average Moslem. The words: *For each of you We have appointed a law and traced out a path, and if God had so willed, He would have made you one community*[4] remain for him little more than a dead letter, and the same may be said of many other verses such as: *For every community there is a Messenger*[5], and the already quoted *Verily We have sent Messengers*

exceptionally privileged, it is clearly providential that the above saying of Christ should be taken by most Christians in an exclusive sense as referring to one manifestation of the Word only (see Frithjof Schuon, *The Transcendent Unity of Religions*, ch. II, § 6–8), and that the average Moslem, while not denying other religions, is inclined to relegate their validity to pre-Islamic times.

[1] Unless one is compelled to do so in virtue of some special function, or other exceptional circumstances. A great contemporary of the Shaikh, Pope Pius XI, said in confidence to Cardinal Facchinetti whom he had just appointed Apostolic Delegate to Libya: 'Do not think that you are going among infidels. Moslems attain to Salvation. The ways of Providence are infinite.' These words, spoken so many years ago, have only been made public recently, in *L'Ultima*, Anno VIII, 75-76, p. 261 (Florence, 1954).

[2] Qoran, II, 115.

[3] *Dīwān*, p. 10.

[4] Qoran, V, 48.

[5] X, 47.

before thee. About some of them have We told thee, and about some have We not told thee, and *Verily the Faithful*[1] *and the Jews and the Sabians and the Christians—whoso believeth in God and the Last Day and doeth deeds of piety—no fear shall come upon them, neither shall they grieve.*[2] But the Sufi, who methodically seeks to permeate his whole being with the Qoran, cannot fail to be interested, potentially, in all other Heaven-sent religions as manifestations of Divine Mercy, as God's *Signs on the Horizons.*[3] I say 'potentially' because he may never come into direct contact with other religions, and in any case he will be more or less bound to retain outwardly the prejudices of the great majority of his co-religionaries so as to avoid creating a scandal. But in so far as these prejudices are his own, they will be like fetters of gossamer upon his outlook, ready to be brushed away at a mere touch.

According to Berque, 'the Shaikh was always hungry for knowledge about other religions. He seemed to be quite well informed as regards the Scriptures and even as regards the patristic tradition. The Gospel of St. John and the Epistles of St. Paul appealed to him in particular. As an extremely subtle and penetrating metaphysician, he was able to reconcile plurality with unity in the Trinitarian conception of three persons in a consubstantial identity. . . . He rejected it none the less, but his understanding of it made some people think that he adhered to it.'[4]

At the time when the Shaikh left the 'Īsāwī Ṭarīqah, and when he and his friend Al-Ḥājj Bin-'Awdah were searching for a spiritual path, there were several different branches of the Darqāwī Ṭarīqah[5] firmly established in the province of Oran to which Mostaganem belongs, not to mention many branches

[1] Moslems

[2] V, 69.

[3] *We shall show them Our Signs on the horizons and in themselves until it be clear to them: He is the Truth.* (XLI, 53).

[4] Berque, p. 739.

He was in fact accused by some of his enemies of believing in the Trinity (*ibid.*, p. 735).

[5] According to Depont and Coppolani, *Les Confréries religieuses musulmanes*, pp. 510-1, there were over 9500 members of this brotherhood in Algeria at that time. In Mostaganem itself there were three Darqāwī zāwiyahs, and it was no doubt from one or more of these that the Shaikh Al-Būzīdī met with opposition

of other orders. Yet he says: 'Although we considered it an absolute necessity to take as a guide someone who was generally recognized as a Master by those who could judge, we had little hope of finding such a one'.[1] Fifteen years later, at the death of the Shaikh Al-Būzīdī, there was still the same quantity rather than quality among those who offered guidance.

In one of his poems he declares:

'I hid the truth[2] on a time and screened it well
And whoso keepeth God's Secret shall have his reward.
Then when the Giver vouchsafed that I might proclaim it,
He fitted me—and how I know not—to purify souls,
And girded upon me the sword of steadfastness,
And truth and piety, and a wine He gave me,
Which all who drink must needs be always drinking,
Even as a drunk man seeketh to be more drunk.
Thus came I to pour it, nay, it is I that press it.
Doth any other pour it in this age?'[3]

The sight of the relatively wasted efforts of so many fervent souls unconsciously following 'blind guides' made the Shaikh more and more outspoken as regards his own function and indirectly—sometimes even directly—as regards the false pretentions of others.[4]

There is little doubt that he felt himself to be the renewer (*mujaddid*) which the Prophet had promised for every century.[5] The last one had been unquestionably the great Shaikh Ad-Darqāwī himself. The Shaikh Al-ʿAlawī says: 'I am the pourer, the renewer',[6] and: 'Proclaim, O chronicler, the name of ʿAlawī after Darqāwī, for God hath made him his successor'[7] His poems were not published until just after the first world war,

on his return from Morocco. Berque wrongly says that he was a member of the Habrī branch of the Darqāwīs, whereas in actual fact he was not a descendant of Shaikh Muhammad al-Habrī but as it were his younger brother, both being disciples of Muhammad ibn Qaddūr of Morocco.

[1] *Raudah*, p. 12.

[2] The truth of his own supreme spiritual realization.

[3] *Dīwān*, p. 35. The whole poem is translated on p. 207.

[4] For lines which he addressed to a spiritual imposter, see p. 198 f.

[5] 'God will send to this community at the head of every hundred years one who will renew for it its religion' (Abū Dā'ūd, *Malāhim*, 1).

[6] *Dīwān*, p. 30, 1.6.

[7] *Dīwān*, p. 45, 1.6.

though they had a wide circulation in manuscript. But the jealousy of the various heads of zāwiyahs was probably roused not so much by anything he said or wrote as by the fact that they found themselves being deserted by their own disciples.

The Shaikh was at this time in his early forties. Berque who met him about ten years later says: 'A remarkable radiance emanated from him, an irresistible personal magnetism. His glance was quick, clear and extraordinarily attractive. . . . He was very affable and courteous, unassertive, full of tact and delicacy, anxious to avoid any friction . . . and at the same time one was conscious of a great tenacity of purpose in him, a subtle flame which consumed its object in a few moments'.[1] One of his disciples wrote: 'When he was talking he seemed almost negligent, as though he was relying upon help from outside, and at the same time he mastered men's hearts and brought them by force to the point of what he was saying'[2] Another wrote: 'He spoke to everyone according to his intellectual capacity and particular disposition, and when he was speaking it seemed as if the one he was speaking to was the only one he cared for in all the world.'[3] His presence was such that when he went out he was liable to draw men irresistibly after him down the street.[4]

As might have been expected, the greatest opposition to him came at first from the heads of the Darqāwī Zāwiyahs in the neighbourhood. This was brought to a climax when after about five years he decided to make himself independent of the mother zāwiyah in Morocco and thus distinct from the other Algerian branches of the order, and to name his branch *Aṭ-Ṭarīqat al-ʿAlawīyat ad-Darqāwīyat ash-Shādhilīyah.*

One of his motives for taking this step was that he felt the need to introduce, as part of his method, the practice of *khalwah,* that is, spiritual retreat in the solitude of an isolated cell or small hermitage. There was nothing very drastic in this, for if remembrance of God be the positive or heavenly aspect of all mysticism, its negative or earthly aspect is retreat or drawing away from other than God. The Tradition 'Be in this world as a

[1] pp. 692-3.
[2] *Shahā'id,* p. 137.
[3] *Shahā'id,* p. 141.
[4] *Ibid.,* p. 95.
[5] *Rauḍah,* p. 29.

stranger, or as a passer-by' has already been quoted, and one of the most powerful aids to achieving this permanent inward spiritual retreat is bodily withdrawal which, in some form or another, perpetual or temporary, is a feature of almost all contemplative orders. In some Sufic brotherhoods—the Khalwatī Ṭarīqah, for example—it was the tradition to make retreat in a special hermitage. But in the Shādhilī Ṭarīqah and its branches, the spiritual retreat had usually taken the form of withdrawal to the solitudes of nature, after the pattern of the Prophet's retreats in the cave on Mount Hira, and though inevitably the *khalwah* must have been used on occasion, to introduce it as a regular methodic practice was something of an innovation for the descendants of Abu 'l-Ḥasan ash-Shādhilī. However the Shaikh no doubt found this form of retreat more practicable than any other in view of the conditions in which most of his disciples lived. We have already seen that he himself had suffered for want of a definite place where he could be alone, and that it was part of his method to supervise at times very closely the invocation of his disciples, which presupposed that the disciple in question would be within easy reach of him.

'Abd al-Karīm Jossot[1] quotes the Shaikh as having said to him:

'The *khalwah* is a cell in which I put the novice after he has sworn to me not to leave it for forty days if need be. In this oratory he must do nothing but repeat ceaselessly, day and night, the Divine Name (Allāh), drawing out at each invocation the syllable *āh* until he has no more breath left.

'Previously he must have recited the Shahādah (*lā ilāha illa 'Llāh*, there is no god but God) seventy-five thousand times.

'During the *khalwah* he fasts strictly by day, only breaking his fast between sunset and dawn. . . . Some fuqarā obtain the sudden illumination after a few minutes, some only after several days, and some only after several weeks. I know one faqīr who waited eight months. Each morning he would say to me: "My heart is still too hard", and would continue his *khalwah*. In the end his efforts were rewarded.'[2]

[1] See p. 30, note 1.

[2] Berque, pp. 753-4, quoting an article by Jossot, *Le Sentier d'Allah*, which I have been unable to trace.

His action in making himself independent seems to have created, for the moment, a disproportionately violent ill-feeling. Every obstacle was put in his way, and no effort was spared to detach from him the Shaikh Al-Būzīdī's former disciples, now his by oath of allegiance. Moreover he had no time to earn his living and was extremely poor, sometimes to the point of having to sell his household goods, for he could not bring himself to ask his disciples for anything and they did not always perceive that he was in difficulties. But although some of the Shaikh Al-Būzīdī's disciples did in fact fall away from him, new disciples began to flock to him from elsewhere, including even one or two heads of zāwiyahs together with their followers. His opponents among the Darqāwīs must have been somewhat disconcerted when the great-grandson of Mawlāy Al-ʿArabī ad-Darqāwī himself came from the mother zāwiyah in Morocco and took the Shaikh as his Master. Here follows an extract of a letter from him:[1]

'What I saw in the Shaikh and his disciples compelled me to cleave to his presence, and in longing for a possible means of opening my inward eye I asked his permission to invoke the Supreme Name. Until then I had simply been an initiate of the order and nothing more, but I had heard that my ancestors used to rely on the Ṭarīqah as a means of direct attainment, not merely of attachment to a spiritual chain. After I had practised the invocation of the Name according to his instructions, I had certain experiences which compelled me to persevere in it, and before long I had direct knowledge of God . . . If I served the Shaikh as a slave for ever and ever, I should not have given him back a tenth part of a tenth of what I owe him. In a word, it was what compelled my great-grandfather to follow Sidi Mawlāy ʿAlī Al-Jamal which compelled me to follow Shaikh Sidi Aḥmad Bin-ʿAlīwah. . . . I paid no attention to those of my family who blamed me for following him, for they did not know the truth of the matter. . . . But when I explained things to my uncle, Sidi Mawlāy ʿAbd ar-Raḥmān[2], he showed no opposition to my following the Shaikh. On the contrary, he

[1] Muḥammad ibn Aṭ-Ṭayyib ad-Darqāwī.
[2] The head of the mother zāwiyah.

often gave me to understand that he had no objection.'[1]

The ill-feeling against the Shaikh on the part of other zāwiyahs was short-lived, and only went on here and there spasmodically in the case of one or two hereditary marabouts who were in danger of losing their influence altogether. But he had now to face the attacks of the enemies of Sufism, and before long he became one of their chief targets. The publication of his poems was the signal for a general attack, in various newspapers and periodicals, on him and on the Ṭarīqah in particular and on Sufism in general. As regards himself, hostility seems to have concentrated especially on a passage in one of the early poems written many years before the death of his Master. He says of it: 'Everything has a cause, and the cause of those verses was that one day I was overwhelmed by a great longing for the Prophet. Then I fell asleep, and in my sleep I saw him in front of me. I was at that time in a state very different from the one in which you see me now, and he stood there, haughty and aloof, whilst I, in all abasement and humility before him, addressed him with those verses, and when I woke I wrote them down.'[2] The offending verse was:

'If I should die of longing, rejected, what excuse will save thee?'

He was accused of disrespect towards the Prophet for daring to address him with anything in the nature of a threat. In view of the utter devotion expressed in the poem as a whole the accusation can scarcely have been in good faith, but the Shaikh seems to have felt that he had in fact been guilty of a certain impropriety. The offending passage was left out of the second edition, and although several of his disciples wrote vigorous defences for the press, he would not allow any of these to be published,[3] nor would he himself answer any of the personal

[1] *Shahā'id*, pp. 151-3. When he left Mostaganem, the Shaikh said to him: 'If you owe me anything, pay me back by giving your family their due, especially your uncle' (*ibid.*, note 5).

[2] *Shahā'id*, p. 56, note 1.

[3] Several years later, however, he allowed one of his Tunisian disciples to publish a large collection of testifications as regards himself by Moslems of note and authority from various Islamic countries, together with many extracts from letters in praise of him and the 'Alawī Ṭarīqah in general. It was compiled by Muḥammad ibn 'Abd al-Bāri', entitled *Kitāb ash-Shahā'id wa'l-Fatāwī*, and published at Tunis in 1925.

attacks. The nearest he came to doing so was to write to the editor of one of the hostile papers, An-Najāḥ (after greetings):

'You have unsheathed your blade and thrust at my honour and reputation with the vigour of a man whom nothing will daunt, and I took it all as springing from jealousy for the religion and the desire to defend it, until the writer was led on to abuse and insults. And all these too I accept and place upon my head, if they were truly meant in defence of the honour of the Prophet. *If God knoweth good in your hearts, He will requite you with good.*[1] but if not, then *I submit my case unto God. Verily God is the Seer of His slaves.*[2,3]

It was in the same year, 1920, that he wrote the first of his vindications of Sufism.[4] This was in answer to a pamphlet entitled *A Mirror to show up Errors* by a teacher in the Religious College at Tunis, whose criticisms were so petty and childish that one might be surprised that the Shaikh should have bothered to answer them at all. But he no doubt realized that they had a significance which went far beyond their immediate author and that they were nothing less than particular crystallizations of a general hostility which could not be ignored. Since most people are apt to be irritated by what they do not understand, any critic of mysticism, however crude and unintelligent his arguments may be, can be almost certain today that his words will awaken a chorus of agreement from quite a large portion of the community, not only from those who are anti-religious but also—and perhaps above all—from a certain class of believers.

It is one of the excellencies of Islam that there is no laity and that every Moslem is in a sense a priest, spiritual authority being shared by the community as a whole. On the other hand it is one of the excellencies of Christianity that it has a definitely constituted spiritual authority consisting of a small minority

[1] Qoran, VIII, 70.
[2] Qoran, XL, 44.
[3] *Shahā'id*, p. 214, note 1. This was published in *An-Najāḥ* itself, which later published a long article in praise of the Shaikh and his disciples (*Shahā'id*, pp. 55-61).
[4] *Al-Qaul al-Ma'rūf*. The quotations from it which follow are from pp. 38-76, with omissions.

of men whose lives are dedicated to religion, the other-worldliness of their office being stressed in various ways and in general by the fact that its function does not extend to the domain of the temporal power, inasmuch as Christ said: 'My Kingdom is not of this world'. But although these excellencies have been responsible, or partly responsible, for centuries of spiritual well-being in both religions, they come in the end to cast their shadows, which are in Christianity the stifling and choking of the spiritual authority by the laity, who push it further and further into a remote corner of the community from which it can barely function and from which it sometimes seeks to emerge by pandering to mundane triviality, and in Islam the existence of a large number of very limited individuals who imagine that the whole religion is within their grasp and that what lies outside the scope of their own meagre understanding is necessarily outside the pale of Islam itself. The author of 'the Mirror' is a striking example of the extreme exoterism that any Moslem mystic is liable to be confronted with. One of his tirades ends with the words: 'Islam is nothing other than the Book of God and the Wont of His Messenger.' To this the Shaikh replied:

'Who told you that the Sufis say that Islam is based on any principles other than these? They say, however, that in the Book of God there is doctrine which is beyond most men's attainment. The Sultan of the Lovers[1] said:

'There lieth a lore beneath the words of the text too subtle to be grasped by the farthest reach of sound intelligences.'[2]

'It may well be that one who cleaves to externals can see nothing in the Book of God but what his own intelligence, such as it is, can apprehend and that he may belie what goes beyond this without realizing that in knowing the outside of the Book only he is as one who knows a fruit by nothing but its peel—and beyond that lies "what no eye hath seen and what no ear hath heard and what the heart of man cannot conceive." Let him examine himself: if what his heart hides is more precious than what his tongue tells of, then he is *one whom his Lord hath made certain*;[3] but if not, then he has missed far more than he has gained. . . . The Prophet said: "Knowledge of the inward is one

[1] See p. 46, note 2.
[2] At-Tā'iyyat al-Kubrā, 1. 675.
[3] Qoran, XI, 17.

of the Secrets of God. It is wisdom from the treasury of His Wisdom which He casteth into the heart of whomsoe'er He will of His slaves"[1] and "Knowledge is of two kinds, knowledge in the Heart which is the knowledge that availeth, and knowledge upon the tongue which is God's evidence against His slave".[2] This shows that secret knowledge is different from the knowledge that is bandied about.

'Abū Hurairah said: "I have treasured in my memory two stores of knowledge which I had from God's Apostle. One I have divulged; but if I divulged the other ye would cut my throat".[3]

'In saying: "Islam is nothing other than the Book of God and the Wont of the Apostle", it is as if you said: "Islam is what *I* understand of the Book and the Wont, and no more" . . . which means that you set your own innermost perceptions on a level with the innermost perceptions of the Companions—nay, of the Prophets! . . .

'The Prophet said: "The earth shall never be found lacking in forty men whose Hearts are as the Heart of the Friend[4] of the All-Merciful".[5] One has only to study the traditions to find that they tell us explicitly that there is within the community an elect to whom God has revealed the secrets of the Book and the Wont, and where else is this body of men to be found save amongst the Rememberers, who are marked out for having devoted their lives to God? It was of such as them that Dhu 'n-Nūn al-Miṣrī[6] said: "In my travels I met a slave girl and asked her whence she came. She said: 'From men *whose sides shrink away from beds*.'[7] Then I asked her whither she was going, and she said: 'To *men whom neither bartering nor selling diverteth from the remembrance of God*' "[8]'

Like many others before him, the author of the 'Mirror' did not fail to criticize the Sufic practice of dancing, not only

[1] Suyūṭī, *al-Jāmi' aṣ-Ṣaghīr*.

[2] *Ibid.*

[3] Bukhārī, *'Ilm*, 42

[4] Abraham.

[5] This Tradition is given by Suyūṭī (*Al Jāmi' as-Ṣaghīr*) in a slightly different form.

[6] An Egyptian Sufi, d. 860.

[7] Qoran, XXXII, 16.

[8] Qoran, XXIV, 36.

because it had not been the practice of the Prophet and his Companions but also on the grounds that the Prophet had forbidden dancing altogether. Opinions differ about this last point; but although we do not know exactly what the Companions did in their Sessions of Remembrance, or Circles of Remembrance as they are called in some Traditions, it seems unlikely that they had any deliberate practice resembling the sacred dance described by Dr Carret.[1] None the less, it is difficult to believe that they did not make some spontaneous rhythmic movements of the body while reciting their various litanies and invoking the Divine Name. Given the Arab genius for rhythm, a practice so simple and elemental as the Darqāwī-ʿAlawī *dhikr* could have crystallized in one generation[2]; and once such practices had been established as they were bound to be, in the natural course of events, it is understandable that certain Shaikhs, as for example Jalāl ad-Dīn ar-Rūmī, the founder of the Maulawī Order of Sufis who are better known to the West as 'the Whirling Dervishes', should have incorporated into the *dhikr* some of the movements, together with the music, of traditional local

[1] See pp. 20-1.

[2] This possibility was brought home to me by the following incident. I was driving from Mecca to Medina with a group of lecturers and students from the Universities of Cairo and Alexandria. Some of the students were 'Moslem Brothers'. The founder of their movement, Shaikh Ḥasan al-Bannā', had a respect for the Sufis, but many of the younger generation tended to be not unlike the author of the 'Mirror' in their conception of Islam, and only a few days previously I had been drawn into an argument with some of them about Sufism, which I had felt bound to defend against their criticisms. As we drew near to Medina one member of the party began to chant an invocation of Blessings upon the Prophet. Soon we all joined in, and then four or five of these Moslem Brothers who were sitting together began to sway rhythmically from side to side. At first it was not very noticeable, but gradually the rhythm of the chant became more and more marked and the swaying more and more purposeful and vigorous. Finally the driver called out that if they did not stop they would overturn the car. They had almost certainly never performed such a *dhikr* before and probably never would again, unless they made another visit to Medina. But the Sufis visit Medina in spirit every morning and evening. In this connection it may be remarked in passing—for it is very significant as regards the place of Sufism in the religion as a whole—that the average Moslem pilgrim becomes, in his practices, something of a Sufi for the brief period of his pilgrimage. This is particularly noticeable on the Day of Arafat, for every tent on the sacred hill-top is like a zāwiyah and the very air vibrates with the perpetual murmur of the Qoran and litanies on every tongue. But when they return to their various countries they relapse for the most part into 'ordinary life', not having that aspiration to nearness which sustains the Sufi upon his path and makes every day for him a 'Day of Arafat'.

dances which by heredity flowed as it were in the blood of his disciples and had therefore a more immediate appeal for them.

None the less, the subjection of the body to a rhythmic motion is never, for the Sufis, any more than an auxiliary; its purpose is simply to facilitate *dhikr* in the fullest sense of remembrance, that is, the concentration of all the faculties of the soul upon the Divine Truth represented by the Supreme Name or some other formula which is uttered aloud or silently by the dancers. It was explained to me by one of the Shaikh's disciples that just as a sacred number such as three, seven or nine, for example, acts as a bridge between multiplicity and Unity, so rhythm is a bridge between agitation and Repose, motion and Motionlessness, fluctuation and Immutability. Fluctuation, like multiplicity, cannot be transcended in this world of perpetual motion but only in the Peace of Divine Unity; and to partake of this Peace in some degree is in fact that very concentration which the *dhikr* aims at. Knowledge of this virtue of rhythm[1] is part of man's primordial heritage, and all men possess it instinctively whether they are aware of it or not.

The sacred dance of the Sufis enters into a more general category of practices which are summed up in the Arabic word *tawājud*. In defence of them the Shaikh quotes from one of the more eminent exoteric authorities of Islam, Ibn Qayyim al-Jauziyyah:[2]

'*Tawājud* is seeking to induce a state of ecstasy (*wajd*) through

[1] Rhythm, like other cosmic and potentially sacred forces, such as those used in magic for example, is capable of being perverted into the wrong direction. It is therefore of vital importance to distinguish between 'white rhythm' and 'black rhythm' and there is no doubt as to which of the two is more familiar to the modern Western World. Needless to say the words 'white' and 'black' are used here without any ethnological significance. To judge from what little one has the opportunity of hearing, the rhythm of most Africans in their native state is eminently 'white'.

[2] d. AD 1350. In his youth he had been a violent critic of the Sufis, but towards the end of his life he came to venerate them. The change appears to have taken place during a period which he spent in prison, where 'he busied himself with reciting the Qoran and pondering and meditating, whereby much good was opened up to him and he had many spiritual intuitions and veritable ecstasies. It was in virtue of this that he ventured to expound the doctrine of the Gnostics' (quoted from Ālūsī's life of Ibn Qayyim by Rashīd Riḍā in his preface to Madārij as-Sālikīn, II, p. 6).

deliberate effort, and opinions differ as to whether it is legitimate or not. The truth is that if one's effort is for the sake of enhancing one's reputation it is wrong, but if it is for the sake of obtaining a *ḥāl* (the partial and transitory realization of a spiritual degree) or *maqām* (the integral and permanent realization of a spiritual degree), it is justified.'[1]

Ibn Qayyim quotes in defence of legitimate *tawājud* the saying of the Prophet: 'Weep, and if ye weep not, then try to weep'[2] which makes one think of the Jews wailing at the 'Western Wall' and the Red Indians going out into the wilds of nature to lament,[3] and similar modes of *tawājud* in other religions. It would be true to say, however, that in the aspen-like soul of the mystic there is nearly always some spiritual motion, however slight, so that the effort in question, instead of being a new departure, is in most cases merely the exaggeration of an initial degree of ecstasy which the mystic fears to lose and wishes to increase. *Tawājud* thus means, 'rushing out to meet ecstasy half way', and that is why the Shaikh makes no distinction between the effort and the achievement in his reply to the criticisms of the 'Mirror'.

He says: 'God commended the people of the Book[4] for their rapture, mentioning one of its aspects with the highest praise: *When they hear what hath been revealed unto the Prophet, thou seest their eyes overflow with tears from their recognition of the Truth.*[5] Does not this point to a sudden impact of movement within the believer through his remembering God and listening to His words? Has He not said moreover: *If We caused this Qoran to descend upon a mountain, thou wouldst see the mountain lying prostrate with humility, rent asunder through fear of God....*[6]

[1] This is a paraphrase of Ibn Qayyim. The full text in question is on p. 43 of pt. 3 in the *Manār* edition of the *Madārij*.

[2] Ibn Mājah, *Iqāmah*, 176.

[3] A mystic contemporary of the Shaikh, a man only 6 years older than him but very far removed in space, said in an unforgettable description of the Red Indian ritual lamentation: 'Until now I had only been trying to weep, but now I really wept. . . .' (*Black Elk Speaks*, by J. G. Neihardt, p. 187).

[4] The Jews and Christians.

[5] Qoran, V, 83.

[6] Qoran, LIX, 21

Why then can you not excuse hearts for being rent and bodies for swaying from side to side at what causes the rending of mountains? It is simply because you do not find within yourself what others find, for there are hearts, as indeed He has mentioned, *as hard as stones or even harder*[1]; or else it is because you have mentioned the Name of God and recited His Book merely by rote. . . . The Imam Ash-Shāfiʿī heard someone reciting: *This is a day on which they speak not, nor are they permitted to proffer excuses*,[2] whereupon he fainted and was carried to his house. But such occurrences do not call for much explanation, seeing that awe and rapture have caused even the death of many of our pious ancestors[3]. . . . Have you never read or heard His Words: *Only those are believers whose hearts thrill with awe at the remembrance of God*[4], and did you not know that the Prophet mentioned as being amongst his people "folk who enter Paradise and whose hearts are as the hearts of birds".[5] Where are we to find those referred to in these utterances if not among the Rememberers? No doubt you tell yourself that you are one of them. So answer me this, with God as your witness: Are you one of *those who remember God much*[6], or of those *whom neither bartering nor selling diverteth from the remembrance of God*, or of those *whom neither their possessions nor children divert from the remembrance of God*[7], or of those *who remember God standing and sitting and reclining upon their sides*,[8] or of those *whose hearts thrill with awe at the remembrance of God*, or of *those whose eyes overflow with tears when they hear what hath been revealed unto the Prophet*, or of those about whom the Prophet said: "The solitary ones take precedence, they who are utterly addicted to the remembrance of God",[9] or of those who are called mad through acting on the Prophet's injunction:

[1] Qoran, II, 84.

[2] Qoran, LXXVII, 35-6.

[3] *See* Hujwīrī, *Kashf al-Mahjūb*, ch. XXV; in Nicholson's translation, pp. 396-7.

[4] Qoran, VIII, 2.

[5] Muslim, *Jannah*, 27; Ibn Hanbal, II, 331.

[6] Qoran, XXXIII, 35.

[7] Qoran, LXIII, 9

[8] Qoran, III, 191.

[9] This Tradition is to be found, with very slight variations, in nearly all the canonical books, e.g. Muslim, *Dhikr*, 1.

"Multiply remembrance of God until they say: 'Madman!' "[1] or of those who are called pretenders because they act on his injunction: "Multiply remembrance of God until the hypocrites say: 'Verily ye are pretenders' "[2]? Tell me, I beg you, which group you belong to. Are you one of the sayers or the said? . . .

'If the grace of ecstasy is beyond you, it is not beyond you to believe that others may enjoy it. . . . None the less I do not say that dancing and manifestations of ecstasy are among the essentials of Sufism. But they are outward signs which come from submersion in remembrance. Let him who doubts try for himself, for hearsay is not the same as direct experience.'

The Prophet is said to have considered that of all his family the one who resembled him most was his cousin Jaʿfar to whom on one occasion he said: 'Thou art like me both in looks and in character,'[3] whereupon no words could express Jaʿfar's pleasure, and he danced in the Prophet's presence.

One of the last precepts given to the Shaikh Ad-Darqāwī by his Master, Shaikh ʿAlī al-Jamal, was that he and his followers should continue to follow the example of Jaʿfar ibn Abī Ṭālib in dancing to the Glory of God.[4]

Against the 'Mirror's' affirmation that 'anyone who considers dancing to be legal is an infidel', the Shaikh Al-ʿAlawī mentions the dancing of Jaʿfar, and also the dancing of a delegation of Abyssinians before the Prophet on one occasion in the mosque at Medina. But he adds:

'Do you imagine that the Sufis hold dancing to be absolutely lawful, just as you hold it to be absolutely unlawful? . . . It behoves the learned man not to pass any judgement about it until he knows what is the motive behind it, lest he forbid what God has allowed'.

Then, since going to meet ecstasy halfway is in reality answering a Divine Summons, he dismisses the question with

[1] Ibn Ḥanbal, III, pp. 68 and 73.
[2] Suyūṭī, *Al-Jāmiʿ aṣ-Ṣaghīr*.
[3] Ibn Ḥanbal, I, 108.
[4] For a list of these last precepts, see Rinn, *Marabouts et Khouan*, p. 233.

the following verses, which are attributed to Ibn Kamāl Pasha:

In wooing rapture there is no blame,
And none in swaying to and fro.
Thou risest if one call thy name
And on thy feet dost hurrying go.
He whom his Lord hath summonèd
May then go hurrying on his head.

He continues: 'Every lover is shaken at the mention (*dhikr*) of his beloved . . . and if love crept through the marrow of your bones, you would long to hear the mention of God, even from an infidel, and you would say, as the Sultan of the Lovers said:

"Mention of her is sweeter to me than all words else,
Even when alloyed by my censurers with their
blame of me."[1]

'Then you would know what it is to thrill with awe, and you would see whether you could retain the mastery over yourself or not. Have you not read in the Book of God about the women who cut their hands when Joseph came before them. *They said: Peerless is God's Glory! This is not of humankind.*[2] Now if such as this could happen through contemplating created beauty, why should not something of the kind happen at the contemplation of the Beauty of its Creator, when He appears in all the Splendour of His Greatness?

'Remembrance is the mightiest rule of the religion. . . . The law was not enjoined upon us, neither were the rites of worship ordained but for the sake of establishing the remembrance of God. The Prophet said: "The circumambulation round the Holy House, the passage to and fro between Ṣafā and Marwah[3],

[1] Ibn al-Fāriḍ's *Mīmiyyah* which begins *Adir dhikra man ahwā*, l.3.

[2] Qoran, XII, 31.

The Qoran tells here how Potiphar's wife invited some of the women of Egypt to her house so that, having seen Joseph for themselves, they would understand why she loved him and would excuse her. When he appeared before them they were so amazed at his beauty that they cut their hands in mistake for their food.

[3] Two rocks in Mecca (the wall of the Great Mosque comes near to Ṣafā, after which one of its gates is named) between which Hagar passed in search of water for herself and Ishmael. To pass between them seven times is one of the subsidiary rites of the Pilgrimage.

and the throwing of the pebbles were only ordained as a means of remembering God"[1]; and God Himself has said: *Remember God at the Holy Monument.*[2] Thus we know that the rite of stopping there was ordained for remembrance and not especially on account of the monument itself, just as the stay at Muna was also ordained for remembrance, not on account of the valley, for He has said: *Remember God during the appointed days.*[3] Moreover concerning the ritual prayer He has said: *Perform the prayer in remembrance of Me;*[4] and you will find other examples if you look through the Book. In a word, our performance of the rites of worship is considered strong or weak according to the degree of our remembrance of God while performing them. Thus when the Prophet was asked what spiritual strivers would receive the greatest reward, he replied: "Those who remembered God most". Then when questioned as to what fasters would be most rewarded he said: "Those who remembered God most", and when the prayer and the almsgiving and the pilgrimage and charitable donations were mentioned, he said of each: "The richest in remembrance of God is the richest in reward".

Among the already referred to last precepts given by the Shaikh ʿAlī al-Jamal to the Shaikh Ad-Darqāwī was the recommendation that he and his disciples should follow the example of the Prophet's Companion Abū Hurairah and wear their rosaries round their necks. The Shaikh Al-ʿAlawī made an exception for his more Oriental disciples and allowed them, if they wished, to carry their rosaries in their hands in conformity with the general practice of their countries. But he himself and his Algerian and Moroccan disciples, like the other Darqāwīs, continued to follow the injunction of the Shaikh ʿAlī al-Jamal. Their large flat wheel-shaped wooden beads make strikingly virile necklaces, very different from the smaller more delicate round-beaded Middle-Eastern rosaries

[1] Tirmidhī, *Ḥajj*, 64.

[2] Qoran, II, 198. This is a mound at a place called Muzdalifah where the Pilgrims spend the night after the day on Mount Arafat, and where each gathers 49 pebbles with which to stone Satan, represented by 3 stone pillars in the valley of Muna (between Arafat and Mecca) where they spend the next three days.

[3] Qoran, II, 203.

[4] Qoran, XX, 14.

which are often made of amber or mother-of-pearl and which are usually carried in the hand.

Both Western and Eastern rosaries have usually ninety-nine beads with a piece at the end called the *alif*, about the length and shape of a finger, to make up the hundred, this being the number most often specified by the Prophet for the recitation of formulae. When a formula is to be repeated a thousand times the Sufis often put ten pebbles or other objects in front of them, one of which they remove after each hundred. As to the shorter litanies each formula is usually repeated thirty-three times, and to facilitate this most rosaries have a small *alif* or other shaped division mark after the thirty-third bead and another after the sixty-sixth.

Beads were not used in the time of the Prophet, and therefore the author of the 'Mirror' added the rosary to his list of 'reprehensible innovations.'

'What is the difference,' replied the Shaikh, 'between counting with date-stones (for which you say there is a precedent) and counting with beads or any other ritually clean objects. You have affirmed that some of the Companions counted with pebbles instead of date-stones. Perhaps you object to beads because they are strung on a cord. But tradition reports that Abū Hurairah had a knotted cord[1] with a thousand knots in it and that he did not go to sleep until he had told it. Does not this come very near to the bead-strung rosary that is used today? And do you think that Abū Hurairah would have left his rosary behind if he had gone on a journey, for example, or that if the Prophet had seen him carrying it in his hand, or wearing it round his neck he would have censured him? Personally I do not think so—but God knoweth best.

'You complain that the rosary is shaped like a cross. By all that is marvellous, what has the form of a rosary to do with the cross? However, "the eye of hatred ferrets out faults". But if

[1] Necessity is the mother of invention, and since the Prophet continually recommended the repetition of formulae a specific number of times (the canonical books abound in Traditions to that effect), and since all are not equally good at counting on the fingers, as the Prophet himself appears to have done, without being distracted by the effort of counting from the formula itself, it would be strange if not a single one of the Companions had been able to devise so simple and practical an expedient as a knotted cord. There is no need to look further than this for the origin of the rosary in Islam.

a man must needs avoid, in what he eats and drinks and beholds, anything that comes anywhere near to being shaped like a cross, then your own form, in virtue of which you are a human being, comes far nearer to a cross than a rosary does. For you said of the rosary: "If the two division marks are long, then its resemblance to the cross shows up very clearly indeed".[1] But however long they may be, your own resemblance to the cross shows up far more clearly. If you stand up and stretch out your arms sideways, you will have no need to look for the cross in the rosary, for you will find it in yourself[2], and then you will be obliged to put an end to your own existence or at least take care never to see yourself, lest your sight should fall upon something that resembles a cross. But if God doomed you to make comparisons as regards the rosary, why did you liken it to the cross rather than to the garlands with which the Arabs used to garland both themselves and whatever they intended to give as an offering when they visited the Holy House of God, as a sign to prevent anyone from doing harm to the wearer of them. These garlands are ropes made of plaited rushes and the like, and God has praised the Arabs for this practice'.[3]

The 'Mirror' went on to qualify as hypocrites all those who use rosaries. The Shaikh replied:

'Even if we admit that there is no lack of hypocrites amongst those who use rosaries for glorifying God, there is certainly no lack of sincere worshippers either, so how can we possibly pass a general judgement? Have you everyone's conscience within your grasp? Probably if you asked the possessor of a rosary what is his intention in wearing it round his neck, he would say: "I find it prevents me from keeping company with fools and from

[1] The two short division marks of the Shaikh's rosary can be seen in plate II. To look anything like a cross, they would have to be not only much longer, but also exactly level.

[2] For many Moslems the cross is just something in the nature of an enemy flag; but for the Sufis it is a symbol of the highest significance. René Guénon dedicated his *Symbolism of the Cross* (Luzac & Co., 1958) to the memory of an older contemporary of the Shaikh Al-'Alawī, an eminent Egyptian Shādhilī Shaikh, 'Abd ar-Raḥmān 'Ulaish, to whom, as he (Guénon) says: 'I owe the first idea of this book.' Later he quotes him as having said: 'If Christians have the sign of the Cross, Moslems have its doctrine.'

[3] Qoran, V. 97.

entering places of ill repute, so I have put it here as a fetter upon my soul, for it says to me as clearly as if it could speak: 'Keep thy duty unto God. Thou are not one to commit flagrant acts of disobedience.' Is this anything but a pious intention? Similarly, if you questioned one who carries a rosary in his hand, he would probably say: "I hold it so that it may remind me of God whenever I forget to remember Him; for I have heard that the Prophet said: 'How excellent a remembrancer is a rosary!'[1]". Is this anything but a pious intention? . . . Similarly there are those who carry rosaries by way of imitating devout men, hoping to be eventually of their number, and this also is a pious intention. Then there are a few of those whom you described as hypocrites, *and they only remember God a little.*[2]

'It is such verses as this last which compel the Sufis to steep themselves in remembrance and to be quite open about it and to abound in it, so that they may pass out of the category of "little" into that of "much", thus escaping altogether from the qualification of hypocrites which is remembering God only a little. May God inspire both us and you to remember Him much—and to think well of His Saints!

'Then you started a new chapter: "Another error is imitating the infidels" . . . and you mentioned a number of innovations which are indeed to be avoided . . . but it was clear to me that you were just treading out the ground for an onslaught, with all your fury, upon the tombs of the righteous and those who visit them. If you had really aimed at stopping the imitation of the infidels, you would have written a chapter urging the need to guard against the scourge of foreign customs which now holds us in its grip and which is taking its unresisted course amongst our sons and our womenfolk. You would have urged us to keep to Islamic precedents and Arab ways, but instead of this you made pronouncements which for the most part could serve no purpose except to stir up discord amongst us.

'As to your pretext for stopping visits to tombs on the ground that the average Moslem believes that the dead Shaikh who is visited has power to give or withhold, etc., I do not think that

[1] Quoted from Dailamī's *Musnad al-Firdaus* by Suyūṭī in his *al-Minḥah fī 'ttikhādh as-subḥah*. See *al-Ḥāwī li 'l-Fatāwī*, II, pp. 139-44.

[2] Qoran, IV, 142. It is the Shaikh who adds this Qoranic definition of hypocrisy.

such a belief exists in any single member of the community. Moslems in general simply believe that there are intermediaries between them and God, and they seek their help in time of need,[1] for they have not yet reached the spiritual state you claim to have reached yourself, in which all mediation is abolished, and so they have recourse to what is nearer to God than they are, and that is all.

'As evidence of the profitlessness of visiting the dead you quoted the words of Ibn ʿArabī: "Verily the dead man is of no avail, for to avail is to act, and his action hath been suspended." Now I do not say that there is any mistake in these words of his, but I do say that there is a mistake in your understanding of what he meant. The dead man is of no avail as regards the training of the disciple and his furtherance upon the path of God. It is scarcely possible to receive the benefit of guidance without the companionship of a living man. But as to the benefit which is sought when one takes as intermediaries and intercessors with God the elect of His creatures, and when one seeks blessings at their shrines, this the Law gives us no option but to acknowledge, for the Law-giver has on the contrary allowed us to seek grace through what is altogether lifeless, such as the Black Stone and the Holy House, let alone forbidden us to do so through undefiled spirits and bodies whose substance is pure light.

'At any rate, you have played your part most dutifully; for having gone beyond all bounds in reviling the members of the Sufi brotherhoods and in cautioning people against keeping company with them, and having demonstrated that no good can come of associating with them while they are still alive, you were afraid lest someone might imagine that there might be some benefit in visiting them when they were dead, so you said: "Ibn ʿArabī said: 'Verily the dead man is of no avail.' " Then it became clear—and it is in fact the gist of your whole treatise—that both alive and dead they are good for nothing. This

[1] For example, round the tomb of Al-Ḥusain (the younger of the Prophet's two grandsons) near the Azhar in Cairo there revolves a circle of suppliants and pilgrims from early morning until late at night. Parents frequently bring sick children into the sanctuary and pass their hands over the outside of the shrine and then over their children's faces and heads. None of them asks the Saint himself to work the cure. But one often hears the prayer: 'O Lord Ḥusain, ask thy mother to ask her father to ask God to cure my child.'

is your judgement; and the Final Judgement is God's.'

Many of the features of the Shaikh's few months' travel after his Master's death are very typical of his life as a whole, and this is especially true of his visit to Tunis, with the somewhat furtive entry into the town to avoid meeting profane acquaintances, the dream about members of Sufi brotherhoods coming to him, his staying four days in the house until they actually came, and his finally going out with them and meeting and teaching many others. Particularly characteristic is his lack of plans as regards details and his continual reliance upon inspiration, in one form or another, to tell him what to do. Thus although he was by nature exclusive and aloof, and disinclined to mix with those who were not fuqarā, he never allowed a general rule to interfere with the particular law of each moment which came to him through the dictates of the Spirit, and it was certainly these dictates rather than his own inclination that imposed upon him a function which went far beyond the confines of his zāwiyah.

Ibn 'Abd al-Bāri' writes: 'Once when the Shaikh was in Algiers he was followed on his way to the Great Mosque by a crowd of over a hundred, men who, far from being initiates were mostly no more than Moslems in name. When they reached the door of the mosque he told them to go in with him, which they did. Then he told them to sit down, and sitting down himself in their midst he preached to them. When he had finished they turned to God in repentance and gave the Shaikh their oaths and made covenants with him that they would never revert to their former state.'[1]

He also mentions[2] that when the Shaikh stayed for a few days in the country, it sometimes happened that almost the whole countryside would come to him for initiation. If they did not aspire to follow the path, they came for the 'initiation of blessing'. Another disciple writes: 'You would find sitting in front of him hundreds, nay, thousands, with heads bowed as if birds were hovering round them and hearts full of awe and eyes wet with tears, in silent understanding of what they heard him say.'[3]

[1] *Shahā'id*, p. 95, note 1.
[2] *Ibid.*, p. 140, note 2.
[3] *Ibid.*, p. 140

Another writes: 'I went to a Shaikh in Bijāyah and took initiation from him after he had prescribed for me, as a condition of this, a considerable number of daily litanies. I persevered in reciting them regularly, and after a while he ordered me to fast every day and to eat (after sunset) only barley bread soaked in water. I kept to this also, and then he transmitted to me the seven Divine Names[1] especially used for invocation in the Khalwatī Ṭarīqah. Then after a few days he ordered me to go and give guidance to others and as soon as I heard this from him I shuddered with dismay and disappointment, for I knew that this was not what I had been looking for. I had only received from him certain vague indications which I did not understand the meaning of, and when I told him of this he sharply forbade me ever to make such confessions again either in front of him, or in front of my fellow disciples for fear that it should cause them misgivings. . . . I left this Shaikh and set about looking for one more worth cleaving to the company of, until by the Grace of God I came into contact with this supreme Master Shaikh Sidi Aḥmad Al-'Alawī through the intermediary of one of his disciples,[2] who prepared me by giving me *Al-Minaḥ al-Quddūsiyyah* to read. Then when the Master himself came to our part of the country[3] I renewed my initiatory oath of allegiance to him, whereupon he transmitted to me the invocation of the Name as practised by his followers, and told me I could invoke it wherever possible, in secret solitude or openly, in company. He stayed in our country for thirteen days, and in that time about two thousand men, women and boys entered the Ṭarīqah. Then after he returned to Mostaganem I went to him there and he sent me into *khalwah*. I stayed there for six days, and gained from this all that I had previously hoped for'. The Shaikh's visit to those parts was in 1919. The last quoted disciple, writing five years later, during which time he had become a Muqaddam, says that in the Shaikh's name he had received more than six thousand into the order and supervised their spiritual retreats, not counting those who stop short at the 'initiation of blessing.' He adds that many among these

[1] These are: (i) *Lā ilāha illa 'Llāh* (there is no god but God), (ii) *Allāh*, (iii) *Huwa* (He), (iv) *Al-Ḥaqq* (the Truth), (v) *Al-Ḥayy* (the Living), (vi) *Al-Qayyūm* (Self-Sufficient), (vii) *Al-Qahhār* (the Irresistible). See Rinn, pp. 300-1.

[2] That is, he received initiation from one of his Muqaddams.

[3] 'Arsh al-Ja'farah in the province of Constantina.

thousands had been given permission to guide others, remarking that 'it was not the Shaikh's practice to authorize anyone to give guidance except after his soul had been purified and his inward eye had been opened to the Divine Light.'[1]

Most of the Shaikh's Muqaddams represented him in their own towns or villages, but some of them travelled from place to place. One of these tells how the Shaikh sent him and others to travel among the tribes in desert places, forbidding them to accept any invitations to meals except in so far as was absolutely necessary. He told them to ask for nothing except water for the ablution. When questioned about their reluctance to accept hospitality they used to say: 'We have only come to you so that you may take guidance from us upon the path or at least that you may give us your oaths always to perform the prayers at the right time with as much piety as you can muster.'[2]

In short, the Shaikh's life might well lead Massignon to revise his judgement that the school of Ibn 'Arabī (to which the Shaikh Al-'Alawī unquestionably belongs) 'put an end to the outward radiation of Islamic mysticism throughout society as a whole.'[3]

The book from which most of these last quotations are taken contains many letters from the Shaikh's disciples, describing their relationship with him, and most of these letters end with a mention of the spiritual realization which they achieved at his hands, 'the opening of the Heart to the Divine Light.' Not infrequently the realization is spoken of in absolute terms; and in most cases he appears to have relinquished his guidance as though the path were ended. In general the letters seemed to me strangely incompatible with what he said to Dr Carret about the extreme rarity of full spiritual realization. I mentioned this to one of his disciples, and I forget the exact words of his reply but the gist of it was as follows:

'No doubt the fuqarā tended to speak of their realization in too absolute a way; but it is true that very many of them had at least some realization, and the whole zāwiyah was vibrant

[1] *Shahā'id*, pp. 122-4.
[2] *Ibid.*, p. 158
[3] *Essai*, p. 80.

with spiritual drunkenness. The Shaikh demanded that the disciple should be as wax in his hands, and he was quite ruthless in his method. He would put them in *khalwah* for weeks at a time if need be, and sometimes for months. For many of the fuqarā, even for most, this was difficult to endure; but what might have been intolerable in other circumstances was made relatively easy because the Shaikh knew how to provoke 'a state of spiritual concentration.'[1] None the less, some of the fuqarā would come out of *khalwah* almost in a state of collapse, dazed in both body and soul, but the Shaikh was indifferent to this provided that some degree of direct knowledge had been achieved. Moreover the faqīr would usually recover his balance very soon, while at the same time a complete break had been made between him and his former life. Some of them for example had been to all appearances just ordinary manual labourers for whom, apart from their work, life had meant no more than begetting children and sitting in cafes. But now their interests were all centred upon God, and their great joy was to perform the *dhikr*.'

'But why', I asked, 'did not the Shaikh always continue his guidance rigorously until the end of the path?'

'Because in a sense a faqīr can be his own guide after a certain point has been reached. Besides in the case of most of his disciples the Shaikh knew that he had already, by a special Grace, achieved as it were the impossible. That the soul should be open to the Divine Light, even with so small an opening as to allow only a glimmer to pass through, was enough to satisfy the utmost aspirations and capabilities of the vast majority for the rest of their life on earth. It remained for them to treasure what they had gained and to consolidate it, which was not difficult thanks to the protective surroundings of the traditional civilization in which they lived. It was these surroundings which neutralized the dangers inherent in such a method.'

According to Berque the Shaikh was accused of hypnotizing his disciples, and Berque himself adds that in his opinion the accusation was not unjustified. But whatever word one uses for what the Shaikh himself often refers to as his 'wine', there

[1] These last four words translate the single word *ḥāl* which is used by the Sufis in a very wide sense, extending sometimes beyond a state of concentration to one of illumination.

can be no doubt that it was quite different from hypnotism in the ordinary sense, and that in some respects it was the very opposite. For although he demanded that his disciples should be 'as passive as a corpse in the hands of the washer of the dead', this passivity was not in the least mediumistic. On the contrary, it presupposed on the part of the disciple an undercurrent of extreme spiritual activity which was destined in the end to rise to the surface and to replace the activity of the Master. As he himself says in describing his own Master's method, which he inherited: 'In all this the Shaikh would watch over him and strengthen him in the *dhikr* degree by degree until he finally reached a point of being conscious of what he perceived through his own power, and the Shaikh would not be satisfied until this point was reached.'

Reliance on the inspiration of the moment is one of the mystic's essential features, and in its full maturity this reliance is no less than an aspect of the supreme spiritual state which is the goal of all mysticism. Although the term *Al-Insān al-Kāmil* ('Perfect Man' or 'Universal Man'), which is used by the Ṣufis to denote this state, infinitely transcends human nature ('man' being used here above all symbolically to indicate the Perfection in whose image he was created), it none the less includes, on the earthly plane, an integral human perfection, which implies not only a static flawlessness but also, dynamically, a perfect reaction to every circumstance of life, that is, a reaction which is in complete conformity with the Will of Heaven; and when there is no other means, legal or traditional, of knowing where the 'wind' lies, such a reaction can only be achieved by following the inspiration of the moment. The Shaikh was fond of quoting the verse:

> Submit unto Salmā[1], go whither she goeth,
> And follow the winds of Fate, turn whither they turn[2].

[1] A woman's name symbolizing a Divine Attribute, perhaps Wisdom as in Ibn 'Arabī's *Tarjumān al-Ashwāq*, IV.

[2] *Minaḥ*, p. 42. This verse has its place in the Shaikh's heritage, for when Aḥmad Zarrūq, one of his spiritual ancestors, took a last farewell of his Master, Aḥmad al-Ḥaḍramī and asked him for a final precept, he simply replied: 'Submit unto Salmā . . .', and having finished the line, would say no more. See 'Abd Allāh Gannūn, *Mashāhīr Rijāl al-Maghrib, Aḥmad Zarrūq*, p. 11.

Similarly he remarks that the inward essence of *islām* (submission to the Divine Will), an essence to which only the elect can penetrate, is *istislām* (going to meet the Divine Will in utter compliance)[1].

It is in virtue of his *istislām*, which denotes a perpetual state of expectant but serene readiness to act at a moment's notice, that the fully realized mystic is the most practical[2] of men. This truth was impressed upon Berque by his visits to Mostaganem. He quotes Delacroix as having remarked that 'most great mystics have had the gift of creative action'[3] and of the Shaikh Al-ʿAlawī he himself says: 'His faith was full to overflowing and communicated itself to others in a cascade of lyrical eloquence. But at the same time he retained a keen sense of facts and how to make the best of them. He belonged to that class of men, often to be met with in North Africa, who can pass without transition from deep thought to action, from the mysteries of the next world to the life of this, from the vast sweep of ideas to the smallest details of native politics'[4].

It was his practicality, in view of the ignorance and limited understanding of great numbers of those who were attached to him, which prompted him to write, in addition to his more profound and abstruse works, one or two very simple expositions of the elements of Islam[5], which differ none the less from the ordinary exoteric catechisms in that they always have an opening, explicitly or implicitly, on to the domain of esoterism. It was a principle of the ʿAlawī Ṭarīqah that the first thing to be done with a novice was to teach him his ordinary religious obligations according to his capacity.

Another result of the Shaikh's acceptance of facts, however much they might go against his own natural inclinations, was that in 1922 he started a religious weekly newspaper, *Lisān*

[1] *Minaḥ*, p. 151.

[2] The wide-spread opinion to the contrary springs partly from failure to understand what mysticism is and, in consequence, from counting as mystics those who are not or those who have only a touch of the mystic about them, and partly from the fact that true mystics never consider this world as a self-sufficient whole but only as a fragment of the Universe. What seems to be practical from a worldly point of view may be grossly unpractical from a more universal point of view, and *vice versa*.

[3] *Études d'histoire et de psychologie du mysticisme.*

[4] p. 693.

[5] See Appendix A (6, 11, 13)

ad-Dīn, which in 1926 he replaced by another with a wider scope, *Al-Balāgh al-Jazā'irī*. Both were published in Algiers. *Al-Balāgh* in particular, which was continued for a few years even after the Shaikh's death, served a double purpose. We have already seen that it had been part of the Shaikh Al-Būzīdī's method to insist on his disciples 'recognizing the truth and acknowledging it whatever it might be', and that 'he had gone on giving them the means of doing this until it had become second nature to them.' The Shaikh Al-'Alawi was as well aware as his Master had been that no purification is complete if it does not include the purification from false ideas as well as from other psychic impurities, and one of the purposes of *Al-Balāgh* was to bestow as far as possible on his disciples a just and objective outlook in every respect. For example, although he continually and strenuously opposed the activities of Christian missionaries in Algeria and other Islamic countries, he none the less defended them against many of the usual attacks and pointed out that for the most part far from being the conscious political instruments of their respective countries they were continually exhorting their governments to make sacrifices as regards material interests. 'But why', he adds, 'do not these missionaries care more for the spiritual welfare of their own people?'[1]

Apart from his disciples, Al-Balāgh was for the community at large. It was his means of preaching a renovation of Islam in all its aspects, not puritanically, as one who seeks to strip his religion of everything that goes beyond his understanding, but on the contrary seeking to safeguard its dimension of breadth and above all to restore what it had lost of its dimension of depth.

'If Islam could speak,' he writes, 'it would complain to God, enumerating all the evils which assail it.'[2] But he asserts continually that of all the dangers which beset Islam, by far the greatest come from certain Moslems, and he makes it no secret that he is referring to those exoteric authorities of the group known as As-Salafiyyah who claimed to be 'reformers', a word which often aroused his anger and sarcasm, prompting him to quote from the Qoran: *And when it is said to them: 'Cause not*

[1] Jan. 9, 1931.
[2] April 17, 1931.

corruption in the land', they say: 'We are nothing if not reformers.' Nay, unknown to themselves they are workers of corruption.[1] This group was particularly hostile to the Sufi brotherhoods whom they looked on as one of the most powerful factors for the maintenance of those 'superstitions' which they aimed at eradicating, and their weekly paper, *Ash-Shihāb,* which was published at Constantina, often contained attacks on Sufism.

To one of these the Shaikh replied at some length, and published his reply as a serial in *Al-Balāgh.* The general situation, which the reader is never allowed to forget, is summed up in the following verses:

O thou that buttest the high mountain,
Seeking to dislodge it with thy horns, take pity,
Not on the mountain, but on thy head.

Then after examining somewhat unmercifully the text of *Ash-Shihāb,* he goes on to the main part of his treatise which is to show that the Sufis have been venerated by all the authoritative classes of the community from the first century of Islam until the present day. This he demonstrated by an anthology of quotations, mostly from very eminent exoteric authorities, in praise of Sufism, and one cannot help feeling that the editors of *Ash-Shihāb* must have regretted having provoked it. At one point the Shaikh himself breaks in:

'There is no religious authority or man of learning in Islam who has not a due respect for the path of the Folk, either through direct experience of it[2] in spiritual realization, or else through firm belief in it, except those who suffer from chronic short-sightedness and remissness and lack of aspiration and who *prefer to take what is inferior in exchange for the superior.*[3] As for the believer of high aspiration, his soul by its very nature strains yearningly upwards towards what lies beyond these conditions that surround us, in the hope that he may chance upon some spiritual perfume or holy breath of inspiration which has strayed from the next world and which will be as a

[1] II, 11-2.
[2] There were many Qadis and Muftis among his own disciples.
[3] Qoran, II, 61.

lamp in his hand to light him upon his path. God says: *Whoso striveth after Us, verily We shall lead them upon Our paths*[1], and indeed the true believer looks unceasingly for one who will take him to God, or at the very least he looks for the spiritual gifts which lie hidden within him, that is, for the primordial nature which he has lost sight of and in virtue of which he is human. It is characteristic of man that his soul should tend upwards beyond those inclinations to cleave to the earth which are what connects him with the lower animal species.'

One of the last quotations in the anthology is from Muhammad 'Abduh,[2] who was both Grand Mufti of Egypt and Rector of the Azhar University:

The Sufis are concerned with the cure of Hearts and purification from all that obstructs the inward eye. They seek to take their stand in Spirit before the Face of the All-Highest Truth until they are drawn away from all else by Him, their essences being extinguished in His Essence and their qualities in His Qualities. The Gnostics amongst them, those who have come to the end of their journey, are in the highest rank of human perfection after the Prophets[3].

After quoting from one or two authorities of his own generation, the Shaikh draws his treatise to a close:

'I do not deny, my brother, the existence of many intruders among the Sufis—only too many—who deserve censure, and if you had concentrated on these, no one could have blamed you. Moreover you would have had a good deed to your own credit, while doing us, in particular, a service at the same time. What offended us was your vilification of the way of the Folk altogether, and your speaking ill of its men without making any exceptions, and this is what prompted me to put before you these quotations from some of the highest religious authorities. At the very least they should impel you to consider

[1] Qoran, XXIX, 69.
[2] d. 1905.
[3] His gloss on the word *Ṣūfī* in his edition of Badī' az-Zamān al-Hamadhānī's *Maqāmāt*, p. 29.

your brothers the Sufis as members of the community of true believers, every individual of whom both we and you are bound to respect. The Prophet said: "Whoso prayeth our prayer and useth our orientation and eateth of our sacrifices, the same is a Moslem, and he is under a pact of protection from God and His Messenger. So cause not the pact of God to be violated." '[1,2]

Apart from criticisms in print, the Shaikh also had visits from those who felt that some of the 'Alawī practices were un-Islamic.[3] One such visitor objected to the practice of repeating over and over again the Divine Name *Allāh* without any 'grammatical context'. For him the Qoranic insistence on *dhikr Allāh* meant prayer to God or praise of God, and nothing more. Generally speaking, it may be said that the need for a more concentrated mode of worship in addition to and beyond prayer and praise in the ordinary sense is felt or not, and understood or not, according to the depth or shallowness of the centre from which one's deepest worship springs. If as in most cases this centre is nearer to the mind, which is the faculty of analysis, a more analytical form of worship will meet the needs of the worshippers. But the deeper the centre, the nearer it will be to the Heart, which is the faculty of synthesis. Litany comes as it were from midway between the Heart and the head. The speed and rhythm with which its formulae are repeated confers on them a synthetic quality, although in themselves they nearly always express analytical thought. Beyond litany is invocation in the sense of the word *dhikr*. This is a cry from the Heart, or from near to the Heart[4], and

[1] Bukhārī, *Ṣalāt*, 28

[2] *Risālat an-Nāṣir Ma'rūf*, pp. 127-8.

[3] Occasionally such visits took an unexpected turn: Sidi 'Alī aṣ-Ṣadaqāwī, one of the Shaikh's most devoted disciples tells us that he first visited the Shaikh to criticize him (*Shahā'id*, p. 104); and the compiler of the *Shahā'id* adds that he now sees many among the disciples who had first come to the zāwiyah with hostile intentions.

[4] Particular circumstances may suddenly lay bare, in the soul, a centre far deeper and far nearer the Heart than anything it had been conscious of before. A case in point is that of three men who were marooned in Greenland during the war for 11 days, and eventually saved, although at one time they had their hopes suddenly raised from near desperation only to be dashed again.

'The mood of the three marooned men changed from ecstasy to doubt and misgiving, and then to desperation. It seemed that the ship on which their last no 'raiment' is more perfectly suited to such a cry than a single Divine Name.

In answer to his critic the Shaikh published as a serial in *Al-Balāgh al-Jazā'irī* a short treatise[1] on the repetition of the Name *Allāh*. Here are a few extracts:

'You know, my brother, that every name has an influence which attaches itself to the soul of him who mentions it even if it is not one of the Divine Names. For example, if a man repeat several times the word "death", he will feel an imprint upon his soul owing to the mention of that name, especially if he persists in it, and there is no doubt that this imprint will be different from that which is experienced from mentioning "wealth" or "glory" or "power".

'Any reasonably sensitive man will be conscious of the influence upon his soul of the name that he mentions, and if we admit this, we are bound to believe that the Name of God also produces an influence upon the soul as other names do, each one leaving the particular imprint that corresponds to it. I think you are aware that a name is ennobled with the nobility of him who is named inasmuch as it carries his imprint in the hidden fold of its secret essence and its meaning.'[2]

He quotes from Ghazālī's commentary on the Divine Names with regard to the Name Allāh: 'That which the slave getteth from this name is deification (*ta'alluh*), by which I mean that his heart and his purpose are drowned in God, so that he seeth naught but Him.'[3]

---

hope rested had been abandoned. There was no sign of life on board.

'For the next three hours they knelt in the sunshine, praying continually. There was only one prayer they all knew, and they chanted it together unceasingly, as children recite a memorized lesson, uncomprehendingly.

' "Our Father, which art in heaven . . ." they chanted right through to the end, and then straightway back to the beginning again, hundreds of times, as though rescue depended absolutely on their maintaining an unbroken stream of prayer.'

(*Sunday Express*, January 25th, 1959.)

A child's recitation of lessons often falls *short* of the mind. But if these men prayed 'uncomprehendingly', that is, if they did not analyse what they were saying, it was because although the form of their prayer was analytical, the centre it sprang from lay far *beyond* the mind—beyond prayer in the ordinary sense, and perhaps even beyond litany.

[1] *Al-Qaul al-Mu'tamad.*

[2] *Al-Qaul al-Mu'tamad*, pp. 5-6.

[3] *Al-Maqṣad al-Asnā*, p. 38 (Cairo, A.H. 1322)

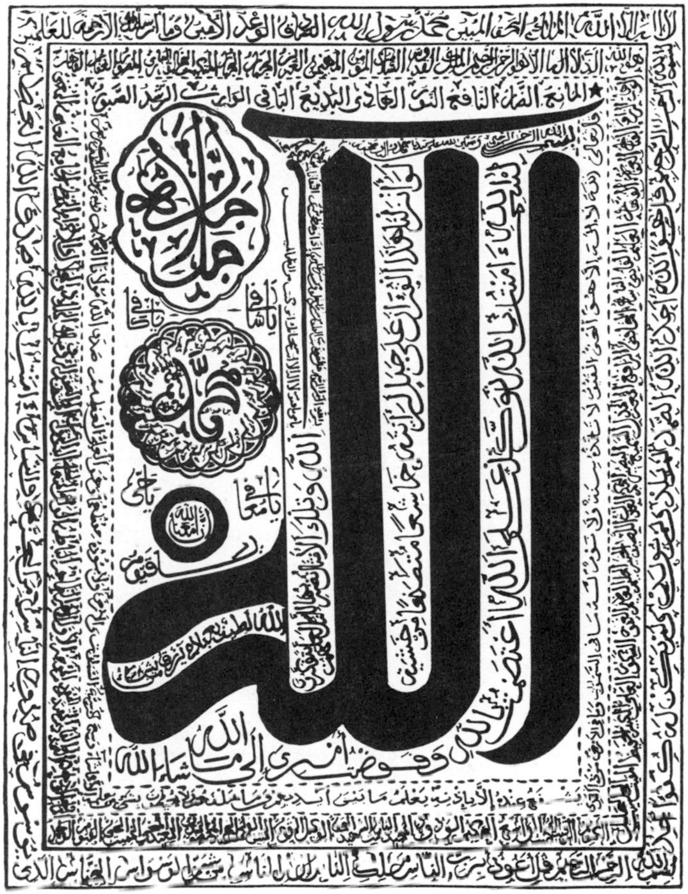

The Supreme Name *Allāh*, surrounded by other Divine Names and verses from the Qoran. The four letters of *Allāh* are, reading from right to left, *alif*, *lām*, *lām*, *hā'*. Between the last two a second *alif* is pronounced but not written.

The following argument is typical of the Shaikh, both as regards its somewhat disconcerting unexpectedness and also as an example of his readiness to meet his critics on their own ground.

'The question of invocation is of wider scope than you imagine. A sick man lay groaning in the presence of the Prophet and one of the Companions told him to stop and to be patient, whereupon the Prophet said: "Let him groan, for groaning is one of the Names of God in which the sick man may find relief".'[1]

'Now suppose that the sick man had been repeating the Name of Majesty *Allāh! Allāh!* instead of *Ah! Ah!*, would that Companion's objection have been justified. . . ?

'This is surely enough to make a man think well of the rememberers, whatever their method of remembrance. But supposing that all I have said so far does not convince you as a logical proof, then it is only fair to say that the question is one about which we must agree to differ. In other words, it is a matter for *ijtihād*[2], and on what pretext, my brother, would you compel us to accept your way of thinking and subscribe to your *ijtihād* when we have done nothing to compel you to subscribe to ours?'[3]

He goes on to quote what various authorities have said about the invocation of the Name, as for example: 'Abū Ḥāmid al-Ghazālī said: 'First of all I sought to make my way upon the path of the mystics with many litanies and much fasting and prayer. Then when God had proved the sincerity of my purpose, He decreed that I should meet one of His Saints, who said to me: "My son, rid thy heart of all attachment save unto God, and go apart by thyself and say with all thy powers of concentration *Allāh Allāh Allāh*".'[4] He also said, I mean Ghazālī: "When thy thoughts are muddied with other than God, thou hast need of the negation *lā ilāha*[5]. But once thou hast

[1] Suyūṭī, *Al-Jāmi' aṣ-Ṣaghīr*.
[2] See p. 44.
[3] *Al-Qaul al-Mu'tamad*, pp. 13-4.
[4] Quoted from Ibn 'Ajībah's commentary on Ibn al-Bannā' at-Tujībī's *Al-Mabāḥith al-Aṣliyyah*. See also Ghazālī's *Mīzān al-'Amal*, pp. 44-5.
[5] 'There is no god . . .', the negative and therefore illusion-destroying half of the affirmation of Divine Unity, *lā ilāha illa'Llāh*, 'there is no god but God'.

withdrawn from all things in contemplation of Him who is the Lord of all, thou takest thy rest in *Say Allāh, and leave them to their idle prating*'[1]. Then he said: 'When thou hast finished recalling that which never was and art busied with the remembrance of Him who ever is, thou sayest *Allāh* and takest thy rest from all else.' He also said: 'Open the door of thy Heart with the key of thy saying *lā ilāha illa 'Llāh* and the door of thy Spirit by saying *Allāh*, and lure down the bird of thy Secret by saying *Huwa Huwa*[2,3].

Apart from the Shaikh's vindications of Sufism, *Al-Balāgh* contains some of his attacks on the so-called 'Reformers' for their continual yielding to the modern age at the expense of the religion. At the same time he exhorts the heads of zāwiyahs to practise what they preach. As regards the world in general he takes his stand against all anti-religious movements and in particular against communism. For Moslems he stresses the importance of raising the general level of knowledge of classical Arabic. He denounces the practice of becoming naturalized French citizens[4]. Again and again he points out the dangers of westernization, that is, of adopting European habits of thought and life, and in particular he condemns those Moslems who wear modern European dress[5].

As a spiritual guide, and therefore a supreme psychologist, he knew that clothes, which are the immediate ambient of the human soul, have incalculable powers of purification and corruption. It is not for nothing that the contemplative and other orders of Christianity, like those of Buddhism for example, have kept throughout the centuries to a dress that was designed and instituted by a spiritual authority bent on choosing a garb compatible with the wearer's dedicated life. Moreover, generally speaking, apart from such examples, one may say that in all theocratic civilizations, that is, in all

[1] Qoran, VI, 91.

[2] 'He is He', or else it may be understood as a repeated invocation of the Divine Name 'He'.

[3] *Al-Qaul al-Mu'tamad*, p. 15.

[4] By becoming a French citizen an Algerian Moslem becomes altogether subject to French law, whereas non-French Algerian Moslems are entitled to remain, at any rate in certain respects, subject to Qoranic law.

[5] For the various references to *Al-Balāgh*, see Berque, pp. 718-28.

civilizations but the modern one, dress has been more or less dictated by the consciousness that man is the representative of God on earth, and nowhere is this truer than in the Islamic civilization. In particular the Arab dress of North-West Africa, the turban, burnus and jallabah, which has remained unchanged for hundreds of years, is an unsurpassed combination of simplicity, sobriety and dignity, retaining these qualities even when in rags.

Al-Balāgh was strenuously attacked by the modernists and also, as was to be expected, by the Salafiyyah reformist group, and *Ash-Shihāb*, kept up an almost undiminished hostility until 1931, when the editor, Bin-Bādis, happened to come to Mostaganem, and both he and the Shaikh were invited to a wedding feast. Although the Shaikh was in bad health at the time—it was barely three years before his death—he accepted the invitation since it is against the wont of the Prophet to refuse to go to a wedding, and having come face to face there with the editor in question, he invited him to the zāwiyah. In the next number of *Ash-Shihāb* there appeared the following item of news:

'A supper was given by Shaikh Sidi Aḥmad Bin-'Alīwah and it was attended by some of the leading men of Mostaganem, together with about one hundred of the Shaikh's pupils. The Shaikh himself was exceedingly cordial and gracious to the point of serving some of the guests with his own hands. . . . After supper verses from the Qoran were recited, and then the Shaikh's pupils began to chant some of the odes of 'Umar ibn al-Fārid which they did so beautifully that their audience was greatly moved.[1] The pleasure of the evening was further enhanced in between the singing by literary discussions about the meaning of some of the verses; and among the many examples of courtesy shown us by our host the Shaikh, I was particularly struck by the fact that he never once touched on any point of disagreement between us by so much as a single allusion that might have compelled me to express my opinion or to defend it. Our conversation all turned on those many questions about

[1] Berque (p. 753) quotes the Shaikh as having said to him: 'Music is not crippled with the dry bones of words. Liquid and flowing like a stream, it carries us into the Presence of God.'

which we are in perfect agreement, avoiding those few points about which our opinions differ.'

By this time the Shaikh had zāwiyahs not only all over North Africa[1], founded by himself in person—he often made short journeys of the kind described in his autobiography—or by one of his Muqaddams, but also in Damascus, in Palestine (at Jaffa, Gaza and Faluja), in Aden, Addis Abbaba, Marseilles, Paris[2], the Hague and Cardiff[3]; and from all these outlying zāwiyahs there was a continual stream of pilgrims to Mostaganem.

I will let the following quotation[4] bring this summary account of the Shaikh's life to a close:

'The idea which is the secret essence of each religious form, making each what it is by the action of its inward presence, is too subtle and too deep to be personified with equal intensity by all those who breathe its atmosphere. So much the greater good fortune is it to come into contact with a true spiritual representative of one of those forms (worlds which the modern West fails to understand), to come into contact with someone who represents in himself, and not merely because he happens to belong to a particular civilization, the idea which for hundreds of years has been the very life-blood of that civilization.

'To meet such a one is like coming face to face, in mid-twentieth century, with a mediaeval Saint or a Semitic Patriarch, and this was the impression made on me by the Shaikh

[1] As early as 1923 he was quoted in the *Echo d'Oran* (Sept. 13th) as having said that he had at least 100,000 disciples. Four years later Probst-Biraben wrote in *Revue Indigène* that he had more than double this number (Berque, p. 766).

[2] In 1926 he was invited to preach the fi st sermon and lead the first prayer at the inauguration of the Paris Mosque. Berque quotes from a letter by a Fransciscan Father who saw him, surrounded by several of his disciples, 'sitting on a sheep-skin on the second class deck of the boat which took us to Marseilles' (p. 737).

[3] For an account of the 'Alawī Zāwiyah at Cardiff, see *Yemeni Arabs in Britain* by R. B. Serjeant in the *Geographical Magazine*, August, 1944. The Shaikh had many Yemeni disciples, mostly seamen, who established zāwiyahs at various ports of call including not only Cardiff but also subsequently, after his death, at Liverpool, Hull and South Shields, and inland at Birmingham.

[4] *Rahimahu Llah* by Frithjof Schuon in *Cahiers du Sud*, Août-Septembre, 1935.

Al-Ḥājj Aḥmad Bin-ʿAlīwah, one of the greatest Masters of Sufism, who died a few months ago at Mostaganem.

'In his brown jallabah and white turban, with his silver-grey beard and his long hands which seemed when he moved them to be weighed down by the flow of his *barakah* (blessing), he exhaled something of the pure archaic ambiance of Sayyidnā Ibrāhīm al-Khalīl[1]. He spoke in a subdued, gentle voice, a voice of splintered crystal from which, fragment by fragment, he let fall his words. . . . His eyes, which were like two sepulchral lamps, seemed to pierce through all objects, seeing in their outer shell merely one and the same nothingness, beyond which they saw always one and the same reality—the Infinite. Their look was very direct, almost hard in its enigmatic unwaveringness, and yet full of charity. Often their long ovals would grow suddenly round as if in amazement or as if enthralled by some marvellous spectacle. The cadence of the singing, the dances and the ritual incantations seemed to go on vibrating in him perpetually; his head would sometimes rock rhythmically to and fro while his soul was plunged in the unfathomable mysteries of the Divine Name, hidden in the *dhikr*, the Remembrance. . . . He gave out an impression of unreality, so remote was he, so inaccessible, so difficult to take in on account of his altogether abstract simplicity. . . . He was surrounded, at one and the same time, with all the veneration that is due to saints, to leaders, to the old, and to the dying.'

[1] 'Abraham the Friend (of God)'.

PART TWO

THE DOCTRINE

CHAPTER V

ONENESS OF BEING

'Since Mysticism in all ages and countries is fundamentally the same, however it may be modified by its peculiar environment and by the positive religion to which it clings for support, we find remote and unrelated systems showing an extraordinarily close likeness and even coinciding in many features of verbal expression. . . . Many writers on Sufism have disregarded this principle; hence the confusion which long prevailed.'

In the light of this timely remark by Nicholson[1], no one should be surprised to find that the doctrine of the Oneness of Being (*Waḥdat al-Wujūd*), which holds a central place in all the orthodox mysticisms of Asia, holds an equally central place in Sufism.

As is to be expected in view of its centrality, some of the most perfect, though elliptical, formulations of this doctrine are to be found in the Qoran, which affirms expressly: *Wheresoe'er ye turn, there is the Face of God*[2]. *Everything perisheth but His Face.*[3]

All that is therein[4] *suffereth extinction, and there remaineth the Face of thy Lord in Its Majesty and Bounty*[5].

Creation, which is subject to time and space and non-terrestrial modes of duration and extent which the human imagination cannot grasp, is 'then' (with reference to both past and future) and 'there', but it is never truly 'now' and 'here'. The True Present is the prerogative of God Alone, for It is no less than the Eternity and Infinity which transcends, penetrates and embraces all durations and extents, being not only 'before' all beginnings but also 'after' all ends. In It, that is, in the Eternal Now and Infinite Here, all that is perishable has 'already' perished, all that is liable to extinction has 'already' been extinguished leaving only God, and it is to this Divine

[1] *A Literary History of the Arabs*, p. 384.
[2] II, 115.
[3] XXVIII, 88.
[4] In the created universe.
[5] LV, 26-7.

Residue, the Sole Lord of the Present, that the word *remaineth* refers in the last quoted Qoranic verse. From this verse, amongst others, come the two Sufic terms *fanā'* (extinction) and *baqā'* (remaining)[1] which express respectively the Saint's extinction in God and his Eternal Life in God, or rather *as* God.

The doctrine of Oneness of Being is also implicit in the Divine Name *al-Ḥaqq*, the Truth, the Reality, for there could be no point in affirming Reality as an essential characteristic of Godhead if anything other than God were real. The word 'Being' expresses this Absolute Reality, for it refers to That which is, as opposed to that which is not, and Oneness of Being is the doctrine that behind the illusory veil of created plurality there lies the one Divine Truth—not that God is made up of parts[2], but that underlying each apparently separate feature of the created universe there is the One Infinite Plenitude of God in His Indivisible Totality.

The Treatise on Oneness[3] says: 'When the secret of an atom of the atoms is clear, the secret of all created things both external and internal is clear, and thou dost not see in this world or the next aught beside God.'[4]

[1] 'The spiritual state of *baqā'*, to which Sufi contemplatives aspire, (the word signifies pure "subsistence" beyond all form) is the same as the state of *moksha* or "deliverance" spoken of in Hindu doctrines, just as the "extinction" (al-fanā') of the individuality which precedes the "subsistence" is analogous to *nirvana* taken as a negative idea'. (Titus Burckhardt, *An Introduction to Sufi Doctrine*, p. 4, published by Muhammad Ashraf, Lahore, 1959—a book which is almost indispensable to anyone who wishes to make a serious study of Sufism and who does not read Oriental texts.)

[2] It is probably failure to grasp this point which is at the root of most Western misunderstandings. Massignon for example says that *Waḥdat al-Wujūd*—which he unhappily translates 'existentialist monism'—means that 'the totality of all beings in all their actions is divinely adorable' (Encyclopaedia of Islam, *Taṣawwuf*). But there is no question here of the *sum* of things being any more divine than each single thing. The least gnat has a secret which is divinely adorable with total adoration. In other words, for those possessed of mystical vision, *there is the Face of God.*

[3] *Risālatu 'l-Aḥadiyyah*, also entitled *Kitāb al-Ajwibah* or *Kitāb al-Alif*. It is ascribed in some manuscripts to Muḥyi 'd-Dīn Ibn 'Arabī and in others to his younger contemporary 'Abd Allāh al-Balyānī (d. 1287), (see the prefatory notes to the French translation by 'Abd al-Hādī in *Le Voile d'Isis*, 1933, pp. 13-4, and to the English translation by Weir, from which I quote, in the *Journal to the Royal Asiatic Society*, 1901, p. 809). It is one of the most important of all Sufic treatises. Hence the large number of existing manuscripts, although until now it has only been published in translations.

[4] We may compare the following Buddhist formulation: 'When a blade of grass is lifted the whole universe is revealed there; in every pore of the skin

If there were anything which, in the Reality of the Eternal Present, could show itself to be other than God, then God would not be Infinite, for Infinity would consist of God *and* that particular thing[1].

This doctrine is only concerned with Absolute Reality. It has nothing to do with 'reality' in the current sense, that is, with lesser, relative truths which the Sufis call 'metaphorical'. Ghazālī says: 'The Gnostics rise from the lowlands of metaphor to the peak of Verity; and at the fulfilment of their ascent they see directly face to face that there is naught in existence save only God and that *everything perisheth but His Face,* not simply that it perisheth at any given time but that it hath never not perished. . . . Each thing hath two faces, a face of its own, and a face of its Lord; in respect of its own face it is nothingness, and in respect of the Face of God it is Being. Thus there is nothing in existence save only God and His Face, for *everything perisheth but His Face,* always and forever . . . so that the Gnostics need not wait for the Resurrection in order to hear the summons of the Creator proclaim: *Unto whom this day is the Kingdom? Unto God, the One, the Irresistible*[2], for this proclamation is eternally in their ears; nor do they understand from His Utterance *God is Most Great* (*Allāhu Akbar*) that he is greater than others. God forbid! For there is nothing other than

---

there pulsates the life of the triple world, and this is intuited by *prajna,* not by way of reasoning, but 'immediately'. (D. T. Suzuki, *Studies in Zen,* p. 94.)

[1] This is implicit in the following formulation of *Waḥdat al-Wujūd* by Al-Hallāj, who literally takes the ground from beneath the feet of those who accuse the Sufis of localizing God (*ḥulūl*).

'It is Thou that hast filled all "where" and beyond "where" too. Where art Thou then?' (*Dīwān,* p. 46, 1.4.)

The Shaikh Al-'Alawī quotes at some length (*An-Nāṣir Ma'rūf,* pp. 112-5) Muḥammad 'Abduh's formulations of the doctrine in question from pt. 2 of his *Wāridāt,* ending with the words:

'Do not think that this is a doctrine of localization, for there can be no localization without two beings, one of which occupieth a place in the other, whereas our doctrine is: "There is no being but His Being." '

Over 2000 years previously the Taoist Chuang Tzu had said: 'A boat may be hidden in a creek; a net may be hidden in a lake; these may be said to be safe enough. But at midnight a strong man may come and carry them away on his back. The ignorant do not see that no matter how well you conceal things, smaller ones in larger ones, there will always be a chance for them to escape. But if you conceal Universe in Universe, there will be no room left for it to escape. This is the great truth of things.' (ch. 6, Yu-Lan Fung's translation.)

[2] Qoran, XL, 16.

Himself in all existence, and therefore there is no term of comparison for His Greatness'[1].

This doctrine is necessarily present whenever there is explicit reference to the Supreme Truth—the Absolute, the Infinite, the Eternal. In Christianity the goal of mysticism is most often conceived of as union with the Second Person of the Trinity. Here the Supreme Truth is not explicit but implicit: who has Christ has indeed All; but for those who follow the path of love this Totality is not usually the direct object of fervour. Yet when it is conceived more directly, then in Christianity also[2] we find inevitably the doctrine of the Oneness of Being.

On the other hand, when the Supreme Truth recedes into the background, then in all religions this doctrine also necessarily recedes, since apart from the Infinite and Eternal Present it is meaningless. No one can hope to understand the formulations of the mystics without bearing in mind that there is liable to be a continual shifting of the centre of consciousness from one plane to another.

One of the first things that a novice has to do in the 'Alawī Ṭarīqah—and the same must be true of other paths of mysticism —is to unlearn much of the agility of 'profane intelligence' which an 'Alawī faqīr once likened, for my benefit, to 'the antics of a monkey that is chained to a post', and to acquire an agility of a different order, comparable to that of a bird which continually changes the level of its flight. The Qoran and secondarily the Traditions of the Prophet are the great prototypes in Islam of this versatility.

Three distinct levels of intelligence are imposed methodically twice a day in the three formulae of the 'Alawī rosary which are (each being repeated a hundred times) firstly asking forgiveness of God, secondly the invocation of blessings on the Prophet, and thirdly the affirmation of Divine Oneness.[3] The first

[1] *Mishkāt al-Anwār*, pp. 113-4 in *Al-Jawāhir al-Ghawālī* (Cairo, 1343 A.H.); in Gairdner's translation, which however I have not followed, pp. 103-5.

[2] 'However vile the dust, however small its motes, the wise man seeth therein God in all His Greatness and Glory.' (Angelus Silesius, *Cherubinischer Wandersmann*).

[3] According to Ḥasan b. 'Abd al-'Azīz, one of the Shaikh's disciples, this triple rosary is used in all branches of the Shādhilī Ṭarīqah (*Irshād al-Rāghibīn*, p. 31). The same formulae are also used, with some variations, by many branches of the Qādirī Ṭarīqah and others. See Rinn, *Marabouts et Khouan*, pp. 183-4, 252-3, 441, 503.

standpoint, which is at what might be called the normal level of psychic perception, is concerned with the ego as such. This is the phase of purification. From the second standpoint this fragmentary ego has ceased to exist, for it has been absorbed into the person of the Prophet who represents a hierarchy of different plenitudes of which the lowest is integral human perfection and the highest is Universal Man (*Al-Insān al-Kāmil*)[1], who personifies the whole created universe and who thus anticipates, as it were, the Infinite[2], of which he is the highest symbol. The disciple aims at concentrating on perfection at one of these levels. From the third point of view the Prophet himself has ceased to exist, for this formula is concerned with nothing but the Divine Oneness.

All mysticism necessarily comprises these different levels of thought, because it is, by definition, the passage from the finite to the Infinite. It has a starting point and an End, and cannot ignore what lies between. It follows that the formulations of any one mystic are unlikely to be all from the same standpoint[3], and this is especially true of the more spontaneous

[1] See Titus Burckhardt's introduction to his *De l'Homme Universel* (translated extracts from Jīlī's *Al-Insān al-Kāmil*), P. Derain, Lyons, 1953.

[2] The first formula of the rosary may also open on to the Infinite, but in a negative sense, for the end of purification is extinction (*fanā'*). The Shaikh Al-'Alawī often quotes the saying attributed to Rābi'ah al-'Adawiyyah, one of the greatest women Saints of Islam (d. 801): 'Thine existence is a sin with which no other sin can be compared' (*Minaḥ*, p. 41). It is this point of view which Al-Ḥallāj expresses in the words: 'Between me and Thee is an "I am" which tormenteth me. O take, by Thine Own *I am*, mine from between us.' (*Akhbār Al-Ḥallāj*, Massignon's edition, no. 50).

[3] The refusal to see that mysticism is never a 'system' and that mystics are consciously and methodically 'inconsistent', taking now one standpoint, now another, has led to much confusion, especially as regards *Waḥdat al-Wujūd*. In his preface to his translation of *Mishkāt al-Anwār* (p. 61). Gairdner says: 'The root question in regard to al-Ghazzali, and every other advanced mystic and adept in Islam, is the question of Pantheism (i.e. *Waḥdat al-Wujūd*, now usually translated, with some advantage, "monism"): did he succeed in balancing himself upon the edge of the pantheistic abyss? . . . Or did he fail in this?' Massignon, for his part, has devoted much of his output to exculpating Al-Ḥallāj from the 'unorthodoxy' in question, that is, to pinning him down to the dualism expressed in certain of his verses, and turning a blind eye to his affirmations of the Oneness of Being, or in other words denying that he ever made the transcension from what Ghazālī calls the metaphor of union (*ittiḥād*) to the truth of the realization of the Oneness (*tawḥīd*) (*Mishkāt*, p. 115). Nicholson pleads for Ibn al-Fāriḍ (*Studies in Islamic Mysticism*, pp. 193-4). Gairdner, feeling that Ghazālī is in great 'danger', pleads for him and by charitable extension for all other Moslem mystics on the grounds that they do not mean

utterances such as those of poetry. But it is natural that spiritual Masters should stress *Wahdat al-Wujūd* above all, because it is the Supreme Truth and therefore the ultimate goal of all mysticism, and also because, for that very reason, it is the point of view that is 'furthest' from the disciple and the one he most needs help in adopting. Relentless insistence upon the doctrine has therefore a great methodic, not to say 'hypnotic value[1], for it helps the disciple to place himself virtually in the Eternal Present when he cannot do so actually. *The Treatise on Oneness* says: 'Our discourse (that is, the formulation of Oneness of Being) is with him who hath resolution and energy in seeking to know himself in order to know God, and who keepeth fresh in his Heart the image of his quest and his longing for attainment unto God; it is not with him who hath neither aim nor end.'

It has been remarked—I forget by whom—that many of those who delight in the poems of 'Umar ibn al-Fārid and Jalāl ad-Dīn ar-Rūmī would recoil from them if they really understood their deeper meaning. The truth is that if the author of this remark and Western scholars in general really understood the deeper meaning of such poetry, that is, if they really understood the doctrine of the Oneness of Being, they would cease to recoil from it. Massignon attacks it because it seems to him to deny both the Transcendence of God and the

---

what they say! (*ibid.*, pp. 62-3). The truth is that all the Sufis are 'dualist' or 'pluralist' at lower levels; but it is impossible that any of them should have believed that at the highest level there is anything other than the Divine Oneness, for though the Qoran changes the plane of its utterance more often even than the Sufis themselves, it is absolutely and inescapably explicit as regards the Eternal that *all things perish but His Face* and *all that is therein suffereth extinction, and there remaineth the Face of thy Lord in Its Majesty and Bounty*. This last word is a reminder that for the Sufis Oneness of Being is That in which there is no loss but only pure gain or, otherwise expressed, That in which all that was ever lost is found again in Infinite and Eternal Perfection. Therefore let those who shrink from this doctrine as a 'pantheistic abyss' or what Nicholson calls 'blank infinite negation' ask themselves if they really understand it.

[1] When Ibn 'Arabī for example criticizes some of the formulations of his great predecessors, such as Junaid and Al-Hallāj, as regards the Supreme State, it is clearly not because he thought that they had not attained to that State, but because the formulations in question are not sufficiently rigorous to be, in his opinion, methodically effective.

immortality of the soul. Yet in affirming the Transcendence and immortality in question he implicitly affirms the Oneness of Being. The difference between him and the Sufis is that he does not follow up his belief to its imperative conclusions, but stops half way. For if it be asked: 'Why is the soul immortal?', the answer lies in Meister Eckhardt's 'There is something in the soul which is uncreated and uncreatable. . . . This is the Intellect.' The soul is not merely immortal but Eternal, not in its psychism but in virtue of the Divine Spark that is in it. The Shaikh Al-'Alawī says in one of his poems:

> Thou seest not who thou art, for thou art, yet art not "thou".

and he quotes more than once Shustarī's lines:

> After extinction I came out, and I
> Eternal now am, though not as I.
> Yet who am I, O I, but I?[1]

As to the Divine Transcendence, I will leave him to show that far from denying It, the doctrine of the Oneness of Being comes nearer than any other doctrine to doing justice to It.

Massignon writes[2] that this doctrine was first formulated by Ibn 'Arabī. It may be that the term *Waḥdat al-Wujūd* was not generally used before his day, but the doctrine itself was certainly uppermost in the minds of his predecessors, and the more the question is studied the further it recedes along a purely Islamic line of descent. The already quoted passage in Ghazālī's *Mishkāt al-Anwār* is closely followed up by: 'There is no he but He, for "he" expresseth that unto which reference is made, and there can be no reference at all save only unto Him, for whenever thou makest a reference, that reference is unto Him even though thou knewest it not through thine ignorance of the Truth of Truths. . . . Thus "there is no god but God" is the generality's proclamation of Unity, and "there is no he but He" is that of the elect, for the former is more general, whereas the latter is more elect, more all-embracing, truer, more exact, and

[1] *Wa-man anā yā anā illā anā?*
[2] Encyclopaedia of Islam, *Taṣawwuf*.

more operative in bringing him who useth it into the Presence of Unalloyed Singleness and Pure Oneness.[1]

The Shaikh Al-'Alawī quotes[2] from the end the *Manāzil as-Sā'irīn* of 'Abd Allāh al-Harawī (d. AD 1088) with regard to the third and highest degree of *Tawḥīd*:

'None affirmeth truly the Oneness of God, for whoso affirmeth It thereby setteth himself in contradiction with It. . . . He, He is the affirmation of His Oneness, and whoso presumeth to describe Him blasphemeth (by creating a duality through the intrusion of his own person)'.

This recalls the almost identical saying of Al-Ḥallāj (d. AD 922):

'Whoso claimeth to affirm God's Oneness thereby setteth up another beside him'[3].

Al-Kharrāz, in his *Book of Truthfulness*, quotes the Companion Abū 'Ubaidah (d. AD 639) as having said:

'I have never looked at a single thing without God being nearer to me than it'[4].

Only one who stops short at the outer shell of words could maintain that there is a real difference between this and the following more analytical formulation from the thirteenth century *Treatise on Oneness*:

'If a questioner ask: "Supposing we see refuse or carrion, for example, wilt thou say that it is God?", the answer is: "God in his Exaltation forbid that He should be any such thing! Our discourse is with him who doth not see the carrion to be carrion or the refuse to be refuse; our discourse is with him who hath insight (*baṣīrah*) and is not altogether blind.'[5]

[1] pp. 117-18. Although written at the end of Ghazālī's life (he died in AD 1111), this treatise is about 100 years earlier than Ibn 'Arabī's *Fuṣūṣ al-Ḥikam*.

[2] *An-Nāṣir Ma'rūf*, p. 99.

[3] Akhbār, no. 49.

[4] Arabic text, p. 59; Arberry's translation, p. 48.

[5] We may compare the following third century BC formulation: 'Tung Kuo Tzu asked Chuang Tzu: "Where is the so-called *Tao*?" Chuang Tzu said: "Everywhere." The former said: "Specify an instance of it." "It is in the ant." "How can *Tao* be anything so low?" "It is in the panic grass." "How can it be still lower." . . . "It is in excrement." To this Tung Kuo Tzu made no reply. Chuang Tzu said: "Your question does not touch the fundamentals of *Tao*. You should not specify any particular thing. There is not a single thing without *Tao*." ' (Chuang Tzu, ch. XXII, Yu-Lan Fung's translation).

Al-Kharrāz's quotation, made about AD 850, spans the first two centuries of Islam with the Qoranic doctrine of Nearness—Identity—Oneness. We have seen that in the early Meccan Surahs the highest saints are referred to as the *Near*, and that what the Qoran means by 'nearness' is defined by the words *We are nearer to him than his jugular vein*. In the following already quoted Holy Tradition this nearness is expressed as identity: 'My slave seeketh unremittingly to draw nigh unto Me with devotions of his free will until I love him; and when I love him, I am the Hearing wherewith he heareth and the Sight wherewith he seeth and the Hand wherewith he smiteth and the Foot whereon he walketh.' It cannot be concluded from this Tradition that this identity was not already there, for the Divinity is not subject to change. The 'change' in question is simply that what was not perceived has now been perceived.[1] These two levels of perception are both referred to in the verse: *We are nearer to him than ye are, although ye see not*[2]. The lower of these two is perception of the merely relative reality of God's absence which is pure illusion in the face of the Absolute Reality of His Presence. For there is no question of relative nearness here. *We are nearer to him than his jugular vein* and *God cometh in between a man and his own heart*[3] mean that He is nearer to him than he is to his inmost self. The Oneness here expressed exceeds the oneness of union.

It may be convenient for certain theories to suppose that these flashes of Qoranic lightning passed unperceived over the heads of the Companions, and that they were only noticed by later generations; but is it good psychology? No men have been more 'men of one book' than the Companions were, and there is every reason to believe that no generation of Islam has ever surpassed them in weighing the phrases of that book and in giving each one its due of consideration. They would have been the last people on earth to suppose that the Qoran ever meant *less* than it said. This does not mean that they would necessarily have interpreted as formulations of Oneness of Being all those Qoranic verses which the Sufis so interpret, for some of these

[1] It has been perceived only because the agent of perception is God, not the mystic. 'I am . . . his Sight', or to use the Qoranic phrase: *The sight overtaketh Him not, but He overtaketh the sight* (VI, 103).

[2] LVI, 85.

[3] VIII, 24.

verses admit more readily of other interpretations. But there are some which do not. If we take, for example, in addition to the already quoted formulations of 'Nearness', the verse: *He is the First and the Last and the Outwardly Manifest and the Inwardly Hidden*,[1] it is difficult to conceive how the Companions would have understood these words other than in the sense of Ghazālī's, "there is no object of reference other than He', though they may never have formulated the truth in question except with the words of the Qoran itself, or with expressions such as Abū 'Ubaidah's: 'I have never looked at a single thing without God being nearer to me than it', or the Prophet's: 'Thou art the Outwardly Manifest and there is nothing covering Thee'[2].

[1] Qoran, LVII, 3.

[2] Muslim, *Da'wāt*, 16; Tirmidhī, *Da'wāt*, 19. This is not incompatible with other Traditions in which he speaks of 'veils' between man and God. It is simply a question of two different points of view, the one being absolute and the other relative.

CHAPTER VI

THE THREE WORLDS

Before considering some of the Shaikh Al-ʿAlawī's own formulations of the doctrine of Oneness of Being, let us consider what he quotes from 'the Shaikh of our Shaikhs, Mawlāy Al-ʿArabī ad-Darqāwī':

'I was in a state of remembrance and my eyes were lowered and I heard a voice say: *He is the First and the Last and the Outwardly Manifest and the Inwardly Hidden.* I remained silent, and the voice repeated it a second time, and then a third, whereupon I said: "As to *the First,* I understand, and as to *the Last,* I understand, and as to *the Inwardly Hidden,* I understand, but as to *the Outwardly Manifest,* I see nothing but created things." Then the voice said: "If there were any outwardly manifest other than Himself I should have told thee." In that moment I realized the whole hierarchy of Absolute Being.'[1]

Ibn ʿĀshir's *Guide to the Essentials of Religious Knowledge*[2], on which the Shaikh's *Al-Minaḥ al-Quddūsiyyah* is a commentary, formulates what must necessarily be attributed to God as follows: 'Being, Beginninglessness, Endlessness, Absolute Independence, Incomparability, Oneness of Essence, of Quality and of Action, Power, Will, Knowledge, Life, Hearing, Speech, Sight.'

The Shaikh comments: 'Here he explaineth what belongeth unto God. See therefore, O slave, what belongeth unto thee, for if thou shouldst qualify thyself with any one of these qualities, thou wilt be contending with thy Lord.

'God's is the prerogative of Being, and Being is the very Self of Him who is. This is Absolute Being which is not to be limited and measured and set on one side. It is not possible

[1] *Minaḥ*, p. 174.
[2] *Al-Murshid al-Muʿīn.*

that there should exist any other being with this Being in virtue of Its Unlimitedness and the Force of Its Manifestation and the Immensity of Its Light. Thou shouldst know that this Being brooketh no denial in the inward eye of the Gnostics, just as sensible objects brook no denial in the sight of those who are veiled. Nay, the appearance of spiritual truth to the Intellect is stronger and more direct than the appearance of the sensible object to the sense. Thus the Manifestation of Absolute Being falleth upon the perception of the Sufi so that he is utterly overwhelmed in his realization of the Infinite. If he trek the vast Beginninglessness he findeth no starting point, and if he then turn unto Endlessness, he findeth no limit and no finality. He plungeth into the depths of Innermost Mystery and findeth no outlet, and he mounteth up throughout the hierarchy of Outward Manifestation and findeth no escape from it, so that in his bewilderment he crieth out for refuge. Then the Truths of the Names and Qualities call unto him saying: "Seekest thou to limit the Essence? Wouldst thou qualify It with dimensions? Thou art in a station which is attended with knowledge of the Secrets of the Names and Qualities. What hast thou to do with created things?" And thereupon he surrendereth himself unto Being, and realizeth that beside It there is neither nothingness nor being.'[1]

As regards the Divine Incomparability he comments: 'Another necessity is God's difference from what is contingent, but this qualification is not one of the supports of the Gnostics, since comparison entereth not into their thoughts. . . . For them the seer is folded up in That which is seen. There is naught that hath being besides God that it might be compared with Him. But this qualification of Incomparability is helpful to those who are veiled—nay, it is the very ark of their salvation.

'The Truth transcendeth all the qualities of contingent things; and if the outer covering be removed for the Gnostics from his Quality of Transcendence amazement falleth upon them, for they find that the Truth transcendeth Transcendence. Then they wish to tell of the marvellous mysteries that are there, but the encumbrances of the letters of the alphabet upon their tongues impede them, and it may be that an utterance cometh forth which resembleth comparison and which

[1] *Minaḥ*, p. 35.

may cause offence in the hearing of those who are veiled, although the utterance is in reality an extreme affirmation of Transcendence.

'None is safe from the snare of qualifying the Truth and making comparisons with regard to It save him who companioneth the Gnostics and treadeth the path of those who realize the Oneness. . . .

'How should one be safe from limiting the Truth who conceiveth It to be far away? And how should one escape beyond the frontiers of ignorance when the created universe still existeth in his sight? . . .

'It is of no avail to affirm His Transcendence with the tongue and to affirm His likeness to other things in the heart. If thou art veiled, in seeming to affirm His Transcendence thou affirmest in fact His likeness to other than Him through thine inability to conceive the Truth of His Transcendence, and if thou knowest Him, in seeming to liken Him to others thou affirmest in fact His Transcendence through the utter obliteration of thy being in His Being. In a word, the Folk's affirmation of His likeness transcendeth the generality's affirmation of His Transcendence.

'Another truth that must be believed of God is His Oneness in Essence, Qualities and Actions, for He is not composed of parts, not multiple.

'The Oneness of the Truth is not to be added unto, for verily It admitteth not of increase even as It admitteth not of diminishment. "God was, and there was naught with Him."[1] "He is now even as He was,"[2] for the Qualities stand not by themselves so as to be independent in their Being or so as to be separated from That which they describe, which is the Essence.

'As to Oneness in Action, this means that it is impossible that there should be any act but the Act of God.

'The Folk may be divided into three groups. The first is the group of those who see that there is no agent but God, thus realizing Oneness in Actions by way of direct intellectual perception, not merely by way of belief, for they see through

[1] Bukhārī, *Khalq*, 1.

[2] It is doubtful if even the most exoteric of dogmatic theologians would venture to deny the truth of this Sufic comment on the above Tradition.

the multiplicity of actions to the One Agent. The second is the group of those who realize the Oneness in the Qualities, that is, that none hath hearing, sight, life, speech, power, will, knowledge save only God. The third is the group of those who realize the Oneness in the Essence and who are veiled from all else inasmuch as the Infinity of the Essence hath been unveiled to them, so that they find no room for the appearance of any created things. They say: "In truth there is nothing there but God", for they have lost all but Him. These are the essentialists and the unifying Gnostics; and all others are veiled and unheeding: they have not tasted the flavour of Oneness nor sensed the perfume of Uniqueness, but they have only heard of this doctrine and they imagine, because it hath fallen upon their ears, that they adhere to it. Nay, they are remote from the Truth and cut off from It.

'As to His Qualities of Power, Will, Knowledge, Life, Hearing, Speech, Sight, these are as a veil over the Essence, for the exceeding force of Its outward manifestation setteth up screens. Thus Power is the veil of the Powerful, Will the veil of the Willer, Knowledge of the Knower, Life of the Living, Hearing of the Hearer, Sight of the Seer, and Speech of the Speaker.

'The Qualities are likewise veiled from sight: thus Power is veiled by the outward manifestations of power, Will by the various impulses, Speech by the differentation of letters and voices, Life by its inseparability from the Essence,[1] Hearing and Sight by the strength of their manifestation in creatures, and Knowledge by its exceeding comprehensiveness in embracing all known things.

'These Qualities are of three different kinds, and each group hath its own specific world. Hearing, Sight and Speech are of the World of Human Sense (*'ālam an-nāsūt*),[2] Power, Will and Knowledge are of the World of the Dominion (*'ālam*

[1] Life, like Intellect (see p. 40), is not strictly speaking of this world but is an outpost of the World of the Spirit in this world, and just as there is continuity between Divine Light and the intellectual spark in man, so also there is a continuity between Divine Being, that is, Divine Life, and the vital spark. It is to this continuity that the word 'inseparability' refers. The other Qualities are also inseparable from the Essence in virtue of Its Omnipresence, but hierarchically they are more remote from it.

[2] The world of matter; he calls it elsewhere *'ālam al-mulk*, the World of the Kingdom.

al-malakūt)[1] whereas Life is of the World of the Domination (*ʿālam al-jabarūt*)[2] and none of them are separate from the Essence in virtue of Its All-embracingness[3] and its Transcendence over all localization.

Now when the people of God speak of the Qualities being dependent upon created things,[4] they mean that They are dependent upon Themselves for Their outward manifestation, inasmuch as existence is woven out of the Qualities even as a mat is woven out of reeds. Thus the Qualities, far from being made up of creatures, are themselves the very tissue[5] of all existing things. Indeed, if thou examine all that is, thou wilt find naught that is an addition to the Oneness of the Divinity—Oneness in Essence, Qualities and Actions.

'The Act is one with the Agent before and after its coming into existence: it appeareth not of itself, but only if He manifest it and be Manifest Himself therein, for things in themselves are nothing.[6]

"By thus enumerating the necessary prerogatives of God, he[7] did not mean to limit them, for the Qualities of the Truth

[1] The world of the soul, which together with the material world makes up what we call 'this world'. Thus, as he remarks later (*Minaḥ*, p. 49): 'The inward aspect of this world is Divine Power, Will and Knowledge, and its outer aspect is Divine Hearing, Sight and Speech—nor is it anything besides this.'

It should be noted that the Knowledge in question is not *maʿrifah* (Gnosis), but *ʿilm* which proceeds from the Divine Name *Al-ʿAlīm*, the Omniscient, and which in man appears as mental knowledge, that is discursive indirect analytical knowledge.

[2] Heaven, the world of the Divine Spirit. The Qoran (XV 29) says of the vivification of Adam: *I breathed into him of My Spirit*. In naming the three worlds, as also in most other points of terminology, the Shaikh follows ʿAbd al-Karīm al-Jīlī (see for example *Al-Insān al-Kāmil*, ch. 39), whereas in earlier treatises, such as Ghazālī's *Iḥyā*, (IV, p. 216), the last two terms are transposed and *ʿĀlam al-Jabarūt* is the intermediary world.

[3] The Sufis often speak of four worlds, of which the fourth is precisely this Ultimate Reality, the world of the All-Embracing Essence, which is called, in relation to the other three, *ʿĀlam al-ʿIzzah*, the World of Sovereign Power.

[4] He is clearly thinking of such paradoxes as Ibn ʿArabī's: 'How is He the Independent (*Al-Ghanī*) when I help Him (by manifesting His Qualities)?'—*Fuṣūṣ*, end of ch. V.

[5] Elsewhere (p. 49) he remarks: 'Take the reeds from out the mat and it will retain neither name nor form.'

[6] He has already said (p. 38): 'He that stoppeth short at the Actions is veiled from direct vision of the Essence, whereas he who knoweth the Essence is veiled only by the Essence'.

[7] Ibn ʿĀshir, whom the Shaikh is commenting.

are unlimited and cannot be circumscribed; he only sought to make his exposition easier for human understanding.'[1]

In his oral teaching the Shaikh used to paraphrase the Shaikh Al-Būzīdī's formulation of these truths as follows: 'The Infinite or the World of the Absolute which we conceive of as being outside us is on the contrary universal and exists within us as well as without. There is only One World, and this is It. What we look on as the sensible world, the finite world of time and space, is nothing but a conglomeration of veils which hide the Real World. These veils are our own senses: our eyes are the veils over True Sight, our ears the veils over True Hearing, and so it is with the other senses. For us to become aware of the existence of the Real World, the veils of the senses must be drawn aside. . . . What remains then of man? There remains a faint gleam which appears to him as the lucidity of his consciousness. . . . There is a perfect continuity between this gleam and the Great Light of the Infinite World, and once this continuity has been grasped our consciousness can (by means of prayer) flow forth and spread out as it were into the Infinite and become One with It, so that man comes to realize that the Infinite Alone is, and that he, the humanly conscious, exists only as a veil. Once this state has been realized, all the Lights of Infinite Life may penetrate the soul of the Sufi, and make him participate in the Divine Life, so that he has a right to exclaim: "I am Allah". The invocation of the name *Allāh* is as an intermediary which goes backwards and forwards between the glimmerings of consciousness and the dazzling splendours of the Infinite, affirming the continuity between them and knitting them ever closer and closer together in communication until they are "merged in identity." '[2]

The Shaikh comments in some detail on the opposites of the Divine Qualities, which are enumerated by Ibn 'Āshir as being impossible with regard to God. I will quote from what he says about nothingness, extinction, death, deafness, dumbness and blindness:

'Here he telleth of what is impossible of God and inevitable

[1] *Minah*, pp. 36-9.
[2] 'Abd al-Karīm Jossot, quoted by Berque, pp. 704 and 750.

for the slave, and by "slave" the Folk mean the world from its zenith beneath the Throne to its nadir at the nethermost fringe of creation, that is, all that started into existence at the word "Be!", all that is "other". So realize, my brother, thine own attributes and look with the eye of the Heart at the beginning of thine existence when it came forth from nothingness; for when thou hast truly realized thine attributes, He will increase thee with His.

'One of thine attributes is pure nothingness, which belongeth unto thee and unto the world in its entirety. If thou acknowledge thy nothingness, He will increase thee with His Being. . . .

'Extinction also is one of thine attributes. Thou art already extinct, my brother, before thou art extinguished and naught before thou art annihilated. Thou art an illusion in an illusion and a nothingness in a nothingness. When hadst thou Existence that thou mightest be extinguished? Thou art *as a mirage in the desert that the thirsty man taketh to be water until he cometh unto it and findeth it to be nothing, and where he thought it to be, there findeth he God.*[1] Even so, if thou wert to examine thyself, thou wouldst find it to be naught, and there wouldst thou find God, that is, thou wouldst find God instead of finding thyself, and there would be naught left of thee but a name without a form. Being in itself is God's, not thine; if thou shouldst come to realize the truth of the matter, and to understand what is God's through stripping thyself of all that is not thine, then wouldst thou find thyself to be as the core of an onion. If thou wouldst peel it, thou peelest off the first skin, and then the second, and then the third, and so on, until there is nothing left of the onion. Even so is the slave with regard to the Being of the Truth.

'It is said that Rābiʿah al-ʿAdawiyyah met one of the Gnostics and asked him of his state, and he replied: "I have trod the path of obedience and have not sinned since God created me," whereupon she said: "Alas, my son, thine existence is a sin wherewith no other sin may be compared."

'Tread then, my brother, the path of those who realize the Oneness and affirm not Being for any but God, for if one of the Folk affirm Being for himself, he is guilty of idolatry. But the generality cannot escape from affirming the existence of other than God, though in doing so they affirm all evils.

[1] Qoran, XXIV, 39.

'Life is not one of thine attributes, for thou art dead in the form of the living, even as a possessed madman who claimeth to be someone that he is not. But if thou wast brought before thy Lord, and threw down thy body even as the body of thy father Adam, He would breathe into thee of His Spirit and create thee in His Form and then mightest thou say without wrong: "I am Alive," having realized thy deadness, whereas previously, in attributing Life unto thyself and giving thyself an independent existence thou wast contending with thy Lord.

'Another attribute of the slave is deafness. Thou art now deaf, O slave, and Hearing is not in thy nature. God is the Hearer, and it is by attributing this faculty unto thyself that thou art deaf. Though thou hast ears, thou hearest not. If thou couldst hear, then wouldst thou hear the Discourse of God at every time and in every state, for He hath not ceased speaking. But where is thy hearing of this Discourse, and where is thine understanding of this Speech? Nay, thou art deaf and art still in the fold of nothingness; but if thou camest out into Being, then wouldst thou hear the Discourse of the All-Worshipped, and if thou couldst hear, then wouldst thou answer. Yet how shouldst thou answer, seeing that dumbness is one of thy qualities? How comest thou to claim Speech which is one of the Attributes of thy Lord? If thou couldst indeed speak, then wouldst thou avail as a teacher, but no one sitteth at the feet of the dumb. If thou wouldst realize thy dumbness, He would increase thee with His Speech, and thou wouldst come to speak with the Speech of God and wouldst hold converse with God, so that thy hearing would be the Hearing of God and what thou wouldst hear would be all from God.

'Blindness, O slave, is another of thine attributes. If thou couldst see, thou wouldst behold His Name *the Outwardly Manifest*, but now thou seest only appearances. Where is thy vision of the Manifestation of the Truth, when things other than Him are clearer in thy sight? Far be it from Him that there should be any veil over His Manifestation![1] It is simply that blindness, thine attribute, hath overcome thee, and thou hast become blind although thou hast eyes, all through attributing Sight unto thyself. But if thou wouldst realize thy blindness and then seek to draw nigh unto Him through such actions as

[1] For the Tradition here referred to, see above p. 130, note 2.

His Good Pleasure accepteth from thee, then He will be thy Hearing and thy Sight, and when He is thy Hearing and thy Sight, then wilt thou hear only Him and see only Him, for thou wilt be seeing Him with his Sight and hearing Him with His Hearing.

'Consider well thine attribute of blindness, and meditate on the wisdom that lieth in attributing it to thyself, and then there will appear upon thee the rays of Sight. Then wilt thou hear what thou heardst not and see what thou sawest not, but this cannot be but by knowing thyself and meditating upon the nothingness that is thine by rights.

'It is God who hath manifested things through His Own Manifestation in them, even as one of the Gnostics hath said:

> 'Thou didst manifest Thyself in things when Thou didst create them.
> And lo! In them the veils are lifted from off Thy Face.
> Thou didst cut man off as a piece from Thy Very Self, and he
> Is neither joined to Thee, nor is he separate from Thee.'[1]'[2]

Ibn 'Āshir formulates 'proofs' of God's Eternity as follows:

'If Eternity were not of necessity His Attribute, then must He needs be ephemeral, subject to change and vicissitude. If extinction were possible, then Eternity would be banished.'

The Shaikh comments: 'In each demonstration he saith: "If so and so were not the case, then so and so would be the case," after the manner of the logicians, and this is suitable for boys who are beginning to learn the doctrine of Islam, but as for the gnostics, who are firm-fixed in the station of face-to-face vision, they dally not with any such teaching as this, being ashamed before God to speak in these terms, let alone to imagine the existence of phase and vicissitude in the Divinity —nay, this is impossible for the brains of the gnostics, and it can find no place in their intelligences where it might be received. Such is the certainty unto which they have attained that they use not logical proof and demonstration even by

[1] 'Abd al-Karīm al-Jīlī's quotation from his own *'Ainiyyah* in his *Al-Insān al-Kāmil*, ch. XXIII (opening).
[2] *Minaḥ*, pp. 39-45.

way of instruction, inasmuch as they are robed with the raiment of nearness in the presence of direct contemplation.

'They understand proof in another sense,[1] however, as for example: if extinction which is pure nothingness, were possible, Pure Being, Eternity's intimate attribute,[2] would be banished. Thus would Eternity be bereft of That which is Eternal, inasmuch as we had spoken of nothingness in Its Presence, whereas not only relative being but also nothingness vanisheth in that Noble Presence. God was, and there was no nothingness and no being with His Being.

'As to pure nothingness, if thou shouldst examine it after thou hadst conceived it, thou wouldst find therein a Truth of His Truths, since no truth is empty of the Truth of the Essence. Even so is the Essence named the Truth of Truths. Thus every impossibility hath, underlying it, a Divine Truth such as is not currently conceived of by men, and that Truth is to be understood from His Saying *Wheresoe'er ye turn, there is the Face of God.*[3] Things lie hidden in their opposites, and but for the existence of opposites, the Opposer would have no manifestation.

'None understandeth what I have just said save him who hath realized the Truth of the Oneness in the Essence and all that this Truth implieth. He that is veiled may take the

[1] Ibn 'Āshir's logic is addressed merely to the reason. But the Shaikh is now referring to supra-rational argument which is addressed to the Intellect and which is intended to provoke a sudden intuitive glimpse of the truth. This intention lies behind most mystic formulations, especially of the kind which are quoted in this and the following chapters. If the path be represented as the opening of a series of doors, the 'proofs' which the Shaikh is speaking of are keys which the spiritual Master gives—key after key—to the disciple; and in the 'Alawī Ṭarīqah, as no doubt in other orders, the saying: 'When the door has been opened, throw away the key' is well known. This saying is never meant to be followed too rigidly, for some keys will open more than one door and must be treasured; but at least it serves to show that the attitude of the mystics towards their own formulations is very different from that of the dogmatic theologians towards theirs, not to speak of the philosophers.

[2] Being is in a sense the 'content' of Eternity and Infinity, and the word 'pure' is a reminder that although in expressing relative truth a distinction may be made between Being and nothingness, in the Ultimate Truth Being is the absolute Positive which precludes all negativity whatsoever, just as Eternity is the Absolute Present which precludes all beginning and end, past and future, and Infinity is the Absolute Totality which precludes all notion not only of 'more' but also of 'less.'

[3] Even by turning one's attention towards 'nothingness' one is inevitably turning one's attention towards God.

Oneness to mean that God is One in that His Essence is not composed, or in that there is no essence like unto It. He perceiveth not that the Oneness refuseth to have the least thing co-existent with it.

'Count not this world as a thing nor believe that it hath otherness or that it is alien to the Divine Presence, for it is no less than one of Its Manifestations, one of Its Secrets, one of Its Lights. *God is the Light of the Heavens and of the earth.*[1]

By way of commentary on this last verse, he follows it with another passage from the Qoran: *Thus did We show unto Abraham the dominion of the Heavens and of the earth, that he might be of those possessing certainty. When the night grew dark upon him, he beheld a planet, and said: 'This is my Lord'. Then, when it set, he said: 'I love not things which set.'*

And when he saw the moon uprising, he said: 'This is my Lord.' Then when it set, he said: 'Unless my Lord lead me, I must needs become one of the folk who have gone astray.' And when he saw the sun uprising, he said: 'This is my Lord. This is greatest.' Then when it set, he said: 'O my people, verily I am innocent of all that ye place beside God. Verily I have turned my face towards Him who created the Heavens and the earth.'[2]

'He did not say *This is my Lord* by way of making comparisons but he spake thus in utter affirmation of God's Transcendence, when there was revealed unto him the Truth of all Truths that is indicated in the noble verse: *Wheresoe'er ye turn, there is the Face of God.* He informed his people of this Truth that they might show piety unto God in respect of each thing. All this was on account of what was revealed unto him of *the dominion of the Heavens and the earth,* so that he found the Truth of the Creator existent in every created thing.[3] Then he wished to impart unto others the knowledge to which he had attained, but he saw that their hearts were turned away from

[1] Qoran XXIV, 35

[2] Qoran VI, 75-9.

[3] Elsewhere (*Unmūdhaj*, p. 11) he quotes the verses:

'Thou didst show Thyself in other than Thee unto mine eyes
Which saw not the other, but rejoiced in Thee Alone.
Even so before me did the Friend invert his glance
When he beheld the light of the planet, moon and sun.'
('Umar ibn al-Fāriḍ, Kāfiyyah, 45-6.)

the pure doctrine of Oneness for which God had singled him out, so he said: *O my people, verily I am innocent of all that ye place beside God.*'[1]

The words *I love not things that set* he explains as follows in another passage:

'Albeit the Truth appear unto His slaves in some forms, yet is He Jealous on behalf of His other forms of manifestation wherein they are unmindful of Him, for the limited form unto which they attach themselves is very often of the most fleeting transitoriness. . . . Abraham was not willing to abide with God in some fleeting forms without recognizing Him in all, and therefore he said: *I love not things which set*, that is, I like not to know God in one thing apart from another lest with the disappearance of that thing I should forget Him. *Nay, I have turned my face*, and wheresoe'er I turn my face, there is the Beauty of God.

'Now Abraham incurred a certain preference for one of his sons, and God tried him for it with an order to sacrifice him, and Abraham showed his obedience, thus proving his sincerity.'[2]

Elsewhere he says: 'It is His Will that thou shouldst know Him in what He will, not in what thou wilt, so go as He goeth, nor seek to lead the way. If thou knewest Him in the Essence, thou wouldst not deny Him in the manifestations thereof. It is His Will that thou shouldst truly know Him, not merely by hearsay.

'The Outwardly Manifest is veiled by naught but the strength of the manifestations, so be present with Him, nor be veiled from Him by that which hath no being apart from Him. Stop not short at the illusion of forms, nor have regard unto the outward appearance of receptacles.

'Do not know Him only in His Beauty, denying what cometh unto thee from His Majesty,[3] but be deeply grounded

[1] *Minaḥ*, pp. 46-8.

[2] *Minaḥ*, p. 71.

[3] Just as the Divine Beauty, being the Archetype of expansion, presides over all outward manifestation, the Divine Majesty presides over the inverse process of contraction, that is, of the reabsorption of all created things in the Essence. In his chapter on Majesty in *Al-Insān al-Kāmil* (ch. 24), Jīlī gives a list of the Names Majestic (*Al-Asmā' al-Jalāliyyah*), amongst which are *Al-*

in all the states, and consider Him well in opposites. Do not know Him in expansion only, denying Him in contraction, neither know Him only when He vouchsafeth, denying Him when He witholdeth, for such knowledge is but a veneer. It is not knowledge born of realization.'[1]

He illustrates these remarks later with regard to the symbolism of the Pilgrimage. Having mentioned that the circumambulation round the Ka'bah signifies being overwhelmed in the Presence of the Oneness, he says that Ṣafā and Marwah, the two rocks[2] outside the Holy Mosque, signify respectively the Beauty and the Majesty.

'The passage of the Gnostics to and fro between these two stations is even as the rocking of the babe in the cradle. It is the Hand of Divine Care which moveth them this way and that, and protecteth them in both states, so that they suffer no trial therefrom, inasmuch as they have already, in virtue of their circumambulation, been overwhelmed in the Presence of the Oneness and have become even as a piece of It. Thus neither Majesty nor Beauty affecteth them inwardly, being already within them, whereas to other than them each is a trial. *We try you both with evil and with good.*[3] For the gnostic the Divine Majesty is none other than the Divine Beauty, and thus doth he delight in them both together. Our Shaikh Sidi Muḥammad al-Būzīdī would often say in moments of suffering "My Majesty is One with My Beauty" and thou wouldst see him even more radiantly happy and more overflowing in wisdom

Qābiḍ (He who contracteth), *Al-Mumīt* (the Slayer), *Al-Mu'īd* (the Bringer-back, the Re-integrator, or the Transformer), Al-Wārith (the Inheritor).

The Divine Beauty displays the world as a symbol of God, whereas the Divine Majesty reveals the limitations of the world inasmuch as it is merely a symbol, and by inheriting 'the reeds out of the mat' (see p. 135, note 5) It finally reduces it to nothing. It is in this sense that all imperfections, all decay, all sufferings, all evils, which are simply phases of a gradual demonstration that 'there is no he but He', may be said to come from the Majesty. They come more directly from the protective shell of time in which this world is wrapped and which serves as a 'filtre' to the action of Majesty. Without this shield there could be no evil, for all appearance of other than God would be reduced to nothing in an instant.

[1] *Minaḥ*, pp. 29-30.

[2] See above, p. 96, note 3.

[3] Qoran, XXI, 35.

than when he was in a phase of Beauty. At one time he was smitten with such agony that one of his legs and one of his arms were paralysed, and when we came unto him, full of sorrow, the first words he spake unto us were: "Since I entered upon the Path I have not found an expression of Truth more eloquent than this: I slept for part of this blessed night, and on waking I touched my arm which is paralysed with the hand of the arm which I can move, and I supposed that it was something other than myself, for being lifeless it did not feel my touch. So I took it to be a foreign body, and I called out to the people of the house to light me a lamp, saying: "There is a snake here with me. I have hold of it." Then when they lit the lamp I found the hand of one of my arms clutching the other, and no snake with me at all nor indeed anything other than myself, so I said: "Glory be to God! This is an example of the illusion that befalleth the seeker ere he hath attained unto Gnosis." See then, my brother, the condition of the Folk, how they delight in God's Majesty inasmuch as they are with Him at all times, not with the manifestations of either Majesty or Beauty, but looking upon expansion and contraction even as they look upon night and day (*We have made the night as a covering and the day for livelihood*[1]), two phases which are necessary for the bodily form, contraction being the attribute of the flesh and expansion that of the Spirit. *God it is who contracteth and expandeth.*[2] Now since the Gnostic is with Him who contracteth, not with the contraction itself, and with Him who expandeth, not with the expansion itself, he is active rather than passive and hath thus become as if naught had befallen him. Be then, O seeker, with God, and all shall be with thee, following thy command. Even so will that which for others is as the fire of Hell become a Paradise for thee, inasmuch as the Hand of Mercy and Grace and Solicitude rocketh thee to and fro, taking care that thou shouldst know no pain, and that thou shouldst want for nothing. Let the Station seek thee: seek it not thou,[3] since it was created for thee, not thou for it. Be

[1] Qoran, LXXVIII, 10-11.

[2] Qoran, II, 245.

[3] He is referring to purity of intention. It is on God exclusively that all spiritual aspirations must be concentrated. In the same sense Rābi'ah al-'Adawiyyah said: *Al-Jār thumma 'd-Dār*, 'the Neighbour first, then His House.'

turned unto God, welcoming all that cometh unto thee from him. Busy thyself with naught but let everything busy itself with thee, and do thou busy thyself with proclaiming the Infinite and saying *there is no god but God*, utterly independent therein of all things, until thou comest to be the same in either state, and art at Ṣafā even as thou art at Marwah. Let Perfection (*Kamāl*) be thine attribute, which is Beatitude in both Majesty and Beauty.'[1]

In another passage, after quoting the following verses by Al-Ḥarrāq:[2]

> The sum of quests is in Thy Loveliness.
> All else we count not worth a glance.[3]
> Nay, when we look we see that naught is there
> Beside Thy Wondrous Countenance.

he comments: 'The Gnostic hath not Gnosis if he know not God from every standpoint and in whatever direction he turneth. The Gnostic hath only one direction, and that is towards the Truth Itself. *Wheresoe'er ye turn, there is the Face of God*, that is, *wheresoe'er ye turn* your senses towards sensible things or your intelligences towards intelligible things or your imaginations towards imaginable things, *there is the Face of God*. Thus in every *ain* (where) there is *'ain*,[4] and all is *lā ilāha illa 'Llāh* (there is no god but God).

'In *lā ilaha illā 'Llāh* all being is comprised, that is, Universal Being and particular being, or Being and that which is metaphorically said to exist, or the Being of the Truth and the being of creation. The being of creation cometh under *lā ilāha* which meaneth that all save God is naught (*bāṭil*),[5] that is, denied, not to be affirmed, and the being of the Truth cometh

[1] *Minaḥ*, pp. 283-5.

[2] Muḥammad al-Ḥarrāq (d. 1845), a disciple of the Shaikh Ad-Darqāwī.

[3] A variant of 'We have only to gaze, naught else' which is a translation of this half line as it stands in Wardīfī's edition of the poem at p. 195 of *Bughyat al-Mushtāq* (Bulaq 1881).

[4] This highly synthetic word means 'eye', 'fountain', 'self', 'origin', and, as here, in a synthesis of all, 'the Divine Essence'.

[5] An echo of the Tradition which he quotes elsewhere (*Al-Qaul al-Ma'rūf*, p. 51): 'The truest word that poet spake is: "Are not all things naught save God?" (Bukhārī, *Manāqib al-Anṣār*, 26). The poet in question is Labīd.

under *illā 'Llāh*. Thus all evils come under the first half, and all that can be praised cometh under the second half.

'All being is comprised in the affirmation of Oneness (*lā ilāha illa 'Llāh*), and thou must comprise it also in naming the noblest of the slaves (in saying *Muhammadun Rasūlu 'Llāh*, Muhammad is the Apostle of God).

'This second testification compriseth the three worlds: *Muhammad* denoteth the World of the Kingdom, that is, the sensible world, and the reference to his Apostlehood is a reference to the World of the Dominion, the inner world of the secrets of abstract conceptions, and this is mediate between the ephemeral and the Eternal; and the Name of Divinity pointeth unto the World of the Domination, the Sea from which both sense and conception are brought forth.

'*Rasūl* (apostle, messenger) is indeed the mediator between the ephemeral and the Eternal, since without him existence would be brought to nothing; for if the ephemeral meeteth the Eternal, the ephemeral vanisheth and the Eternal remaineth.

'When the Apostle was placed in his exact relation unto both, then was the world ordered, for outwardly he is a lump of clay, and inwardly he is the Caliph of the Lord of the Worlds.

'In short, the meaning of the affirmation of Oneness is not complete, nor is its benefit all-embracing, without the affirmation of Oneness in Essence, Qualities and Actions. This affirmation is to be understood from the saying *Muhammadun Rasūlu 'Llāh*.

'When one of the Gnostics saith *lā ilāha illa 'Llāh*, he findeth in reality, not merely metaphorically, nothing but *Allāh*. So do not be content, my brother, with the mere utterance of this noble sentence, for then thy tongue alone, naught else, will benefit, and this is not the end in view. The essential is to know God as He is. "God was and there was naught with Him. He is now even as He was." Know this, and thou wilt rest from the burdens of negation, and naught will remain for thee but the affirmation, so that when thou speakest thou wilt say: *Allāh, Allāh*. But now thy Heart is burdened and its vision is weak. Ever since thou wert created thou hast been saying *lā ilāha* . . . but when will that negation take effect? Nay, it will not take effect, for it is merely a negation with the tongue. If thou wouldst make denial with thine Intellect, that is, with thy Heart and thine innermost Secret, then the whole world would be banished from thy sight, and thou wouldst find God instead of finding thyself, let alone thy fellow creatures. The Folk have denied the existence of other than God and they have found rest and have entered His Fortress, never to leave It, whereas thy negations know no ending. . . .

'Other than God will not vanish at a mere "no" upon the tongue, nor yet through the eye of faith and certainty but only when thou comest unto the station of direct perception and face-to-face vision; and verily *thy Lord is the Uttermost End*[1], unto which all cometh. Then wilt thou need no negation just as thou wilt need no affirmation, for He whose Being is Necessary is already affirmed before thou affirmest Him, and that of which the being is impossible is already naught before thou negatest it. Wilt thou not frequent a physician who will teach thee the art of obliteration, that thou mayest once and for all obliterate everything apart from God, and who will then bring thee into the presence of sobriety where thou wilt find naught but God? Then wilt thou live with God and die with God and be raised with God and dwell *in the abode of truthfulness at the court of an Almighty King*;[2] and all this will be in virtue of thy remembrance and thy Gnosis that *there is no god but God*. Now thou knowest only the mere phrase, and the furthest extent of thy knowledge is that thou sayst: "None is rightly worshipped but God." This is the knowledge of the generality, but what hath it to do with the knowledge of the Folk? Would that thou hadst known the knowledge of the elect before knowing what thou now knowest, for it is this thy present knowledge which cutteth thee off from the other. Wilt thou not deny all upon the hand of a Shaikh eminently practised in the Truth, until there is naught left for thee but God, not merely by way of faith and certainty, but by direct perception? Hearsay is not the same as seeing face to face.'[3]

[1] Qoran, LIII, 42.
[2] Qoran, LIV, 55.
[3] *Minah*, pp. 59-62.

CHAPTER VII

THE SYMBOLISM OF THE LETTERS OF THE ALPHABET

The Shaikh mentions, as we have seen, the reeds of which a mat is woven as symbols of the Manifestations of the Divine Qualities out of which the whole universe is woven. We find a somewhat analogous but more complex symbolism in his little treatise *The Book of the Unique Archetype* (*Al-Unmūdhaj al-Farīd*) *which signalleth the way unto the full realization of Oneness in considering what is meant by the envelopment of the Heavenly Scriptures in the Point of the Basmalah*[1].

He begins by quoting two sayings of the Prophet:

> 'All that is in the revealed Books is in the Qoran, and all that is in the Qoran is in the *Fātiḥah,*[2] and all that is in the *Fātiḥah* is in *Bismi 'Llāhi 'r-Raḥmāni 'r-Raḥīm.*' and 'All that is in *Bismi 'Llāhi 'r-Raḥmāni 'r-Raḥīm* is in the letter *Bā'*, which itself is contained in the point that is beneath it.'[3]

'This Tradition[4] hath been bandied about from pen to pen, and sounded in the ears of the elect and generality, so that one and all they endeavour to probe its hidden mysteries. Nor had I the strength to stand aloof from the throng, which had fired the spirit of emulation within me, so I rose to my feet and groped for a snatch of some of its fragrance. My hands fell on the perfume at its very source, and I brought it out from among the hillocks of the dunes, and came with it before the wisest of the learned. They received it with all honour and magnification, and each one said: *This is none other than a noble*

[1] The formula *Bismi 'Llāhi 'r-Raḥmānī 'r-Raḥīm* (literally 'In the Name of God, the All-Merciful, the Merciful') with which the Qoran opens. Its 'point' is the dot under the letter *Bā'*, (see plate IV).

[2] The first chapter of the Qoran (literally 'the Opening').

[3] These Traditions are quoted by 'Abd al-Karīm al-Jīlī at the beginning of his commentary on them, *Al-Kahf wa 'r-Raqīm,* which was almost certainly the starting point of the Shaikh's treatise.

[4] Presumably he is referring to both Traditions. In the Arabic this preamble is in rhymed prose, from which the Shaikh is seldom far away in any of his writings.

A page from the Qoran. The opening of the Chapter of Mary, from a sixteenth-century Moroccan manuscript (British Museum, Or. 1405). It begins with the *Baslamah,* reading from right to left.

Angel.[1] I said: "Indeed, it is above my station. It is the throw of a stone without a thrower." Then the tongue of my state answered, and said: *Thou threwest not when thou threwest, but it was God that threw.*[2]

'Whenever, in this treatise, I mention one of the names of "other than God", that is on account of the needs of expression. So let not thine imagination conceive "the other" as being truly other, for then wouldst thou miss the good I am seeking to show thee. For verily we bring thee *great tidings.*[3] Incline then unto that through which thou mayest be o'erwhelmed in the Reality, and go thou forth from the relative unto the Absolute. Perchance thou wilt understand what is in the Point, though *none understandeth it save the wise,*[4] *and none meeteth it face to face save him whose destined portion is immeasurably blessed. . . .*[5]

'Whenever I speak of the Point I mean the Secret of the Essence which is named the Oneness of Perception (*Wahdat ash-Shuhūd*), and whenever I speak of the *Alif* I mean the One Who Alone *is* (*Wāhid al-Wujūd*),[6] the Essence Dominical, and whenever I speak of the *Bā'* I mean the ultimate[7] Manifestation which is termed the Supreme Spirit, after which come the rest of the letters, then single words, then speech in general, all in hierarchy. But the pivot of this book turneth upon the first letters of the alphabet on account of their precedence over the others. *The Foremost are the Foremost, it is they who*

[1] Said by the women of Egypt (Qoran, XII, 31) with reference to Joseph (see p. 96, note 2).

[2] In the Qoran (VIII, 17) these words are addressed to Muhammad with reference to his throwing a handful of gravel at the enemy during the Battle of Badr, an act which changed the tide of the battle in favour of the Moslems, who completely defeated a Meccan army three times as large as theirs. This was the first battle of Islam, AD 624.

[3] XXXVIII, 67.

[4] XXIX, 43.

[5] XLI, 35.

[6] It is here that he diverges from Jīlī, in whose treatise the Point stands for the Divinity in All Its Aspects, whereas the *Alif* is the Spirit of Muhammad (Jīlī quotes the Tradition: 'God created the Spirit of the Prophet from His Essence, and from that Spirit He created the entire Universe') that is, the Supreme Spirit, which for the Shaikh is symbolized by the Bā'. But beneath this divergence the doctrine remains the same.

[7] Ultimate, because this Spirit, which is none other than 'Universal Man', contains the whole Universe.

are brought nigh.[1] These are *Alif* and *Bā'*, and they hold in the Alphabet the place that is held by the *Basmalah* in the Qoran, for together they make up *Ab*[2] which is one of the Divine Names. By it would Jesus speak unto His Lord, and he used it when he said: "Verily I go unto my Father and your Father", that is, unto my Lord and your Lord. And now, if thou understandest that these two letters have a meaning that thou knewest not, be not amazed at what we shall say of the Point, and the rest of the letters.

'The Point was in its hidden-treasurehood[3] before its manifestation of itself as *Alif*, and the letters were obliterate in its secret essence until it manifested the inward outwardly, revealing what had been veiled from sight by donning the various forms of the visible letters; but if thou graspest the truth, thou wilt find naught there but the ink itself, which is what is meant by the Point,[4] even as one of us hath said:

The letters are the signs of the ink; there is not one,
Save what the ink hath anointed; their own colour is pure illusion.
The *ink's* colour it is that hath come into manifest being.
Yet it cannot be said that the ink hath departed from what it was.
The inwardness of the letters lay in the ink's mystery,
And their outward show is through its self-determination.
They are its determinations, its activities,
And naught is there but it. Understand thou the parable!
They are not it; say not, say not that they are it!
To say so were wrong, and to say "it is they" were raving madness.
For it was before the letters, when no letter was;
And it remaineth, when no letter at all shall be.
Look well at each letter: thou seest it hath already perished
But for the face of the ink, that is, for the Face of His Essence,
Unto Whom All Glory and Majesty and Exaltation!

[1] Qoran, LVI, 10-1.

[2] Father. It may be noted here incidentally how close the *Basmalah* is in reality to the *In Nomine*. The relationship between the two Names of Mercy in Islam, of which the second only is both Divine and human, is comparable to the relationship between the first two Persons of the Christian Trinity, while the Mercy Itself which is implied in the *Basmalah*, being from both *Ar-Raḥmān* and *Ar-Raḥīm*, that is, 'proceeding from the Father and the Son', is none other than the Holy Ghost.

[3] Referring to the Holy Tradition: 'I was a Hidden Treasure and I wished to be known; and so I created the world.'

[4] The point and the ink are interchangeable as symbols in that writing is made up of a series of points of ink.

Even thus the letters, for all their outward show, are hidden,
Being overwhelmed by the ink, since their show is none other than its.
The letter addeth naught to the ink, and taketh naught from it,
But revealeth its integrality in various modes,
Without changing the ink. Do ink and letter together make two?
Realize then the truth of my words: no being is there
Save that of the ink, for him whose understanding is sound;
And wheresoe'er be the letter, there with it is always its ink.
Open thine intellect unto these parables and heed them!'[1]

'If thou hast understood how all the letters are engulfed in the Point, then wilt thou understand how all the books are engulfed in the sentence, the sentence in the word, the word in the letter, for we can say with truth: no letter, no word, and no word, no book. The word hath indeed no existence save through the existence of the letter. Analytical differentiation proceedeth from synthetic integration, and all is integrated in the Oneness of Perception which is symbolized by the Point. This is *the Mother* of every book. *God effaceth and confirmeth what He will,* and *with Him is the Mother of the Book.*[2]

'The Point is essentially different from the letters. *There is naught like unto Him and He is the Hearer, the Seer.*[3] Even so the Point, unlike the other signs, is not subject to the limitation of being defined. It transcendeth all that is to be found in the letters by way of length and shortness and protuberance, so that the sense cannot grasp it either visually or aurally as it graspeth the letters. Its difference from them is understood, but its presence in them is unknown save unto him whose *sight is like iron*[4] *or who giveth ear with full intelligence*[5], for although the letters are its qualities, the Quality encompasseth not the Essence, not having the universality which is the Essence's own. The Essence hath incomparability as Its prerogative whereas the Qualities create comparisons.

'And yet to make a comparison is in reality the same as affirming incomparability by reason of the oneness of the ink,

[1] 'Abd al-Ghanī an-Nābulusī, *Dīwān al-Ḥaqā'iq*, p. 435. (Cairo, 1889.)
[2] Qoran, XIII, 39.
[3] XLII, 11.
[4] An echo of L, 22.
[5] L. 37.

for though the letters are comparable each to other, this comparability doth not belie the incomparability of the ink in itself, neither doth it belie the oneness of the ink which is to be found in each letter. Here lieth the ultimate identity between striking comparisons and denying the possibility of comparison, for wherever there be any question of comparison, it is always in reality the ink itself which is compared with itself. *He it is who is God in Heaven and God on earth.*[1] Howsoever and wheresoever He be, He is God, so let not that which thou seest of Him in the earth of comparability prevent thee from conceiving of Him as He is in the Heaven of incomparability, for all things are made of both incomparability and comparability. *Wheresoe'er ye turn, there is the Face of God.* This is in virtue of the general Attribute which overfloweth from the Infinite Riches of the Point on to the utter poverty of the letters. But as to that which belongeth unto the Point's Own Mysterious Essence, it is not possible that it should undergo the least manifestation in the letters, nor can any letter, either in its form or its meaning, carry the burden of the Point's innermost characteristics.

'Seest thou not that if thou tracest some of the letters of the alphabet, as for example: ب ت ث thou wilt find for each letter another letter that resembleth it: ت is like ب, for example, and ث is like ت. Then if thou wishest to pronounce one of these letters, thou wilt find a sound that fitteth it exactly, whereas the Point hath no exteriorization that so fitteth it. If thou seekest to utter its truth, thou sayest *nuqṭat*^{un}, and this utterance will force thee to submit unto letters which have nothing to do with the essence of the point—*nūn, qāf, ṭā'* and *tā'*. It is clear, then, that the Point eludeth the grasp of words. Even so is there no word that can express the Secret Essence of the Creator. Therefore whenever the Gnostic seeketh to denote the Divine incomparability in words, that is, when he seeketh to convey what is meant by the Plenitude of the Essence with all Its Attributes, there cometh forth from his mouth an utterance which goeth far wide of its mark by reason of the limitations of language.

'The Point was in its principial state of utterly impenetrable

[1] Qoran, XLIII, 84.

secrecy[1] where there is neither separation nor union, neither after nor before, neither breadth nor length, and all the letters were obliterate in its hidden Essence, just as all the books, despite the divergence of their contents, were obliterate in the letters. As to this reduction of books to letters, it can be perceived by all who have the least intuition. Examine a book, and thou wilt find that naught appeareth on its pages to convey their sense but the twenty-eight letters,[2] which in their manifestation of each word and meaning will be forever reassembling in new formations as the words and meanings vary, until God *inherit the earth and all who are on it*[3] and *all things come unto God.*[4] Then will the letters return unto their principial centre where nothing is save the Essence of the Point.

'The Point was in its impenetrable secrecy with the letters all obliterate in its Essence, while the tongue of each letter petitioned the length, shortness, depth or other qualities that its truth required. Thus the promptings unto utterance were set in motion according to the demands of the Point's attributes which lay hidden in its Essence. Then was determined the first manifestation.

'The Point's first manifestation, its first definable appearance, was in the *Alif*, which came into being in the form of incomparability rather than of comparability, so that it might exist qualitatively in every letter while remaining essentially aloof from them. Moreover, thou shouldst know that the appearance of the *Alif* from the Point was not caused, but the Point overflowed with it. Thus was the primal *Alif* not traced by the pen,[5] nor was it dependent upon it, but sprung from the outward urge of the Point in its principial centre. Whenever

[1] '*Amā*, literally 'blindness', with reference to the blindness of 'other' than It, inasmuch as It is pure, unshared Perception (*Wahdat ash-Shuhūd*).

[2] It must be remembered that the purpose of a mystical treatise is always eminently 'practical', and the practical purpose of this one is in fact indicated in its title (see p. 148). The Shaikh is here inviting his disciples to transpose this operation to the book of Nature in such a way as to see there the 'letters' rather than the 'words'.

[3] Qoran, XIX, 40.

[4] XLII, 53.

[5] The pen symbolizes the Supreme Pen after which Sūrah LXVIII of the Qoran is named. 'Abd al-Karīm al-Jīlī (*Al-Insān al-Kāmil*, ch. 47), says: 'The Prophet said: "The first thing which God created was the Intellect" and he also said: "The first thing which God created was the Pen" Thus the Pen is the first Intellect, and they are two aspects of the Spirit of Muhammad.'

there streamed from it an overflow, there was *Alif*, naught else. It dependeth not upon the pen for its existence, nor needeth it any help therefrom in virtue of its straightness and its transcending all that is to be found in the other letters by way of crookedness or protuberance or other particularity. *He is not questioned as to what He doth, but they are questioned.*[1] As to the other letters, they need the movement of the pen upon them, nor could any of them have appearance except by means of it, on account of their concavity, roundness, and whatever else characterizeth them.

'It is true that the *Alif* also may be made to appear by means of the pen, while yet remaining independent of it and without any disparagement to the transcendence of its station, inasmuch as the pen hath its length and straightness from the *Alif*, nay, it *is* the *Alif*, whose penned appearance is thus through itself for itself.

'The *Alif* is a symbol of the One who Alone is, of Him whose Being no being precedeth. Thus the appearance of the Point as *Alif* is what is called "Firstness'. Before its manifestation it was not so qualified, even as it was not qualified by "Lastness". *He is the First and the Last and the Outwardly Manifest and the Inwardly Hidden.*

If the unique Firstness of the *Alif* be confirmed,[2] then of necessity must Lastness also be reserved for it alone.[3] Thus doth it declare unto the other letters *Unto Me is your return,*[4] one and all. Yea, *unto God come all things*.

"As to the Outward Manifestation of *Alif* in the letters, it is easily perceived. Consider the question well, and thou wilt find that there is no letter whose extension in space is not derived from the *Alif*: the *Ḥā'* for example is nothing other than a hunchbacked *Alif*, whereas the *Mīm* is a circular *Alif*, and such is the manifestation of the *Alif* according to the dictates of its wisdom, in all the letters, but *the sight attaineth not unto Him*, and this is the meaning of the Inward Hiddenness, for it is clear that no one can perceive the existence of

[1] Qoran, XXI, 23.

[2] 'The *Alif*, unlike all other letters, is only one degree distant from the Point, for two points together make an *alif*' (Jīlī, *Al-Kahf wa 'r-Raqīm*, p. 7).

[3] In the inverse process of reintegration.

[4] Qoran, XXXI, 15.

the *Alif* in the circle of the *Mīm* except after much practise, and naught hindereth us from perceiving it but its roundness, that is, its manifestation in a quality that we do not recognize. It itself is the veil over itself. . . .

'The Outward Manifestation of the Truth may be stronger in some visible forms than in others, and this is not difficult to see for him who looketh. Canst thou not detect the *Alif* in some letters as not in others? Not far from its form is the form of the *Lām*, for example; and there is in the *Bā'* of the *Basmalah* that which revealeth the manifestation of the *Alif* therein. But few are they who can easily detect it in the other letters. As to the generality, they are ignorant of the rank of the *Alif*; some know it in its Firstness and are ignorant of it in its Lastness, and there are some who know it in both; but whoso knoweth it not in every letter, small and large, long and short, early in the alphabet and late, verily he seeth not aright, and his perception faileth. If thou hast understood that the *Alif* is manifest in every letter, tell me whether this causeth it to fall short of the dignity of its incomparability wherein it retaineth ever that which belongeth unto it alone. Nay, the essential truth of the *Alif* remaineth as it is, and I see no short-coming on account of its manifestation, which I see rather as one of its perfections. The short-coming—though God knoweth best—is in him who would confine it to one quality, not allowing it to reach out unto another, but constraining it, limiting it, refusing to know it, and reducing it to comparability by making of it a thing like other things. The truth of the knowledge which befitteth its station is that thou shouldst see the *Alif* manifest in every word of every book. All is *Alif*. . . .

'The letter *Bā'* is the first form wherein the *Alif* appeared, and thus it manifested itself therein as never elsewhere. "God created Adam in His Image";[1] and by Adam it is the First Man[2] who is meant, and he is the Spirit of Being. It was in virtue of his having been created in His Image that He made him His

[1] Bukhārī, *Isti'dhān*, 1; and most other canonical books of Traditions.

[2] If God created the human being in His Image, He created *a priori* in His Image man's spiritual prototype, Universal Man, here called 'the First Man', who was the first created thing, This prototype is what the *Bā'* represents; it is only remotely, and by extension, that Bā' can be said to represent Adam in the sense of earthly man, who was the final outcome of creation.

representative on earth, and ordered the Angels to prostrate themselves to him.

'Had not His Beauty shone in Adam's countenance,
The Angels never had bowed down prostrate before him.'[1]

Was their prostration to other than Him? Nay, God pardoneth not him who is guilty of idolatry.

'The *Bā'* of the *Basmalah* differeth from the ordinary *Bā'* both in form as in function. *Verily thou art of a tremendous nature*;[2] and its greatness is none other than the greatness of the *Alif*. *Whoso obeyeth the Apostle obeyeth God.*[3] Seest thou not that elsewhere the *Bā'* is not lengthened, whereas in the *Basmalah* it is lengthened, and its length is none other than the elided *Alif*. *Bism* (بسم) was originally *bi-ism* (باسم), and then the *Alif* in *ism*[4] left its place vacant and appeared in the *Bā'*, which thus took on the form of the *Alif*, just as it fulfilled the function of the *Alif*. Even so did the Prophet say: "I have a time wherein only my Lord sufficeth to contain me", and thou seest that the *Bā'* hath a time, namely in the *Basmalah*, wherein only the *Alif* sufficeth to contain it, both in its form and in its Point[5], albeit the Point of the *Alif* is above it, whereas the Point of the *Bā'* is beneath it. Indeed the *Alif* is none other than the Point itself which is an eye that wept or a drop that gushed forth and which in its downpour was named *Alif*, without any detriment unto itself in virtue of the Integrity of the *Alif* and its flawless Transcendence wherein the Point remaineth in its Eternal Incomparability. *Verily we stand over them Irresistible.*[6] Full descent only took place at the manifestation of *Alif* as *Bā'*, followed by the other letters. If its form had been identical with that of the *Alif*, the *Bā'* would have lost its distinctive characteristics. But the *Bā'* is *Bā'* and the *Alif* is *Alif*: the *Alif* was manifested spontaneously, of its own free will, whereas manifestation was forced upon the *Bā'*.

[1] Jīlī, *'Ainiyyah*.
[2] Qoran, LXVIII, 4 (addressed to Muhammad).
[3] Qoran, IV, 80.
[4] An initial vowel is always written with *alif*.
[5] In many manuscripts of the Qoran the *hamzah* on an initial *alif* is indicated by a large dot as may be seen in plate IV. In plate III this dot is replaced by a star.
[6] Qoran, VII, 127.

Hence the necessity of the difference between its form and that of the *Alif*, lest we should deny the latency of *Alif* in the other letters,[1] or lest we should think that freedom is altogether incompatible with obligation.[2]

'Moreover the Point, which is above the *Alif*, is beneath the *Bā'*, so let this be for us an illustration of the truth that the things of the lower worlds are manifestations of the Point even as are the things of the higher worlds, nor let the manifestation of the Point in the Essence prevent our recognition of it in the Qualities. The Prophet said: "If ye lowered a man by a rope unto the nethermost earth, ye would light upon God."[3] Even so doth the Point beneath the *Bā'* signify the effacement that underlieth all things. *Everything perisheth but his Face. He it is who is God in Heaven and God on earth.* The Point's being above the *Alif* instructeth us that the *Alif* is its state of manifestation; but the *Bā'* is its veil, and therefore doth it lie beneath the *Bā'*, like the hidden treasure beneath the wall that Al-Khiḍr feared would collapse.[4]

'When *Bā'* understood its true relation unto *Alif*, it fulfilled what was incumbent upon it both by definition and obligation.[5] It submitteth unto its definition by cleaving unto the other letters,[6] inasmuch as they are of its kind, unlike the *Alif* which standeth aloof from the letters when it precedeth them, though they attain unto it as a Finality; and verily *thy Lord is the Uttermost End.*'

[1] But for the mediation of the *Bā'* of the *Basmalah*, which on the one hand clearly suggests the *Alif* while on the other hand it is distinguished from it precisely by the lower curve which joins it to the other letters, it would not have been possible for us to see the *Alif* in the other letters. Otherwise expressed, but for the mediation of the Word made flesh, the latent Divinity in men could never be brought out.

[2] Lest we should think that the coexistence of free will and predestination in man is impossible. The *Bā'* is in fact an image of this coexistence, for its resemblance to the *Alif* symbolizes man's relative free will, whereas its difference from the *Alif* symbolizes man's predestination.

[3] A comment, by the Prophet, on the verse: *He is the First and the Last and the Outwardly Manifest and the Inwardly Hidden* (Tirmidhī, *Tafsīr Sūrat al-Ḥadīd*; Ibn Ḥanbal, VI, 370).

[4] A reference to Qoran, XVIII, 77-82.

[5] Referring to the Prophet's fulfilment of the normal functions of the human being, which were his by definition, and of his apostolic obligations.

[6] *Bā'* is joined to the letters on either side of it, *Alif* only to a letter that precedes it.

CHAPTER VIII

THE GREAT PEACE

It has already been explained[1] that rhythm may serve ritually as a bridge from the perpetual fluctuation of this world or, more particularly, of the soul, to the Immutability of the Infinite World of the Divine Peace. In other words rhythm, like the letter *Bā'* through whose mediation the common letters of the alphabet are reabsorbed into the *Alif*, is a symbol of the Prophet as Universal Man, for he personifies the whole created universe, the macrocosm, which is in fact the bridge between the microcosm, the little world of the individual, and the Metacosm, the Infinite Beyond.

This passage from agitation through rhythm to Peace, from microcosm through macrocosm to Metacosm, from individual through Universal Man to God, is traced out not only in the sacred dance of the 'Alawī-Darqāwī Ṭarīqah but also in the rosary. In the dance it is the breathing above all which is subjected to the rhythm. The ordinary rhythm of breathing represents the individual, the microcosm, and the sacrifice of the individual rhythms of the dancers to the macrocosmic rhythm of the dance is a mode of 'repentance' or 'asking forgiveness' which is the first formula of the rosary. The rhythm of the dance itself, the rhythm of the universe, corresponds to the second formula of the rosary, the invocation of Blessings upon the Prophet, through whom the soul is de-individualized and universalized. Beyond its aspect of plenitude, this second formula has also an aspect of extinction or emptiness in the Face of the Absolute on to which it opens, and its final words, which are a prayer for Peace, are in one sense analogous to the end of the dance, when the rhythmic breathing 'expires' and the dancers sink to the ground in repose.

The inward concentration, which is the ultimate aim of the dance, corresponds to the third formula of the rosary, the affirmation of the Divine Oneness in Its Infinite Plenitude.

It was explained to a friend of mine by an eminent Moroccan

[1] p. 92.

Darqāwi, Al-Ḣājj Muḣammad Būsha'rah of Salé, that the rhythmic breathing of a faqīr during the dance is in fact very comparable to the breathing of a man at the point of death, who has already been half reabsorbed into the greater world from which he came and who breathes in and out to a cosmic rhythm which is far beyond his control. But whereas the dying man is passive and more or less unconscious, the faqīr actively and consciously anticipates his death in a ritual death-agony which symbolizes the extinction of all that is not God.

The rhythm to which the breathing is subjected is the rhythm of creation and dissolution, of Beauty and Majesty.[1] Breathing in represents creation, that is, the Outward Manifestation of the Divine Qualities, the flowing of the ink from the *Alif* into the *Bā'* and the other letters of the alphabet; breathing out represents the 'return 'of the Qualities to the Essence; the next intake of breath is a new creation,[2] and so on. The final expiring symbolizes the realization of the Immutability which underlies the illusory vicissitudes of creation and dissolution, the realization of the truth that 'God was and there was naught else beside Him. He is now even as He was.'

Since bodily repose after the sacred dance is only a symbol and not the Reality of the inward Peace which is aimed at, and since this Peace altogether transcends motion and rest, presiding alike over the most violent rhythmic movements and over the ultimate repose from them, Its Presence may be realised as well during the dance itself as after it has ceased. The fullest attainment of inward Peace means the shifting of the consciousness from a secondary or illusory centre to the One True Centre, where the subject is no longer the *Bā'* but the *Alif*, no longer the created being but the Creator. This is in fact what is meant by 'concentration'; it follows therefore that for one who is truly concentrated, the symbolism of breathing is necessarily inverted: breathing in becomes the absorption of all in the Oneness of the Essence, and breathing out is the Manifestation of the Divine Names and Qualities. Here lies the highest significance of the dance rhythm, as also of the second

[1] See p. 142, note 5.

[2] According to the Qoran, the span of life is a continuous alternation of presence in creation and absence from it, for in sleep the soul is withdrawn from creation, to be re-manifested on waking (VI, 60).

formula of the rosary. To say that beyond his created plenitude Universal Man has an aspect of total extinction means that beyond this extinction he has an aspect of Absolute Plenitude, for his extinction is simply the measure of his capacity to receive. Nothingness is as it were an emptiness of infinite dimensions, and one of the names of Reality is the All-Bountiful.

In the words of the second formula, which is in full: 'O God, whelm in Glory our Lord Muḥammad, Thy slave and Thy messenger, the unlettered prophet, and his family and companions, and give them Peace', it is the Glory which, from the highest point of view, corresponds to the intake of breath, the whelming of all in the Oneness of the Essence, whereas Peace is the relaxation of breathing out, the remanifestation of the Self, not as man but as God, in the sense of the already quoted lines:

> After extinction I came out, and I
> Eternal now am, though not as I.
> Yet who am I, O I, but I?

The Shaikh Ad-Darqāwī quotes Abū Sa'īd ibn al-A'rābi[1] as having said when asked of the meaning of extinction (*fanā'*):

'It is that the Infinite Majesty of God should appear unto the slave and make him forget this world and the next with all their states and degrees and stations and all memories of them, extinguishing him both from all outward things and also from his own intelligence and soul, and from his extinction therefrom, and from his extinction from extinction therefrom, inasmuch as he hath been utterly o'erwhelmed in the waters of Infinite Realization.'[2]

The Shaikh Al-'Alawī says:

'The Gnostics have a death before the general death. The Prophet said: "Die before ye die", and this is the real death, for the other death is but a change of abode. The true meaning of death in the doctrine of the Sufis is the extinction of the slave, that is, his utter effacement and annihilation. The

[1] d. 952. In his youth he was a disciple of Junaid.
[2] *Ar- Rasā'il ad-Darqāwiyyah*, quire 3, p. 1.

The Shaikh Al-'Alawī. A drawing done from memory, some years after his death, by Frithjof Schuon.

Gnostic may be dead unto himself and unto the whole world, and resurrected in his Lord, so that if thou shouldst ask him of his existence he would not answer thee inasmuch as he hath lost sight of his own individuality. Abū Yazīd al-Bistāmī[1] was asked about himself and he said: "Abū Yazīd is dead—May God not have mercy on him!" This is the real death; but if on the Day of Resurrection thou shouldst ask one who hath died only the general death "Who art thou?" he would answer: "I am so-and-so", for his life hath never ceased and he hath never sensed the perfume of death, but hath simply passed on from world to world, and none graspeth the meaning of the real death save him who hath died it. Thus have the Sufis a reckoning before the Day of Reckoning, even as the Prophet said: "Call yourselves to account before ye be called to account."[2] They laboured in calling themselves to account until they were free to contemplate their Lord, and theirs is a resurrection before the Resurrection.'[3]

The Shaikh continually affirms the spiritual precedence of Prophets over Saints; others have affirmed the superiority of sainthood over prophethood. But the apparent contradiction was resolved once and for all by Ibn 'Arabī:

'If a Prophet maketh an utterance which transcendeth the scope of his function as Law-giver, then he doth so inasmuch as he is a Saint and a Gnostic, for his station as one possessing Gnosis is more universal and perfect than is his station as a Messenger or Lawgiver. Thus if thou hearest any man of God say—or if he is reported as saying—that sainthood is higher than prophethood, his meaning is as we have just explained. Or if he say that the Saint is above the Prophet and the Messenger, he is referring to one person, and meaneth that the Messenger is more universal in virtue of his sainthood than he is in virtue of his apostle-prophethood.[4] He doth not mean

[1] d. 874.

[2] Tirmidhī, *Qiyāmah*, 25.

[3] *Minah*, p. 74.

[4] Elsewhere (*Kalimat Shaithiyyah*) he explains this by remarking that 'apostlehood and prophethood come to an end (with the fulfilment of the mission in question) whereas sainthood knoweth no end.' 'Abd al Ghanī an-Nābulusī, in his commentary, distinguishes between the sanctity of the Prophet and the non-Prophet by speaking of the 'sainthood of prophecy' and 'the sainthood of faith'.

that those Saints who are followers of the Messenger are higher than him.'[1]

It is clearly to the sainthood of the Prophet and not to prophethood in itself that the Shaikh is referring when he affirms the spiritual precedence of Prophets over Saints. None the less this precedence is not an absolute one, for he speaks of the Supreme Station as belonging to 'the Prophets and the elect of the Saints', and he makes it clear that their ultimate equality lies in nothing other than the Oneness of the Essence or in other words the equality of the Essence with Itself, whereas the precedence of the Saints who are Prophets over those who are not lies in receiving a greater plenitude of Divine Manifestation as it were below the level of the Essence, in the realm of the Names and Qualities.

'The Divine Manifestation varieth in intensity from one person to another, nor can any single rule be laid down for it, nor doth it keep to the same mode, but the inward eyes of men are ranged in hierarchy and the secret receptacles are more capacious in some than in others. Even so doth He manifest Himself unto each according to his capacity to receive the manifestations of His Most Holy Beauty in respect of which no end or limit can ever be reached. Know then, in view of these disparities, that such Manifestations of the Names and Qualities and Truths as are vouchsafed unto the holder of the degree of our Lord Muḥammad are beyond the aspirations of the greatest of the Steadfast.[2] Similarly the degree of the Steadfast is beyond the aspirations of the Witnesses of Truth.[3] As to those ejaculations on the part of the greatest of the Gnostics which imply or even definitely claim that they have transcended the degree of the Prophets and Messengers, they are to be explained as follows, and by way of example let us

[1] *Fuṣūṣ al-Ḥikam, Kalimat 'Uzairiyyah.*

[2] This term is taken from the Qoran, XLVI, 35, where it refers directly to the greatest of the pre-Islamic Messengers and by implication also to Muḥammad. But the Shaikh here identifies Muḥammad with the Supreme Spirit.

[3] *Aṣ-Ṣiddīqūn*, the highest of those Saints who are not Prophets. The Shaikh clearly does not set out here to establish a complete hierarchy. Otherwise he would no doubt have mentioned, between these last and the Steadfast, the degree of those Prophets (such as Isaac, Jacob and John the Baptist, for example) who are not Messengers.

take Abū Yazīd al-Bistāmī's "We plunged into a sea while the Prophets remained standing on its shores," and 'Abd al-Qādir al-Jīlānī's "O Companies of Prophets, ye have been given a title, and we have been given that which ye have not been given", and 'Umar ibn al-Fāriḍ's

> 'Haste ye to share my Eternal Union by whose Light
> The tribe's elders are still but the babes I knew in childhood'[1],

and his

> 'All those under thy protection desire thee[2],
> Yet I by myself am worth all the rest,'[3]

and the saying of one of the Gnostics:

' "The steps of the Prophets end where those of the Saints begin."[4] The explanation of these utterances is that the Gnostic hath a time even as the Prophet said: "I have a time wherein only my Lord sufficeth to contain me." Extinction and submersion and annihilation come suddenly upon the Gnostic, so that he goeth out from the sphere of sense and loseth all consciousness of himself, leaving behind all his perceptions, nay, his very existence. Now this annihilation is in the Essence of the Truth, for there floweth down over him from the Holiness of the Divinity a flood which compelleth him to see himself as the Truth's Very Self in virtue of his effacement and annihilation therein. In this state he giveth utterance to such sayings as: "Glory Be to Me!"[5] and "There is no god but I Alone",[5] speaking with the Tongue of the Truth, not with his own tongue, and telling of the Essence of the Truth, not of himself. Such are the demands of the extinction which appertaineth unto this station. We are not to understand that these Saints have transcended the degree of the Prophets. Therefore, my brother, whenever thou hearest of any such utterance on the part of the Shaikhs, interpret it as having

[1] *At-Tā'iyyat al-Kubrā*, l. 760.
[2] All mystics.
[3] *Kāfiyyah*, l. 36.
[4] Al-Ḥakīm at-Tirmidhī (see Massignon, *Essai*, p. 292).
[5] Said by Abū Yazīd al-Bistāmī.

been uttered by them in a state of extinction from themselves and of submersion in the Infinity of their Lord.'[1]

This last quotation is relatively easy to understand, at any rate in theory. More difficult to conceive is the state of the supreme Saint as compared with that of other men at times when his life has not been interrupted by the re-absorption of all his faculties into the Essence.

With regard to one of the Shaikh Al-Būzīdī's disciples, the Shaikh says: 'One of our brethren was troubled and perplexed by the case of Jacob and the grief which he suffered on account of Joseph, according to the words of the Qoran: *His eyes grew white with blindness for the grief that he was suppressing.*[2] He asked me how he could have felt such exceeding sorrow, and how the beauty of Joseph could have diverted his attention from the Truth, and he quoted as an argument the words of Ibn al-Fāriḍ:

> 'If the Beauty of His Face in Jacob's ears they had sounded,
> The beauty of Joseph from Jacob's memory had been banished'[3]

'I humoured him until he had subsided, and then I said to him: 'Jacob's exceeding sorrow was not for the person of Joseph, but because Joseph was for him a place of the Manifestation of the Truth, so that when Joseph was by, Jacob's own presence with God was increased in intensity. The Truth would appear unto Jacob in Joseph even as He appeared unto Moses in Mount Sinai so that Moses could scarce attain unto the Great Intimacy save when he was on the mountain, although God is Present in every place. *He is with you wheresoe'er ye be.*[4] Even thus would the Beauty of the Truth manifest Itself unto Jacob in the form of Joseph, so that he could not endure to part with him, for he had become as the orientated sanctuary of his vision of God. Likewise did the Prophet say: 'I saw God in the form of a beardless youth.' Hence also the prostration of the Angels before Adam, for God created him in His Image, and hence also the prostration of some of the Christians unto

[1] *Minaḥ*, pp. 51-2.
[2] XII, 84.
[3] *Fā'iyyah*, l. 38.
[4] Qoran, LVII, 4.

Jesus even in his lifetime and their attributing unto him the Attributes of Divinity. All these prostrations were unto God, and unto none other than God, for the Manifestation of His Beauty can be so intense in some forms that the human imperfections are obliterated.

'Men of perfect intelligence, the Prophets and the elect of the Saints, know Him who manifesteth Himself in the form, not the form itself, so that their knowledge, far from implying limitation and comparability, is an affirmation of His Transcendence and Incomparability, and when they contemplate Him in any form their vision is attributed unto His Name the Outwardly Manifest.

'Jacob's intimacy with God had been wont to grow exceedingly intense when he beheld his son, and when he lost him direct vision came not so readily unto him. Thus was it that he grieved.

'Thou shouldst know also that although the Truth appeareth unto His slaves in some forms, yet is He Jealous on behalf of those His other forms wherein they are unmindful of Him, for the limited form whereunto they attach themselves is very often of the most fleeting transience. Therefore the Truth trieth those whom He loveth by the sudden disappearance of the form, so that their vision may be deflected from the part unto the whole, as He did with Jacob.'[1]

It is clear from this passage that there is no comparison between the intimacy of the Saint even at its lowest degree, and the remoteness of the mere believer. The words: 'When Joseph was by, Jacob's own presence with God was increased in intensity' show that Jacob was always present with God even when Joseph was not there. Similarly, in another passage, with reference to the state of supreme sanctity, the Shaikh speaks of the Divinity 'taking one of His slaves unto Himself and bringing him into His Presence, where sometimes He revealeth Himself unto Him, and sometimes withdraweth from him.'[2]

That the 'withdrawal' in question is merely as it were a separation within the framework of a union is confirmed a few pages later where, having considered what must and must

[1] *Minaḥ*, pp. 70-1.
[2] *Minaḥ*, p. 20.

not be believed of God, he goes on to consider what may be believed of Him, that is, what is neither inevitable nor impossible. These possibles he divides into the two categories of 'self-evident possibility' (that which is more or less bound to happen on occasion) and 'non-self-evident possibility' (that which is theoretically possible, but improbable):

'An example of self-evident possibility is that a creature should be drawn into the Presence of the Truth and that he should become one of the people of direct contemplation without any previous spiritual effort on his part. An example of theoretic possibility is that God should eject one of His loved ones from among the people of contemplation and nearness and that He should place him amongst those who are cut off from Him and veiled, for this might indeed happen, though none perceiveth the possibility thereof save after due reflection, on account of the strangeness and rarity of such an occurrence among the Folk—may God protect us and all who submit to Him from the like!'[1]

There can be no doubt that the rare 'cutting off' here referred to is altogether different from the regularly repeated 'separation' of beatific sobriety. One must beware however of trusting to the terminology rather than the context, for the Shaikh says that when the Saint's faculties are given back to him after having been utterly absorbed in the Divine Essence, 'it may be that he will say: "I am cut off after being united. I have gone forth once more after I had entered in", until thou mightest think that he had never sensed the fragrance of God's welcome. And yet his Beloved is not hidden from him but hath only let down the thinnest of curtains that He may hear him call unto Him and that He may see him turn unto Him for refuge,[2] and this is what God desireth of the Gnostic, at all times.'[3]

[1] *Minaḥ*, p. 28.

[2] These altogether universal considerations explain why even Śri Ramana Maharshi forsakes at moments his methodically perpetual standpoint of Supreme Identity to say in his hymns: 'Save me . . . and honour me with union with Thyself, O Arunācala!', and 'Smile with Grace and not with scorn on me who come to Thee, O Arunācala!' (see Frithjof Schuon, *Language of the Self*, pp. 52–3, Ganesh-Luzac).

[3] *Minaḥ*, pp. 160-1.

Abu 'l-'Abbās al-Mursī[1] used to pray: 'O Lord, open our inward eyes and illumine our secret parts, and extinguish us from ourselves, and give us subsistence in Thee, not in ourselves.'[2] This extinction from oneself and subsistence in God are precisely what the Shaikh has termed in a previously quoted passage 'death to creation' and 'resurrection in God.' In summing up all that he tells us about the Supreme Station (*Al-Maqām al-A'lā*), that is, the state of 'the Prophets and the elect of the Saints', one may say that the subsistence in God is Absolute Eternal Infinite Oneness, within the framework of which there is room—if one may seek to express the inexpressible—for relative 'separation' and 'reunion'. Subsistence in God during life on earth will normally be extended as it were in hierarchy throughout the three worlds. As we saw in a previous chapter, this hierarchic subsistence in God is affirmed, in ascending order, by the words *Muḥammadun Rasūlu 'Llāh*, and here the possibility of the relative 'separation' within the Absolute Oneness is at its greatest. But when the hierarchy of the three worlds 'melts' into the One World of the Essence, the possibility of even relative 'separation' no longer exists. Moreover this subsistence of 'union' is in a sense always retained even in 'separation', for 'Wheresoe'er be the letter, there with it is always its ink'.

The state of 'extended' subsistence in God, expressed by the words *Muḥammadun Rasūlu 'Llāh*, is further defined by the Shaikh as follows:

'When the Gnostic knoweth God in His Essence and Qualities and is drowned in direct vision thereof, this Gnosis should not take him beyond the prescribed bounds, but he maintaineth a deep-rooted integration of his law-abiding outside with his visionary inside. His separation (*farq*) veileth him not from his union (*jam'*),[3] nor his union from his separation. He beholdeth directly the Truth within him, while the Law is binding upon him from without.'[4]

Elsewhere he says that spiritual perfection demands 'that

[1] The successor of Abu 'l-Ḥasan ash-Shādhilī.

[2] Quoted by the Shaikh ad-Darqāwī, *Rasā'il*, q. 3, p. 2.

[3] He has already 'apologized' for his terminology by quoting Jīlī's: 'He (man) is not joined to Thee, nor is he separate from Thee.'

[4] *Minaḥ*, p. 31.

one should combine outward stability with inward overwhelmedness, so that one is outwardly spiritual effort and inwardly contemplation, outwardly obedient to God's command and inwardly submissive (*mustaslim*) to His Utter Compulsion[1, 2], and that the Supreme State belongs to those 'who combine sobriety (*ṣaḥw*) with uprootedness (*iṣṭilam*)'.[3]

This same double qualification of full spiritual maturity—or virility (*rujūliyyah*) as the Shaikh usually calls it—is expressed in the Glory (*ṣalāh*)[4] and Peace (*salām*) of the second formula of the rosary. He says: 'By *ṣalāh* the Sufis mean the Manifestation of Divine Glory as when God poureth forth His Radiance upon one of His slaves, taking him unto Himself and bringing him into His presence. As for *salām*, Peace, when it is conferred by God on His slaves, it denoteth safety and stability beneath the Glory that hath come over them. One must therefore not ask God for his Glory alone, but for His Glory together with his Peace, nor must one mention the Peace first, for it referreth back unto the Glory, denoting stability and strength beneath it. Now God may manifest His Glory unto some of His slaves and delay the vouchsafing of His Peace, so that the Glory shaketh them with all manner of agitation and turmoil, and causeth them to cry out, and divulge some teaching unto those who are not qualified to receive it. Thus are they wrongfully accused and unjustly condemned, all by reason of the isolation of God's Glory upon them. Therefore if God wisheth to preserve them and to preserve others through them, He immediately followeth up His Glory with His Peace, whereupon their agitation is stilled and the course of their lives is made straight, so that outwardly they are among creatures and inwardly with the Truth, integrating two opposite states and combining the wisdom of each. They are the heirs of the Prophets, and they refer unto this noble station as drunkenness and sobriety, or extinction and

[1] That is, inwardly predestined and outwardly having free will (we see here, as always, that the mystics carry in themselves the solutions to the so-called 'problems' of religion) which needs, as complement, another of his formulations about this state, namely that its possessor is 'inwardly free (because he is none other than Destiny) and outwardly enslaved' (*Minaḥ*, p. 117).

[2] *Minaḥ*, p. 199.

[3] *Minaḥ*, p. 208.

[4] This word can only be so translated when God is the agent.

subsistence, and the like. Thus by drunkenness they mean God's manifesting His Glory unto them, whereas sobriety is Peace after being utterly overwhelmed in the direct vision of their Lord. Now it is the special prerogative of the Prophets that God's Peace should come upon them together with His Glory, or immediately after It; but as for His Saints, some of them are characterized by the manifestation of His Glory without his Peace, and some die in this state, whilst others (the heirs of the Prophets) return unto their senses while remaining inwardly firm-fixed in drunkenness.'[1]

This return is as if the Divine Centre should flood the whole circle of creation, filling it with 'uncreatedness'—as indeed It has never ceased to fill it—as far as its outermost circumference, where lie the sharpest illusions of 'other than God'. It is to this 'meeting of the finite with the Infinite' (it can scarcely be spoken of without some such contradiction in terms) that Ghazālī alludes in his already quoted words:

> 'Each thing hath two faces, a face of its own and a face of its Lord; in respect of its own face it is nothingness, and in respect of the Face of God it is Being.'

The Shaikh also refers to the same mystery, in so far as it concerns the 'circumference' of the Saint, when he says in one of his poems:

> All glorification of me cometh short
> Of the measure, as doth all contempt.[2]

What cannot be 'contemned' enough is his apparently independent individual self, which is a pure illusion:

> Think it not me thou seest here
> Clad in human qualities.[3]

But since for most men this 'face of nothingness' is his only reality, he is bound to speak on occasion with the 'voice of

[1] *Minaḥ*, pp. 20-2. This is also the main tenor of his little treatise *Dauḥat al-Asrār*.
[2] *Dīwān*, p. 31.
[3] *Ibid.*, p. 17.

nothingness',[1] as when he says: 'I am going at last to take my rest in the Presence of God' or, with reference to the Face of Being. 'It is easier to live with than it was.'

What cannot be 'glorified' enough is the Divine Self, which has become forever his immediate centre of consciousness, and of which he writes:

Thou who seekest to know my wisdom
Unto God address thy questions,
For mankind knoweth me not.
Hidden are my states from them.
Seek me as thou drawest nigh
To Him, beyond the state of slavehood,
For in the created universe
No residue of me remaineth. . . .
A river, I, of the o'erflowing
Mercy of the All-Merciful
In flood on earth for men to see[2]

[1] Christ spoke with the 'voice of nothingness' when he said: 'Why callest thou me good? There is none good but one, that is, God' (*St. Matthew*, XIX, 17).

[2] *Dīwān*, p. 17.

CHAPTER IX

GNOSIS

In considering what is possible and what is not, the Shaikh mentions as an example of 'self-evident impossibility' the impossibility of relegating the Essence, that is, of setting It on one side. It follows, without being immediately obvious, that the eye of the body, whose normal objects of vision are earthly things, cannot see the Essence as distinct from the world of the senses, for this would mean relegating the Essence to other than this world. He mentions this as an example of 'non-self-evident impossibility', an impossibility which had not been evident to Moses, for instance, when he asked to see God.[1]

'When Moses asked to see God distinctly, apart from the world, He answered him: *Thou shalt not see Me*, for I am not outside the world nor am I in it; I am neither separate from it, nor joined unto it. *Gaze upon the mountain: if it stand firm in its place, then shalt thou see Me*. And *when his Lord manifested Himself unto the mountain*, and the shadow gave place to the substance, and separation attained unto union, and the mountain and all other places were levelled out of sight, *Moses fell down senseless*, for 'between' had been obliterated and 'where' had vanished, and the eye had been refreshed with the Eye.'[2, 3]

The difference between the Manifestation of the Truth to the mountain for the sake of Moses and to *the Lote Tree of the Uttermost End*[4] for the sake of Muhammad would seem to be that whereas Moses was unprepared—hence the extreme violence attendant upon the vision—Muhammad was fully

[1] Qoran, VII, 143. It is from this verse (in italics) that the Shaikh quotes in the following paragraph.

[2] Or Essence; that is, the human eye of Moses had been replaced by the Divine Eye.

[3] *Minah*, p. 28.

[4] This celestial tree, which Muhammad saw on his Night Journey (see p. 35, note 3) marks the summit of the created universe.

prepared inasmuch as on the Night Journey he was altogether in the next world, which meant that his outward eye was spontaneously and perfectly co-ordinated with his inward eye. But the Shaikh affirms that it is none the less possible for the outward eye, while still 'in this world', to see the Truth, provided that it can first achieve a perfect co-ordination with the inward eye.[1]

'The outward eye is the ray of the inward eye and the faqīr should not open his outward eye (in the hope of seeing Reality) until the connection hath been established between it and his inward eye. When, in virtue of this connection, his outward eye hath become pure inward vision, then will he see the Lord of the verse *Naught is like unto Him* with all his faculties,[2] just as he will also hear Him with all his faculties, even as one of us hath said:

> I am all eyes when He appeareth before me
> Even as when He converseth with me, I am all ears.'[3,4]

The Qoran mentions two visions which the Prophet had of the Truth during the Night Journey, one with the inward eye, the Heart, and one with the outward eye. The vision of the Lote Tree was the second of these, and it is described as follows:

Verily he saw Him at another revelation by the Lote Tree of the Uttermost End. Even here is the Garden of Ultimate Refuge.

[1] During this life the Saint's 'resurrection in God' is a resurrection of the soul, not yet of the body. But through the co-ordination just referred to, he may also have foretaste of the resurrection of the body.

[2] He has already been quoted as teaching that the Intellect is as an outpost of Divine Sight, and he has just extended the continuity still further by saying that the ray of the Intellect virtually reaches as far as the outward eye. In speaking now of all the outward faculties he means that they are all as differentiated 'rays' or branches of the Intellect which, being a synthesis, may be called 'inward eye', 'inward ear', etc., according to the context. The co-ordination of the outward eye with the inward eye implies that the other outward faculties will also be co-ordinated with their intellectual archetype; and in virtue of this co-ordination each outward faculty will take on something of the versatility of synthesis which normally belongs to the Intellect alone, so that, for example, the touch, smell and taste will become as it were endowed with both vision and hearing.

[3] 'Alī, the grandson of 'Umar ibn al-Fāriḍ, '*Ainiyyah* l. 32.

[4] *Minaḥ*, p. 174.

When there enshrouded the Lote Tree That which enshroudeth, the eye wavered not nor did it transgress. Verily he beheld, of all the Signs of his Lord, the Greatest.[1]

In his commentary[2] on these verses, the Shaikh says: 'This vision was with the eye of the senses, whereas the previous one had been with the eye of the intelligence. Now the genitive after Lote Tree is possessive, and what is meant is the Lote Tree of Him at whom all things reach their end. *Verily thy Lord is the Uttermost End.* The Lote Tree here signifieth the whole of manifestation which groweth out from its root in Him. Thus is it also named the Tree of the Universe.

'This vision was more excellent than that which preceded it in virtue of its union of separate elements and its integration of widely scattered fragments. Thus He said: *Even here is the Garden of Ultimate Refuge*, meaning that the Lote Tree marketh a finality of Gnosis, and that he who attaineth unto this point is enshrouded by the Lights of the Divine Presence—nay, the whole world is enshrouded, so that he seeth naught without seeing therein God. This is explained in the words *When there enshrouded the Lote Tree That which enshroudeth*, that is, when it was enfolded and covered by the all-enshrouding Lights of the Divinity, so that the whole hierarchy of created beings disappeared, the majestic and the lowly, in the manifestation of the Lights of the Names and Qualities. *God is the Light of the Heavens and of the earth.* It was through the appearance of These, which is referred to in the words *at another revelation*, that Muḥammad attained unto more through the vision of the outward eye than through the vision of the Heart alone. His outward eye was at its vision one with his inward eye, and therefore did God praise him with the words: *His eye wavered not, nor did it transgress*, that is, the outward eye wavered not from what the inward eye beheld, nor did it transgress by going beyond the bounds and turning its attention away from that wherein the Truth manifested Himself unto him, but it kept its gaze upon Him in each several thing. . . .

'Now the Truth is not to be seen by any outward eyes whatsoever except their sight be inverted and have taken on

[1] LIII, 13-8.
[2] *Lubāb al-'Ilm fī Sūrat Wa'n-Najm*, a commentary on the whole Chapter of the Star, in which these verses occur.

the function of the inward eye, even as the sight of Muhammad's outward eye had been inverted and become one with his inward eye. The *Rūh al-Bayān*, citing *At-Ta'wīlāt an-Najmiyyah*,[1] saith that his other-worldly sight was united with his earthly sight so that with the former he beheld the Inward Aspect of the Truth in respect of His Name *the Inwardly Hidden*, and with the latter he beheld the Outward Aspect of the Truth in respect of His Name the *Outwardly Manifest*.

'Now what if thou askest: 'What impedeth others also from seeing Him with the outward eye in this world, inasmuch as nothing can come between the sight and His Outward Manifestation? And in what consisteth the special privilege of the Prophet's vision?", my answer is that the cause of the impediment is not that the Truth refuseth to allow the sight to fall upon His Essence. The sight's lack of vision is the natural result of its lack of preparation. As one of the greatest of us hath said, what preventeth vision of the Truth in this world is that the creatures recognize Him not. They have eyes, yet they see not, that is, they know not that what lieth before their gaze is the Truth, being veiled from Him by naught else but their own obtuseness. The special privilege of the Prophet cometh from his being more perfect than others in intellectual penetration. He knew with all certainty that the sight cannot attach itself unto nothing, and that therefore no object of sight can be void of the Outward Manifestation of the Truth, for things in themselves are naught. Thus there came over him the vision of the outward eye, nor is anyone who hath inherited the least share of the Prophet's penetration cut off from the Truth's Outward Manifestation in things.

'The Heart's vision was hierarchically nearer to the Truth than was the vision of the outward eye, which could never have achieved the union of separate elements and the integration of widely scattered fragments if the universe had not been enshrouded by the all-enshrouding Lights of Unification which are lit from the tree of *Wheresoe'er ye turn there is the Face of God.*[2] Whoso attaineth unto This hath reached an End

[1] By the Sufi Ahmad as-Samnānī (d. 1336).

[2] He is here commenting indirectly on the Verse of Light (Qoran, XXIV, 35): *God is the Light of the Heavens and of the earth. His Light* (on earth) *is like a niche, wherein is a lamp; the lamp is of glass; the glass is like a shining planet.*

beyond which there is no passing, and Muhammad's attainment thereunto is indicated in the words *Verily he beheld, of all the Signs of his Lord, the Greatest.* We know from this last word that the Sign in question was not of the category of created beings nor yet of the Manifestations of the Names and Qualities,[1] but it can have been no less than the direct vision of the Lights of the Holy Essence. Thus was this state greater than all his other states, and of it he said: "I have a time when only my Lord sufficeth to contain me," and in this connection also did he say: "Increase me, O Lord, in marvelling at Thee."

'What I have said about the possibility of the outward eye gazing at the Truth in direct vision is so exceedingly improbable in the opinion of most of those who make a claim to learning, let alone those who make no such claim, that some may even consider it as being against reason and also against the Law. Such was the opinion of the Muʿtazilites,[2] and they were satisfied that this conclusion was necessary on the grounds that what is seen must be localized in order that the sight may fall upon it. They were not fully alert unto the inevitable corollary of this, that the Sight of the Truth would be prevented from fixing Itself upon created beings, on the ground that Its doing so would presuppose Its localization upon the object seen. Thus in following them we should be attributing a lack of perception unto God—High Exalted is He above all such incapacity! The remedy is not to speculate about the spiritual state in question, but to leave it unto its masters, for indeed the mysteries thereof are beyond the scope of most intelligences.'[3]

It is lit from a sacred olive tree that is neither of the East nor of the West, the oil whereof well nigh blazeth though the fire have not touched it—Light upon Light! God leadeth to His Light whom he will, and God citeth symbols for men, and God is the Knower of all things.

Inasmuch as it is *neither of the East nor of the West,* the sacred olive is the tree of *wheresoever ye turn . . . ,* that is, the tree of Gnosis.

[1] He has already said that at the manifestation of *That which enshroudeth* 'the whole hierarchy of created things disappeared . . . in the manifestation of the Lights of the Names and Qualities.' These were evidently a transitional preparation for the Supreme Lights of the Greatest Sign. To use another of his metaphors, it may be said that for the words to be re-absorbed into the Point they must first be re-absorbed into the letters.

[2] A rationalistic heretical sect of early Islam.

[3] *Lubāb,* pp. 8-10.

CHAPTER X

THE RITUAL PURIFICATION

It is a general principle of Sufism that a thorough grounding in exoterism is indispensable as a preparation for entry upon the esoteric path; and in the Darqāwī Ṭarīqah, at the time when the Shaikh wrote *Al-Minaḥ al-Quddūsiyyah*,[1] all novices were made to learn by heart Ibn 'Āshir's *Guide to the Essentials of Religious Knowledge* as a means of ensuring that they had a minimum of religious instruction.

This little verse treatise is divided into three parts, one for each of the three planes of the religion—*īmān*,[2] *islām*, *iḥsān*, that is, theology, canon law (including ritual obligations), and mysticism. *Al-Minaḥ al-Quddūsiyyah* is only one of many commentaries on it. But it differs from the others in that it transposes the two lower planes of the religion on to the highest plane, reintegrating *īmān* and *islām* in *iḥsān*[3] by giving a purely mystical interpretation both to the doctrine and the rites. When the Shaikh finally comes to the last part, that is, to Ibn 'Āshir's exposition of Sufism he says: 'Until now I have but taken my bearings from the poem, regardless of what may have required comment in its details of expression, but now I propose to follow it literally, word for

[1] As we have seen, he wrote the first version during the Shaikh Al-Būzīdī's life-time, but subsequently revised it before publication.

[2] If it be asked why Ibn 'Āshir does not take them either in ascending or descending hierarchic order, the answer is no doubt that he follows the order which is natural for an exposition, treating of doctrine before ritual, and leaving until the end what does not concern everybody.

[3] Of *iḥsān* he says: 'It is the finality of what precedeth it, that is, the finality of submission (*islām*) and the finality of faith (*īmān*). Therefore is it named excellence (*iḥsān*) in the sense of perfecting a thing or being an adept at it, and whoso hath no foothold in the Station of Excellence, his submission unto God cometh short of the measure.' (*Minaḥ*, p. 79). In other words *iḥsān*—or Sufism —is an extra dimension, of depth or of height, added to *islām* and *īmān*. *Iḥsān* itself may also be considered as susceptible of taking on an extra dimension, and thus he says (p. 77) that whereas the beginning of *iḥsān* is *murāqabah* (vigilance), its end is *mushāhadah* (direct contemplation). Elsewhere (p. 151) he remarks that the inward aspects of *islām*, *īmān* and *iḥsān* are respectively *istislām* (see p. 169), *īqān* (certainty) and '*iyān* (face-to-face vision).

word.'[1] But he does not dwell much on this part of the poem since he has already commented on it implicitly in what has gone before.

The symbolism of a rite is its very essence, without which it would lose its ritual quality. A prostration of the body, for example, which does not signify inward effacement is a mere physical act, and the same applies to an ablution which does not signify inward purification. Definitions of the degree of inward effacement and purification respectively symbolized by the rites of prostration and ablution will vary according to each person's powers of conception; and so it is with all other rites. Ghazālī mentions that the pilgrim's doffing of his sandals before his ritual entry upon the Pilgrimage, signifies, like Moses' doffing of his in the Holy Valley[2], stripping oneself of this world and the next; but he adds: 'Yet if thy soul taketh flight before this symbolism, seek comfort in His Words: *He sendeth down water from heaven so that the valleys are in flood with it, each according to its capacity*,[3] for the commentaries tell us that the water is Gnosis and that the valleys are Hearts.'[4]

He follows this up with a passage in which he may be said to speak with the voice of all true mystics as regards the symbolic interpretation of sacred texts:

'Whoso taketh unto himself the outward or literal meaning alone, abstracting it from the whole, is a materialist (*ḥashwī*), and whoso taketh unto himself the inward meaning alone, abstracting it from the whole, is a pseudo-mystic (*bāṭinī*), but whoso combineth the two is perfect. Even so did the Prophet say: "The Qoran hath an outside and an inside, like a wall with a watch-tower above it." Or perchance it was 'Alī who said this, since its lineage stoppeth short at him. My meaning is that Moses understood that in being told to doff his two sandals he was being told to strip himself of the two worlds, so he obeyed the command outwardly by doffing his sandals and inwardly by doffing the worlds. Such is the true relationship:

[1] *Minaḥ*, p. 313.
[2] Qoran, XX, 12.
[3] Qoran, XIII, 17.
[4] *Mishkāt al-Anwār*, p. 128.

one must pass to and fro, from the one to the other, from outward word to inward secret.'[1]

Almost all the Sufi writers have referred in their poems or treatises to the inner meaning of the Islamic rites, some only in passing, others with more insistence.[2] But it is very possible that the Shaikh was the first—and that he will prove to be the last—to write a comprehensive commentary which gives a metaphysical interpretation of the smallest details of ritual not merely as regards what is obligatory (*farḍ*), but also as regards what is recommended (*mandūb*), permitted (*mubāḥ*), strongly discouraged (*makrūh*) and forbidden (*ḥarām*).

In commenting on Ibn ʿĀshir's verse:

'Purity is thine through water which naught else hath changed'

he says: 'Purity is reached through Absolute Water, the Water of the Unseen, that is, the Limpidity with which the visible world is flooded,[3] Limpidity which is variegated in Its manifestation, One with Itself in Its seeming multiplicity, Self-manifested, Hidden through the intensity of Its manifestation, Absolute in Its relativity—this is the Water which is free from any taint and which availeth for purification; and of It hath one of the Gnostics said:

'With the Water of the Unseen make thine ablution
If thou hast the Secret, and if not, with earth or stone.'[4]

[1] *Ibid.*, pp. 128-9.

[2] See, for example, Ghazālī, *Iḥyā'*, III-VII; Ibn 'Arabī, end of *Fuṣūṣ al-Ḥikam*; Jīlī, end of *Al-Insān al-Kāmil*.

[3] He means, in other words, the ink with which the letters are flooded (see above, pp. 150-1) that is, the Divine Essence.

[4] Sha'rānī, in his life of Abu 'l-Mawāhib ash-Shādhilī (*Ṭabaqāt, II*) attributes these verses to Ibn 'Arabī, and quotes Abu 'l-Mawāhib's commentary: 'The meaning of ablution is the purification of the limbs of the qualities of the Heart from the defilements of mental conceptions; and the Water of the Unseen is Pure Unification (*Tawḥīd*). If thou have not direct access unto It in Its Purity, then cleanse thyself with the clean earth of logical demonstration, (see also E. J. Jurji, *Illumination in Islamic Mysticism*, pp. 80-1).

Of this earth-purification which the Law allows to take the place of the ablution if one cannot find water, or if one is not well and fears some harm from using water, the Shaikh says (p. 111): 'He who feareth to lose the balance of his soul should perform the earth-purification, keeping to the outside of the

This is the Water of the Unseen which availeth for purification, and all other water in relation unto it is as dry sand, not to be used except when this Water hath been lost. In order to qualify for use in this special rite of purification, water must be free from any taint. This restriction excludeth the waters of the sensible world and the psychic world, since both these waters have suffered change from their original state. It is the Water of the Spirit which fulfils all that the definition requireth, for This is indeed Absolute, being free from any taint, and remaining ever as It was, not adulterated by anything, not flavoured by anything, not added to anything, not restricted by anything, with naught above It and naught beneath It. Here lieth the Truth of Absoluteness and it is only This that deserveth the name Water. By It, naught else, may one attain to purification from the existence of "other". Thou shouldst know, moreover, that the springs whence this Water floweth are the Hearts of the Gnostics, and therefore he that aspireth unto purification must seek out their tents and wait humbly at their doors. If he findeth this Water,[1] then let him look to the three qualifications[2] and if these be fulfilled he hath gained what he sought. But if he findeth that it hath suffered change from what it originally was inasmuch as something hath adulterated it, then it must be judged according to the cause of adulteration, even as our author hath said:

> If it be changed by aught unclean, 'tis thrown away
> But if by aught that's clean, 'twill serve for common use.

The meaning of "changed by aught unclean" is that it hath been

---

Law and constraining himself to do deeds of piety until he be cured of his ailment. The same holdeth good also of him who findeth no water, that is, who findeth no one to initiate him into that Unification which is the prerogative of the elect.' Elsewhere (p. 106) he says that earth represents 'the Lore of Certainty' (*'Ilm al-Yaqīn*), that is, mental knowledge of the doctrine, whereas water represents 'the Truth of Certainty' (*Ḥaqq al-Yaqīn*), direct intellectual perception, Gnosis, and he quotes 'Ali ibn al-Fāriḍ (the grandson of 'Umar): 'Pass on unto the Truth of Certainty, transcending all that others tell thee, and thine own mind which is a barrier. (*'Ainiyyah*, 1. 45).

[1] That is, if he believes that he has found it, namely, if he finds one who appears to be a spiritual Master in the fullest sense.

[2] These are that it should be Absolute, free from any taint (that is, free from any presence other than its own), and remaining ever as it was,—in other words, Absolute, Infinite, Eternal.

tainted by a lower soul that claimeth independent existence, for if the lower soul hath imparted its flavour unto the water, then hath the being of that water become as nothingness, and it will serve neither for worship nor yet for common use, but is thrown away and shunned. But if he findeth that it hath been changed in one or all of its attributes by something clean, then it will serve for common use, not for worship; and the meaning of "common use" is that it will serve as a means of helping one to carry out the obligations of the religion and to avoid what is forbidden and to perform voluntary acts of piety such as fasting and keeping vigil and the like; but it will not serve as a preparation for worship,[1] which is a means of entering the Presence of God and beholding Him. The purity needed for this is not to be attained save by finding the Real Water. In short, there are three kinds of water, unclean, clean and Pure: he that hath the unclean water is one whose water is adulterated with love of this world and excess of inclination unto it, and he that hath the clean water is one whose soul is permeated with such exceeding love of the next world as hath turned him away from loving its Creator, whereas he that hath the Pure Water is he who is wholly unadulterated and untainted, having no desire and no quest apart from his Lord, and not consenting to be aught apart from Him. The worship of such is unto God through God, even as one of them hath said:

Some worship through their fear of Hell,
Seeing in salvation an ample boon,
And others worship that they may dwell
In Paradise, and bask till noon
In the meads, then drink of Selsebil.[2]
I keep not Heaven or Hell in view.
For naught I'll change my Love: Thou me
In spirit, blood, bone, breath, through and through
Hast penetrated. Even so
A thorough friend must thorough be.'[3]

[1] It will serve as a means to the relative purity necessary for salvation, but not as a means to the Absolute Purity of the Prophets and their heirs, who alone know what worship is in its highest sense, which he defines later.

[2] A Fountain in Paradise (see Qoran, LXXVI, 18).

[3] From the basic Arabic root *khā'-lām-lām* are derived the words *takhallul* (intimate penetration) and *khalīl* (intimate friend). These verses are attributed to Rābi'ah al-'Adawiyyah.

'This is the Truth[1] of the Water's Limpidity and Purity, so that he who findeth It not suffereth privation indeed. Therefore let him who hath intelligence spare no pains in his quest for It, nor be content with aught else, and let him take It even there where he findeth It, though it cost him all his fortune and his very soul.

'Water is not spoiled if it hath been changed by nothing other than stagnation. Hence the exception:

> But if the change be but from long association
> With something clean, if for example it be muddied
> With red clay, count it pure, as also melted ice.

'He maketh exception in this verse for water that hath suffered change only through stagnation and for water that hath melted after being frozen. The exception of stagnancy holdeth good for the intermediary world, whose water was first of all excluded for its being changed from what it originally was; but since this change was through stagnation, it may serve not only for common use but also for worship, yet not for worship unless the Real Water be lost.[2]

'Also included in the exception is the sensible world,[3] but

[1] He means that this is the secret of Its irresistible effectiveness, referring to what the last three verses express of the All-Penetrating Omnipresence of the Divine Spirit which is everywhere and yet at the same time 'no where' since Its Purity transcends all localization. Elsewhere (p. 46) he says: 'When God hath revealed unto them (the Gnostics) the Presence of Eternity and they have beheld the World of Limpidity, they find there the true meaning (by comparison) of ephemerality, for the ephemeral is in a state of constant change, whereas the Archetype is Pure Limpidity unclouded by any turbidness of fluctuation.' Then he quotes Ibn al-Fāriḍ's line about the Eternal Archetypes of all four elements. (*Khamriyyah*, l. 22): Limpidity, not water; Subtlety, not air; Light, not fire; Spirit, not body.

[2] By 'stagnation' he is referring to a Ṭarīqah which has become 'static' because it has no longer a Shaikh who can offer guidance in the fullest sense, but only one who, not being an heir of the Prophets, cannot dispense the Real Water, though he remains none the less orthodox (the water has not been tainted by any alien body). The Real Water is virtually there, in the doctrine (which being primarily addressed to the mind belongs precisely to the intermediary world) and also in the spiritual chain and the rites, and it may be actualized at any moment by special Grace. But such Grace could only be hoped for if one had entered that 'stagnant' brotherhood as a last resort, not if one had wilfully avoided a Shaikh whose Heart flowed with the Real Water.

[3] Yet more remote, beyond the stagnation of the mental world, lies the crystallization of the sensible world. But failing more direct means, virgin

only on condition that it hath melted after its crystallization, in which case it must be considered as Absolute, for the Archetype is Absolute, and to return unto the Archetype is to be once more the Archetype, as the poet of the *'Ainiyyah* hath said:[1]

> The world is nothing other than a berg of ice.
> And thou art of the water that from its sides is flowing.
> Nor is the ice, if we grasp the truth, other than its water.
> Though it be deemèd ice in the doom of the Law
> Yet at the ice's melting is that doom revoked,
> And it is deemèd water, even as in truth it is.'[2]

The purpose of the ablution in Islam is the removal of inward impurity, symbolized by various modes of outward impurity or, in cases of doubt, supposed outward impurity, which necessitate the ablution before one can proceed to the ritual prayer. The Law only defines the outward or symbolic impurity; the conception of what it symbolizes will vary as spiritual aspirations vary. At the highest level its conception is expressed in the already quoted saying of Rābi'ah al-'Adawiyyah: 'Thine existence is a sin with which no other sin can be compared.'

'The meaning of defilement (*ḥadath*)', continues the Shaikh, 'is ephemeral existence (*ḥudūth*), that is, the existence of other than God. This is not ousted from the heart of the Gnostic, and its film is not removed from his inward eye to be replaced in his sight by Eternity, save through his finding the Water and his Purification therewith. Except he be purified by It, he is far from the Presence of his Lord, unfit to enter It, let alone to sit therein. Likewise the slave will not cease to suppose the existence of defilement in all creatures until he have poured

nature (the untainted 'orthodoxy' of the sensible world) has powers of purification for one who can 'absolve' it by reducing it to the Essence, that is, by transforming it, through intellectual penetration, to the flood of Limpidity which it really is.

[1] Jīlī, *Al-Insān al-Kāmil*, ch. 7, says: 'God hath said: *We created the heavens and the earth and all that is between them with naught but Truth* (Qoran, XLVI, 3). Even so is the world like ice and the Truth—Glorious and Exalted—is the Water which is the Origin of this ice. Thus is the name 'ice' but lent unto that crystallization, whose true name is Water.' Then he quotes from his own *'Ainiyyah*, the lines which follow above.

[2] *Minaḥ*, pp. 83-6.

this Absolute Water over their outward appearance. Without It he will not cease to condemn them, and how should his verdict be revoked when he seeth their defilement with his eyes, and when his Heart believeth in the independent existence of creation? Far be it from him to take the outward appearance of things for other than he seeth it to be, and to deem them pure, as if the cause of his condemning them had vanished from his sight. How should he deem them pure, when he seeth their transgression, disobedience, disbelief, hypocrisy, idolatry, contentiousness and the like—how, until he hath changed this standpoint for one which is altogether beyond his experience? On seeing the letter *Shīn*,[1] should he say that it is *Zain*?[2] Nay, he telleth of what he seeth, naught else. Jars only ooze out what is inside them. Thus passeth he judgement upon most creatures that they are guilty of defilement, nor is this verdict rescinded from his Heart, nor is the stain of guilt removed from existing things but through purification with this Absolute Water. Once purity hath been achieved, that is, once he hath washed the outward appearance of things in this Water—nay, once he hath washed his own sight therein, since as for the things they are already pure before they be purified—then will his eyes tell him that his verdict was false, and he will come to see what he had never seen before.'[3]

In distinguishing between the two ablutions, the greater and the lesser, he says that the purity obtained through the lesser, which only involves washing certain parts of the body, signifies extinction in the seven Qualities of the Truth—Power, Will, Knowledge, Life, Hearing, Sight and Speech. This purity, he says, 'is current among both the generality of the Sufis and the elect, unlike the Great Purity which is only for the Prophets and the greatest of the Saints.'[4] To each one of these, when he has obtained the purity of complete extinction signified by the washing of the whole body in the greater ablution, 'the Truth appeareth on a sudden, immediately he hath finished his ablution, and this Vision cometh unto him in Its Totality, with neither limitation nor interruption nor revealing of one part

[1] This suggests also the word *shain* which means 'deformity'.
[2] In many dialects the letter *Zāy* is *Zain*, which also means 'ornament'.
[3] *Minaḥ*, p. 86.
[4] *Minaḥ*, p. 87.

without another, nay the Truth appeareth unto him in All His Manifestations so that he knoweth, by directly seeing it and living it, the verity of His saying *Wheresoever ye turn, there is the Face of God*. Even so did our author speak of the necessity of "rubbing the water all over the body", inasmuch as the Truth's Manifestation embraceth all beings, the higher and the lower, the majestic and the beautiful. Thus doth he attain unto the Station of Intimate Friendship (*khullah*)[1] in that he is permeated with the love of his Beloved, mingled with His Blood and Flesh, both without and within, whence the necessity of "wetting through and through (*takhlīl*)[1] the hair", that the Gnostic may be as thoroughly drenched with the Love of the Truth as is his hair with the water.'[2]

[1] See page 180, note 3.
[2] *Minaḥ*, pp. 97-8.

CHAPTER XI

THE RITUAL PRAYER

Since ablution in its highest sense means the attainment of a state beyond which it is impossible to go, it might be wondered, on first thoughts, what is left for the ritual prayer to symbolize. But what is One in the World of Reality is multiple in 'the world of symbols' as this world is often called, for here the Divine Light is as it were reflected in innumerable mirrors, some of which catch only one of Its aspects, some more. The Supreme Station is symbolized, according to one or more of Its aspects, in every fundamental rite of every religion, when that rite is considered in its highest aspect.[1] The same may even be said of each different part of any composite rite such as the Islamic prayer which consists of a series of ritual acts. It is possible to consider each act either in itself or in relation to the other acts which precede or follow it, that is, either as a complete symbol or as part of a symbol—or as both. This complexity, inherent in all symbolism,[2] is what makes—or helps to make—mystical texts often so difficult for modern Western minds. But the Shaikh assumes that the relatively synthetic intelligences for which he is writing will grasp this complexity as something which is second nature to them, so he says nothing at all to explain it. What appear to be inconsequences or even contradictions in his interpretation of the movements of the ritual prayer are simply caused by the presence of two symbolisms together in his mind at once. For although he is mainly considering the movements of the prayer as mutually related parts of a whole, he never altogether forgets the supreme significance of each movement in itself. In other words—to use a manner of expression which conforms to his—the Water of the Unseen is never very far from the

[1] It is not difficult to see, for example, how this applies to each of the Seven Sacraments of the Church.

[2] This complexity is none other than the complexity of the Universe itself, symbolism being the science of the relationship between the different levels of existence, as Ghazālī explains in the last quoted passage from *Mishkāt al-Anwār*, pp. 177f.

surface and is continually welling up in a spring which floods the whole exposition with the Absolute. This is true of all his writings and confers on them a ritual quality, making them particularly comparable to the prayer itself during which the Absolute continually wells up in flood through the repetition of *Allāhu Akbar*, God is Most Great, at each ritual act[1] except one. As he himself says, the purpose of this repetition by the worshipper is that 'all his moments should be saturated with consciousness of the Absolute Greatness of God.'[2]

Of the *Fātiḥah* he says: 'This is the intimate discourse which is specifically demanded of the worshipper in the Divine Presence when he standeth before his Lord and when the Secrets of the Divinity flow over him in flood. Whoso attaineth unto this Divine Manifestation, on him do the Lights of the Holy Presence shine clear, and he hath reached a state of nearness beyond which there is no going.[3] Naught remaineth

[1] The movements of the prayer are:

(a) Standing up and facing the direction of Mecca, with the hands raised, palms forwards, on either side of the head, the thumbs almost touching the ears and the finger tips more or less on a level with the top of the head.

(b) Saying *Allāhu Akbar*.

(c) Lowering the hands to the sides or clasping them on the breast (this point differs according to the different schools of law—see Appendix A, 10) and reciting the *Fātiḥah* (the opening chapter of the Qoran) followed by some other passage from the Qoran to be chosen by the worshipper.

(d) An obeisance, in which the hands are placed on the knees, so that the back is horizontal.

(e) Rising to full height from the obeisance with the words 'God heareth whoso praiseth Him'. (All the other movements of the prayer, including the obeisance itself, are made to the words *Allāhu Akbar*).

(f) A prostration, which is made by kneeling and placing the forehead on the ground with the hands palm-downwards on either side of it.

(g) Rising from the prostration to a sitting position.

(h) A second prostration.

These movements make up one prayer cycle which is repeated a different number of times according to the different prayers. At the sunset prayer three such cycles are prayed, at night four, at dawn two, at noon four, and at mid afternoon four. At the end of the second cycle of each prayer the sitting position is resumed after (h) for the recitation of a formula dedicating oneself to God and asking for Peace. This is done also at the end of the final cycle, whereupon, instead of standing up for a new cycle, the worshipper seals the prayer from the sitting position with a turn of the head to the right and the words *As-Salāmu 'alaikum*, Peace be on you.

[2] *Minaḥ*, p. 135.

[3] A few pages later (p. 116) he speaks of this stance at the beginning of the prayer as being 'far from the Truth' as compared with the nearness of prostration.

thereafter but the exchanging of confidences. The Folk name this the Station of Intimate Discourse, and in it the ears of the Gnostics are delighted by what is spoken unto them by the Lord of the worlds.'[1]

Then he draws us back to the significance of this in relation to the rest of the prayer rather than as a whole in itself by letting his expression of the Absolute end with a hint that there is more to come and that what has been gained is only a foretaste, not yet an Eternal Possession:

'The best that they hear from their Divine Protector is: "Leaveth this nearness aught to be desired?", whereat he who is immersed in the Lights of contemplation answereth: "Nay indeed, and therefore *Praise be to God, the Lord of the Worlds*,"[2] inasmuch as he hath been favoured beyond others and hath gained what his imagination had been powerless to conceive, even as one of them hath said:

> I gained my Desire beyond my highest hopes.
> O that It were mine, utterly and forever![3,4]

In considering the prayer as a whole he gives a summary account of it as follows:

'When he hath made good his entry into the rite of the prayer (by raising his hands and saying *Allāhu Akbar*) and when the Lights of Divine Manifestation have shone visibly upon him, he beginneth to draw himself in little by little and his first shrinkage is the letting down of his hands to his sides or putting them on to his breast, after they had been on a level with the top of his head. All this is through his approach unto the Truth, and the nearer he approacheth the more he draweth himself in. First it is demanded of the worshipper that he raise himself unto his full height and lift his hands before the

[1] *Minaḥ*, p. 112.
[2] The first words of the 'intimate discourse' which is spoken at this part of the prayer.
[3] Ibn al-Fāriḍ, *Lāmiyyah* (Ushāhidu ma'nā ḥusnikum . . .) l. 5.
[4] *Minaḥ*, pp. 112-13.

Manifestation of the Truth upon him. But when some degree of union hath been achieved and he hath begun to approach nearer and nearer unto the Truth, his stature is changed and his existence is brought low and beginneth to be folded up *like the folding of a written scroll*,[1] all on account of his nearness unto the Truth, until he attaineth unto the extremity of nearness, which is in the state of prostration. The Prophet said: "The slave is nearest his Lord when in prostration." At his prostration he descendeth from the stature of existence unto the fold of nothingness, and the more his body is folded up, the more is his existence folded up, even as one hath said:

> My existence hath come to naught in my vision, and I have parted
> From the 'I' of my vision, effacing it, not affirming it[2]

'Before his prostration the Gnostic had the upright stature of existence, but after his prostration he hath become extinct, a thing lost, effaced in himself and Eternal in his Lord.'[3]

It has already been mentioned that among the movements of the prayer there is one obeisance followed by two prostrations. Having specified that the obeisance signifies 'effacement of the actions and also of the qualities (in the Divine Actions and Qualities)', he says of prostration:

'When the worshipper hath obtained the degree of prostration and hath been extinguished from existence, he prostrateth himself a second time that he may be extinguished from that extinction. Thus is his (second) prostration identical with his rising up from (the first) prostration, which rising signifieth subsistence.'[4]

The Shaikh means that symbolically this rising and falling must be considered as simultaneous; each is an extinction of

[1] Qoran, XXI, 104.
[2] Ibn al-Fārid, *At-Tā'iyyat al-Kubrā*, l. 212. The poem continues:
'I embraced what I perceived, and effaced mine own perceiving'
that is, I embraced the Object of my vision and effaced its subject.
[3] *Minaḥ*, pp. 156-7.
[4] *Minaḥ*, p. 114.

the extinction in that each represents a purely positive 'result' of the extinction: the rising means subsistence, whereas the second prostration crowns that subsistence with the crown of Divinity. If we take his already quoted verse:

> Thou seest not who thou art, for thou art, yet art not 'thou'.

then it may be said that the rising means *thou art* whereas the second prostration means *yet art not 'thou'*. Referring to the simultaneity of these two positions, he continues:

> 'He is prostrate with regard unto the Truth, upright with regard unto creation, extinct (even as a Divine Quality is extinct) in the Transcendent Oneness,[1] subsistent in the Immanent Oneness. Thus is the prostration of the Gnostics uninterrupted, and their union knoweth no separation. The Truth hath slain them with a death that knoweth no resurrection. Then He hath given them Life, Endless Life, that knoweth no death.'[2]

With regard to the perpetuity of the prostration, the Shaikh draws our attention to the fact that it is recommended (*mandūb*) that on rising from prostration to the sitting position the worshipper should not *lift* his hands from the ground and place them on his knees but that he should *draw* them up to his knees. He interprets this recommendation as being 'lest one wrongly imagine that after the worshipper prostrateth himself, that is, after he hath been put out of existence and hath taken hold of the Rope of the Essence which is the sum of his desires, on rising he relinquisheth, by lifting his hands, all that he hath gained . . . whereas from this recommendation it is to be concluded that he who hath reached his Goal keepeth ever hold upon the Rope of God.'[3]

[1] The Transcendent Oneness (*Aḥadiyyah*) is Pure Non-Duality, which excludes all concepts such as those of Essence and Quality, Creator and creation, etc. The Immanent Oneness (*Wāḥidiyyah*) is that more outward Aspect of Non-Duality which embraces, penetrates and unifies all apparent differentiation. Jīlī (*Al-Insān al-Kāmil*, ch. 6) says that *Aḥadiyyah* corresponds to 'God was and there was nothing with him' and that *Wāḥidiyyah* corresponds to 'He is now even as He was.'

[2] *Minah*, pp. 114-15.

[3] *Minah*, p. 162.

After the final prostration before the end of the prayer, the worshipper resumes the sitting position from which, after expressions of devotion to God and invocations of Peace on the Prophet, himself and all the faithful, he seals the prayer by turning his head to the right with the words *As-Salāmu 'alaikum*—Peace be on you!

Of this final sitting position the Shaikh says: 'He must take a middle course when he returneth unto creation, that is, he must be seated, which is midway between prostration and standing, that he may make good his intercourse with creation. For if he went out unto creatures in a state of being prostrate, that is, in a state of extinction and obliteration, he could take no notice of them. Nor must he go out unto creation standing, that is, far from the Truth as he used to be before his extinction, for thus would he go out unto creation as one created and there would be no good in him and none would profit from his return. Even so must he take a middle course, and "midmost is best in all things". It is said: "Long live the man who knoweth his own worth and taketh his seat beneath it!" Now a man gaineth knowledge of his worth only at his obliteration. Thus is a sitting position[1] required of him after his obliteration.'[2]

As to what is displeasing to God (*makrūh*) during the prayer, Ibn 'Āshir mentions, amongst other things: 'pondering on what is inconsistent with awestruck reverence.'

The Shaikh says: 'All pondering is in fact inconsistent with awe-struck reverence which (in its fullest sense) is nothing short of amazement and wonderment at the Essence of God. Meditation may be on things that are made, but not on the Essence, even as the Prophet said: "Meditate upon all things, but meditate not on the Essence lest ye perish." Thought is only used with regard unto what is made, but when the Gnostic hath attained unto the Maker, then is his thought changed to wonderment. Thus is wonderment the fruit of thought, and once it hath been achieved the Gnostic must not swerve from

[1] Sitting is 'beneath' prostration which signifies, beyond obliteration, deification.

[2] *Minaḥ*, p. 116.

it nor change it for that which is its inferior. Nor can he ever have enough of wonderment at God, and indeed the Prophet would say: "O Lord, increase me in marvelling at Thee". Meditation is demanded of the faqīr whilst he be on his journey. One meditateth on the absent; but when He that was sought is Present in Person, then is meditation changed into wonderment.'[1]

He quotes:

Give me excess of love, and thus increase me in marvelling at Thee;
And Mercy have upon a Heart with flame of passion seared for thee;
And when I ask to see Thee as Thou art, make not reply *thou shalt not*[2] but let me see.[3]

Also *makrūh* are 'trifling' and 'looking away'. The Shaikh says: 'Trifling, for the Gnostic, is being busied with that which concerneth him not, once he hath realized the degree of Perfection; and everything except being busied with God is such frivolity and trifling as justifieth neither a turn of the head thereunto nor the waste of a moment of time thereon. The occupations in question may be allowed for the generality, but for the Gnostic they are counted ill. 'The good deeds of the Righteous[4] are the ill deeds of the Near'; and if even good deeds can be faults for them, what of other deeds which directly impair their nobility? It is permissible for them to hang out their lamp of this world, but it must be on their outside, and not within them,[5] for the Gnostics are inwardly ever with God, and if their inward parts were to be busied with aught else, they would be trifling in His Presence.

'As to "looking away", it is as if the Gnostic after realizing the Oneness of God by way of direct vision should turn unto another station or seek for something more than he hath already, as if, for example, he should turn unto working wonders and

[1] *Minah*, p. 168.

[2] God's reply to Moses (see p. 171).

[3] Ibn al-Fāriḍ, *Rā'iyyah* (*Zidnī bi-farli 'l-ḥubb*).

[4] See p. 38.

[5] One of the Shaikh's disciples once said to me that it is impossible for a Saint to be preoccupied inwardly even with being a spiritual Guide, and that he will only accept that function if it be imposed upon him, in which case he is given the means of guidance, without any effort on his part.

should crave that normalities be violated on his account,[1] that he may have power, side by side with the Truth, to destroy him whose destruction he willeth and to make safe him whose security he willeth. If God in His Loving-Kindness go not after him and bring him back unto where he was, then will he perish with those that perish, inasmuch as he sought to exchange the better for the worse, the higher for the lower, and was *not content with one food.*[2] Thus it may be feared for him lest he have to *go down unto Egypt,* the Egypt of souls, inasmuch as he was not content with the Presence of the All-Holy.'[3]

He makes it clear however that such an example would only apply to 'those who make false claim to attainment of sanctity.' As regards the true Saint he says: 'The deeds and words and states of the Gnostics range between what is bounden and what is recommended, not going beyond these. But this they achieve with God's Help, so that if any one of them should purpose to turn away from that which is pleasing unto God and His Apostle, it would be scarcely possible for him, nay, he would be incapable of it, and incapability in this sense is God-sent achievement. Hence it is said that the protectedness (*ḥifẓ*) of the Saints is as the infallibility (*'iṣmah*) of the Prophets.'[4]

Passing on to the funeral rites, he says with regard to the washing of the corpse:

'He in whom there is a residue of life is not washed. Even if he were already on the washing table and it was seen that there was life in one of his limbs, the washer would leave him then and there. Even so the Shaikh proceedeth not to the purification of the disciple so long as there be any residue of lower soul in him, that is, unless he hath realized his death, having reduced unto ashes the fire of his nature. Otherwise he will let him be, so long as he hath any claim to be alive. Therefore doth he require of the disciple who is eager to enter the Presence

[1] Elsewhere (p. 171) he says: 'The working of wonders is not a criterion of sanctity such as the slave may seek from God, but rather doth it impose itself upon the slave (at the right moment)'.

[2] Referring to the Jews whom Moses threatened with return to Egypt when they asked for a change from the manna and quails (Qoran, II, 61).

[3] *Minaḥ*, pp. 169-70.

[4] *Minaḥ*, p. 169.

of God that he should first make every effort to reduce his soul unto nothing and to deal the death-blow to his existence, that he may be passive in the hands of the washer, and lest he be left with all his impurities upon him by reason of his stubbornness and wilfulness and want of passivity. Even so did one of them say:

> If Destiny be propitious and if Fate drive thee
> To a veritable Shaikh, one versed in the Truth,
> Then take pains to please him, and follow his wishes,
> And leave all that ere this thou wast bent on achieving.
> Be thou with him as a corpse in the ablutioner's hands.
> He turneth it at will, while it passive remaineth.[1]

'Thus should the disciple be between the hands of his Master, if he would be purified of all that hath contaminated him and if he would escape from his natural limitations. Then when his purification hath been made good and he is cleansed, so that the light of his Heart hath shone forth from the niche[2] of his existence, he must hide it, for guarding secrets is one of the marks of the perfect Gnostic, just as divulging secrets is a characteristic of the ignorant. Here lieth the meaning of the shroud: he must enshroud the glass of Freedom with the niche of servitude until nothing of the secret of his electhood appeareth save what is necessary. When the death of the soul hath been realized, when it hath been purified from seeing with the eye of the senses and cloaked in a seemly garment, then hath it deserved concealment from prying eyes, and this is what is meant by burial, that is, it hath deserved burial in the earth of obscurity, that its growth thereafter may be beautiful and acceptable unto God, even as the author of *al-Ḥikam*[3] hath said:

' "Bury thine existence in the earth of obscurity, for if a seed be not buried it bringeth not forth in fullness."

'Indeed, there is nothing better for the disciple than obscurity after attainment, and no harm is greater for him than fame at that moment, that is, at the moment of his entry unto God,

[1] Jīlī, *'Ainiyyah*.

[2] Using the symbolism of the Verse of Light. (see p. 174, note 2).

[3] A treatise in the form of aphorisms, by Ibn 'Aṭā' Allāh al-Iskandarī, the successor of Abu 'l-'Abbās al-Mursī.

not afterwards, for after his burial in the earth of obscurity there is no harm in the spreading of his fame inasmuch as the growth hath come after the roots were firm, not before, so that there is no doubt that he will bring forth in fullness.

'Moreover he did not seek manifestation for himself, but it was God who manifested him after his burial. He slew him and entombed him; then, if He will, He raiseth him up; but if He will not, then the Gnostic hath it not in him to raise up his own fame of his own accord, for in this station he is void of preference, desiring neither manifestation nor obscuration and being but as a tool in the hands of the Craftsman, as one of them hath said:

' "Thou seest me as an instrument of which He is the Mover. I am a pen in the Fingers of Fate".'[1, 2]

Analogously, by a symbolism parallel to this last, the realization of Supreme Sainthood is mirrored in the funeral prayer. Just as the body yields up the soul at death, so the soul, at spiritual death, yields up the Spirit. The Shaikh says:

'Bodily death taketh not place without the Angel of Death, and even so spiritual death taketh not place save through the intermediary of a Master who knoweth how to grasp the Spirits of his disciples.

'Whoso understandeth the outcome of spiritual death which is the delight of contemplating the Divinity, how should he not deliver up his soul unto destruction, counting all that he leaveth behind him as a trifle, for trifling indeed, in the eye of him who knoweth what he seeketh, is that which he leaveth behind? Nay, though the soul be precious, yonder lieth That which is more precious than it:

The soul is precious, yet for Thee will I exchange it,
And being slain is bitter, yet in Thy Good Pleasure is it sweet.'

'When the disciple surrendereth himself unto a Shaikh that he may unite him with his Lord, then is the Shaikh bound to

[1] Jīlī, *'Ainiyyah*.
[2] *Minaḥ*, pp. 179-81.

bring him into the Presence of God with a rite whose obligations are four.[1]

'Among the obligations through which this death is fulfilled, and through which the existence of the disciple is folded up, are four affirmations of the Greatness of God. The meaning of this is that the Master should cast upon the hearing of his disciple the four Aspects of Being, the Firstness and Lastness and Outward Manifestation and Inward Hiddenness all at once, cutting short all his arguments and stopping up all loop-holes. Then doth the truth of God's Words *He is the First and the Last and the Outwardly Manifest and the Inwardly Hidden* become so evident that when these Aspects have closed their ranks and the disciple findeth no outlet for want of any gap between them, his Spirit departeth and his body goeth to nothing, inasmuch as the directions of space exist no longer for him through his finding not even so much as the breadth of a finger-tip left vacant by these four Aspects, whithersoever he turneth. Even if he turn unto himself, he findeth that he himself is one of these Aspects, and so it is wherever else he turn, according to His Words *Wheresoever ye turn, there is the Face of God.* Thus when the rapt one turneth his face unto himself and seeth in the mirror of his existence the Face of God, he saith as Al-Ḥallāj said: "In my cloak is none but God"; and it is not the cloak alone which is meant, but all bodies, the higher and the lower, the sensible and the spiritual.

'Then do the Spirits of the disciples vanish, for in the Presence of the Truth's Being they find neither "where" nor "between" in which they might exist.

'He that prayeth over the dead must know how to bring him into the Presence of God inasmuch as he is interceding for him. Thus must he make him beloved of God, that he may be duly received; and then will he himself be one of the dearest of men unto God, even as the Prophet said, speaking with the Tongue of the Truth: "The dearest of men unto Me is he who maketh Me dear unto men, and maketh men dear unto Me."

'So let him be as importunate in prayer as he can, until the

[1] The four necessary elements in the funeral prayer are, in the words of Ibn 'Āshir, 'Four magnifications, prayer, purpose, peace', that is, saying *Allāhu Akbar* (God is Greatest) four times, invoking Mercy on the dead with a resolute purpose, and saying *As-Salāmu 'alaikum* (Peace be on you) as at the end of the ordinary ritual prayer.

Truth let down His Beatitude upon the dead; and He receiveth him not, unless his Master have an utterly resolute purpose.

'When the entry of the dead into the Presence of God hath been fulfilled, then doth the Shaikh bid him set about issuing from that station unto another, which is the synthesis between the two stations, the outward and the inward; and this is expressed by the word Peace.'[1]

[1] *Minaḥ*, pp. 176-9.

PART THREE

FURTHER DIMENSIONS

CHAPTER XII

A SPIRITUAL AFFINITY

'In Islam it is said not only that the Moslem religion is the fulfilment of the antecedent religions and that Muhammad is thereby the "Seal of Prophecy" (*Khātam an-nubuwwah*), but also that the earlier prophetic missions—those of Abraham, Moses and Jesus—were carried "out by mandate from Muhammad"; now this means, not only that in Islam Muhammad is assimilated to the Logos as such—every religion makes such an assimilation in regard to its founder—but also that earlier Prophets exercise a sort of function within the framework of Islam itself, a function of example and, sometimes, of esoteric inspiration.'[1]

It would be true to say that the Prophets of the Old Testament, together with Jesus, John the Baptist and Zachariah, receive a threefold honour in Islam, firstly as Prophets and Messengers of God, secondly as manifestations of the Muhammadan Spirit[2]—for so the Logos is termed—and thirdly as 'brothers' of Muhammad the man. Christians are sometimes astonished at the great reverence shown for some of those towards whom they themselves are almost indifferent. No Moslem will just simply say 'Aaron' (*Hārūn*); it must be, at every mention,[3] no less than 'our Liege-Lord Aaron—on him be Peace!' Moreover the slightest negativity of attitude such as some Christians evince for David and Solomon, by way of example, would be counted as a degree of impiety; and one has seen light-hearted representations of Noah in certain Christian miracle plays which would no doubt have brought the sentence of death down upon their author and their actor anywhere within the confines of the Islamic civilization.

[1] Frithjof Schuon, *Dimensions of Islam*, p. 70 (Allen & Unwin, 1969).
[2] See p. 153, note 5.
[3] Except in abnormal circumstances, as in some of the quotations which follow, where Jesus is referred to in visions without the words 'our Lord'.

The *credo* imposed on the faithful by the Qoran is that they should *believe in God and His Angels and His Books and His Messengers.*[1] *We make no distinction between His Messengers.*[2] It is significant also that one of the greatest of Islamic mystical treatises—the already quoted *Fuṣūṣ al-Ḥikam* of Ibn 'Arabī—should have the Prophets as its theme, each chapter being centred on a particular aspect of the Divine Wisdom and on that Prophet who is its special vehicle. Each Prophet is a *Faṣṣ*, (setting or cavity in a ring or other ornament made to hold a precious stone) specially formed to be the receptacle of the Wisdom in question—hence the title of the treatise, literally 'The Bezels of the Wisdoms'.

As one of the Shaikh's disciples has said, 'the shining of earlier Prophets into Islam lies in the very essence of Islam itself; it is as it were called for by that essence;[3] nor is this a poverty but a rich treasure of the Islamic reality; it is not the religions but the Prophets themselves that shine into Islam, and they do so in a certain sense out of their own *islām*'.

In response to this Prophetic radiance there is, as it were, a complementary shining out of the Saints of Islam towards the pre-Islamic Prophets, in the sense that a Saint may have a special affinity with one or more of the Prophets. The Prophet Muhammad himself was conscious of a strong affinity between Abū Bakr, his constant companion (later, the first Caliph), and Jesus, and between 'Umar (the second Caliph) and Moses.[4] Other Saints throughout the history of Sufism have been conscious of being the heirs of these or of other Prophets; and in the context of this book we may ask: Is it possible to see, in the spirituality of the Shaikh al-'Alawī, the reflection of the light of any one of the Divine Messengers who preceded Muhammad?

This question is answered very convincingly by Michel

[1] An immediate consequence of this is that when a Jew enters Islam he is required to restify not only that Muhammad is the Messenger of God, but also that Jesus is the Messenger of God. Of the iniquities of the Jews mentioned by the Qoran one of the greatest is that *they uttered against Mary a tremendous calumny.* (Qoran, IV, 156.)

[2] Qoran, II, 285.

[3] As Seal (and thereafter summary) of the Religions.

[4] He also likened Abū Bakr to Abraham, and 'Umar to Ṣāliḥ, the Prophet sent to the people of Thamūd, not mentioned in the Bible.

Vâlsan in a most interesting article[1] which he begins with a mention of the first visit made by Dr Carret to the Shaikh in 1920. He quotes a paragraph from the doctor's account of the Shaikh, ending with the words: 'It occurred to me that such must have been the appearance of Christ when he received his disciples at the time when he was staying with Martha and Mary.'

'Further on', continues M. Vâlsan, 'Dr Carret reiterates this idea, saying with reference to the Shaikh, "that Christ-like face". Many readers will see here . . . no more than a summary reference to a notion of sainthood that is generally accepted throughout the Western world. . . . We have reasons for not thinking along the same lines, and many other considerations may help to explain, at least in a certain measure, the "likeness" that is brought out in the doctor's account which, in our opinion, conveys something more subtle than a mere physical appearance.'

M. Vâlsan then refers to events which took place at a particularly crucial point in the Shaikh's life. Readers will remember that on the death of his Master, he announced his intention of going to live in Tripoli, and that when the fuqarā' proved unable to make up their minds to follow anyone else as spiritual guide, the question of a final decision was put off for another week. Meantime many visions were seen by the fuqarā' or by members of their families, and they all pointed clearly to the Shaikh al-'Alawī as successor to the Shaikh al-Būzīdī. Six of these are given in Chapter III.[2] M. Vâlsan draws our attention to four others which are indeed, as he says, highly significant.[3] The first was recounted by the head of the 'Alawī Zāwiyah at Ja'āfirah:

'One of the fuqarā' told us that he had had a vision of the

[1] 'Notes on the Shaikh al-'Alawī' in *Studies in Comparative Religion*, Summer, 1971 (Perennial Books, London). It should be read in full by any who are interested in the questions raised in this chapter.

[2] Pp. 66–6.

[3] I had already read them, though I confess that their special interest had escaped me, but I have now translated them from the Arabic.

moon cloven in two.[1] Then a plank was let down from it on chains, nearer and nearer the earth until it was only a little above us and we could see on it the Master al-ʿAlawī—may God be pleased with him!—and beside him Sayyidnā ʿIsā (our Liege-Lord Jesus)—on him be Peace! Then a crier stood up and cried out: "Whoever wishes to see Jesus—on him be Peace!—with the supreme Master, they are both here, descended from Heaven, so let him come with all speed." Then the earth trembled and shook and all upon it were shaken, and all the people gathered together and asked to mount up beside the Master on that plank, but he said: "Stay where you are, and we will come back to you" '[2]

We may compare this with the following, recounted by Shaikh Ḥasan ibn ʿAbd al-ʿAzīz at-Tilimsānī:

'I had a vision in which I was in the valley of the town of Tlemcen, and it was filled with a large crowd of people who were waiting for the descent from Heaven of Jesus—on him be Peace!—and then a man did descend, and the people said: "This is Jesus", and when I was able to see his face I found that he was the Shaikh Sidi Aḥmad Bin ʿAlīwah—may God be pleased with him!'[3]

Another comparable vision was recounted by the already mentioned great-grandson[4] of the founder[5] of the Darqāwī Tarīqah:

'I saw a group of people who told us of the descent of Jesus—on him be Peace!—and they said that he had already descended, and that he had in his hand a wooden sword with which he struck stones and they became men, and when he struck animals they also became human. Now I was conscious (in my vision)

[1] A sign of the end of the world, and therefore of the second coming of Christ, which is awaited in Islam no less than in Christianity.

[2] *Rauḍah*, p. 138.

[3] *Ibid.*, p. 135.

[4] See p. 86.

[5] Selections from his letters have recently been published in an English translation, *Letters of a Sufi Master, the Shaikh al-ʿArabi ad-Darqāwī* (Perennial Books, London, 1969).

that I knew the man who had descended from Heaven, that he had written letters to me and I to him. Then I made ready to meet him, and when I reached him I found that he was Shaikh Sidi Aḣmad al-ʿAlawī—but in the guise of a doctor, tending the sick, and with him were more than sixty men to help him—may God be well pleased with him!'[1]

Finally there is the vision of Sidi Aḣmad ibn Ḣājji at-Tilimsānī:

'Whilst I was absorbed in the invocation of the Supreme Name I saw the letters of Majesty[2] fill the whole universe, and out of them shone the Prophet himself in a luminous form—may God whelm him in Glory and give him Peace! Then the letters manifested themselves in another shape, and I saw in them the face of Shaikh Sidi Aḣmad Bin-ʿAlīwah, and on it was written Muṣṭafa Aḣmad Bin-ʿAlīwah. Then I heard a voice say: "Witnesses! Observers!" Then the letters were manifested a third time, in the image of the Shaikh with a crown on his head, and while we looked a bird alighted on his head and spoke to me, saying: "Behold, this is the station (*maqām*)[3] of Jesus—Peace be on him!"'[4]

[1] *Raudah*, p. 137.

[2] That is, the letters of the Name *Allah* (see above, pp. 54–5).

[3] See above, p. 93, l.5. It may be noted in passing that the ʿĪsawī Tariqah (see p. 50, note 3) is not named after Jesus directly, but bears his name simply because that was the founder's family name. There is nothing specifically Christic about this particular order. But to revert to what is directly connected with Christ, M. Vâlsan mentions another great Saint of Islam as being also unquestionably of the Jesus type, namely Ḣallāj; it is no doubt partly in virtue of this affinity that Ḣallāj looms so large on the horizon of many Christians.

[4] *Raudah*, p. 145.

CHAPTER XIII

SELECTIONS FROM HIS APHORISMS

Many of the Shaikh's disciples were treasurers of truths which they had heard him speak and which had never been written down; and several years after his death it was decided to collect and publish some of these oral teachings.

The utterances of a spiritual Master are often enigmatic and often paradoxical. An enigma is a challenge to the soul; the need to knock more than once at the door of the formal expression is a reminder that the content also needs to be penetrated, and that it is not merely a surface that can be lightly skimmed. Since wisdom is in fact a hidden treasure, it is not always uneloquent, in the long run, to present it as such. In the case of the paradox, on the other hand, it is the hearer himself who is penetrated. The barbed shaft of the unexpected has power to goad him into a state of spiritual vigilance, and to key his understanding to a higher pitch. Here again the expression corresponds to an aspect of what is expressed, for the truth is in fact strange, and the mind should not be allowed the complacency of supposing that it is familiar with more than a fragment of the truth, seen from a particular angle. The purpose of a Master's teaching is sometimes to throw his disciple off his balance, causing him to relinquish a lower equilibrium for a higher one.

The Gnostics are ranged in hierarchy: the knower of his Lord and the knower of himself; the knower of himself is stronger in Gnosis than the knower of his Lord.[1]

The key to this formulation lies in the duality which is implicit in the Divine Lordship, as in the Name Creator, that is, the

[1] This is the first of the aphorisms given in the above-mentioned anthology, *Ḥikmatu-hu, Sa Sagesse*, where the Arabic is followed by a French translation (often more of a hindrance to understanding than a help) without any commentary.

duality of Lord-slave and Creator-creature. But beyond this is the Oneness of the Absolute which allows no duality to encroach upon Its One-and-only Indivisible Infinitude. In other words, beyond the Personal God is the Transpersonal[1] Self, which is what the Shaikh means by the word 'himself'. We are reminded here of Śri Ramana Maharshi's perpetual question: 'Who am I?' Whoever has answered this question, not merely in theory but by realization, may be called 'the knower of himself'. These considerations serve to explain also the following aphorism which is the negative corollary of the first.

The veiled are ranged in hierarchy: the veiled from his Lord, and the veiled from himself. And the veiled from himself is more heavily veiled than the veiled from his Lord.[2]

The Shaikh is here expressing indirectly the preeminence of esoterism over exoterism. Piety is nothing other than a transparency, in some degree or other, of the veil which lies between the slave and his Lord; and the very fact that exoterism is obligatory for all means that this veil cannot be, normally and by its nature, impenetrable. Otherwise the agnostic and the atheist would not be so blameworthy. But in the vast majority the esoteric doctrine, that is, the doctrine of the Self, which is never totally secret, being always, as it were, 'in the air', awakens no subjective response of spiritual aspiration; in them the Intellect is dormant; the eye of the Heart, which is the organ of Self-perception, is closed. Thus it is true to say that the majority are more heavily veiled from themselves than from their Lord. And indeed if all other veils were removed it could be said, not that the Lord would be a veil over the Self (for the veil over the Subject must be subjective), but that they would still be veiled by their centrifugal aspiration. Spiritual effort must eventually be turned into an inward direction, for 'the Kingdom of Heaven is within you'.

[1] This term, which is far less inadequate than the more commonly used 'Impersonal', is taken from Frithjof Schuon. For a full and profound treatment of the relationship between these two highest 'Divine Presences' see his *Dimensions of Islam,* ch. 11, and also ch. 3.

[2] *Ḥikmatu-hu,* 2.

Whosoever seeketh God through another than himself will never attain unto God.[1]

It is true that the seeker needs to seek through his spiritual Master, without whose guidance he would be in danger of remaining at a standstill. But the task of the Master is above all to thrust the seeker into his innermost Self.

The doctrine of Self-Knowledge is dangerous, the great danger being, as one of the Shaikh's disciples has said, that the seeker, for want of the necessary sense of the Absolute, should unconsciously 'deify a secret fold of the ego', imagining it to be the Self. In this context the sense of the Absolute is, or presupposes, the sense of Transpersonality. Thus Shaikh says:

The *tā'*[2] of the second person spelleth retribution; the *hā'* of the third person spelleth trial; the *nūn* of the first person spelleth duality. The Truth is beyond that.[3]

The pronouns were given to man to express earthly differentiation, not Divine Oneness. If God is 'Thou', then the speaker exists as 'I' and earns retribution. 'Thine existence is a sin wherewith no other sin can be compared.'[4] If God is 'He', then the speaker is banished, excluded or suspended. Nor can 'I' do justice to Supreme Realization, for 'I' can only express a subject, and the Truth cannot be so limited, any more than it can be limited to the object 'He'. 'I' and 'He' are fragments; thus the word 'I', inasmuch as it presupposes a complement to complete it, signifies duality. By saying 'the Truth is beyond that', the Shaikh means that the Supreme Self is the Transcendent Synthesis of all three persons and cannot adequately be denoted by one person alone. The Infinite Sufficiency of this Synthesis is expressed in the Name *aṣ-Ṣamad*.

He that hath realized the Truth of Infinite Plenitude *(aṣ-Ṣamdāniyyah)* findeth no room for otherness.[5]

[1] *Ḥikmatu-hu*, 33.

[2] The letters *tā'* and *nūn*, as prefixes or suffixes in parts of the verb and elsewhere, signify respectively the second and first persons, whereas *hā'* is the consonant of the third personal pronoun.

[3] *Ibid*, 37.

[4] See above, p. 125, note 2.

[5] *Ibid*, 14.

Each of the three persons implies 'otherness', but their Divine Archetype sums up in its Oneness all those relationships which are deployed in fragmentary differentiation between 'I' and 'Thou' and 'He'. The name *aṡ-Ṡamad* is a central jewel in what might be called the crown of Islamic doctrine—and also, in a sense, the crown of Islamic liturgy—the Chapter of Sincerity,[1] which answers the question 'what is God?' in the most Absolute terms, and which begins: *Say: He, God is One, God, the Self-Sufficing in Infinite Plenitude.*

Transpersonality means Ineffability; thus the Shaikh says:

Perfection of courtesy demandeth the maintenance of the veil.[2]

For the Saint to unveil deliberately his Secret would be a violation of what Providence has ordained alike for both macrocosm and microcosm. The veil is the isthmus between the two seas[3] which is not to be overpassed, the two seas being Heaven and earth or, microcosmically, Spirit and soul. Without the isthmus, the earth would be overwhelmed by Heaven, as would the soul by the Spirit. Thus the maintenance of the veil is courtesy to creation, as well as to the Creator.

Yet the seas all but meet; the veil must not be too untransparent, for perfection of courtesy lies in holding the right balance. In one of his poems the Shaikh says: 'I neither divulge nor conceal the Secret[4]', which brings us to another of his aphorisms:

Whoso concealeth the Secret is himself veiled from it, and whoso divulgeth it is vanquished.[5]

The first part of this is explained indirectly in the following:

He whose station is equal to his state, telleth unawares the Secret of God.[6]

[1] Qoran, CXII.

[2] *Ḥikmatu-hu*, 49.

[3] *He hath let loose the two seas; they come together, but an isthmus is between them, and they encroach not beyond it.* (Qoran, LV, 19–30).

[4] Dīwān, p. 37.

[5] *Ḥikmatu-hu*, 45.

[6] *Ibid*, 36.

The state (*ḥāl*) is a Grace that at any time may flow over the mystic, the Arabic term being taken from the already quoted verse of the Qoran which defines that Grace: *God cometh in* (*yaḥūlu*) *between a man and his own heart.* A Saint in the highest sense is one in whom this state has become a station (*maqām*),[1] that is, no longer fleeting but permanent. The Saint is perpetually conscious of God's being nearer to him than his innermost self, and this unremitting consciousness wears thin the veils, so that even his body, especially his face, may show at times a certain transparency, almost as if lit with light, as much as to say 'I am the Truth', as did Al-Ḥallāj when he 'told the Secret of God'. Only he who is himself veiled from the Secret can succeed in hiding it altogether. On the other hand, to 'tell' the Secret is not the same as to 'divulge' it. The divulger is 'vanquished' and blurts it out because, not having the 'station' he has not the capacity to contain it. Very relevant is the already quoted saying of the Shaikh ash-Shādhilī: 'Vision of the Truth came upon me and would not leave me, and it was stronger than I could bear . . . so I asked for strength and He strengthened me.'[2] The strength is none other than the Divine Self which alone has capacity to receive the Truth and strength to bear It. The relationship may be reversed and it may be the Self which is the content, as when the Prophet said: 'I have a time when only my Lord sufficeth to contain me.' In either case, the 'station' of the Saint is his adequacy, in receiving not to spill, and in giving to fill.

This adequacy of Supreme Subject to Supreme Object is reflected throughout all the stages of the spiritual path. The spiritual act, in particular the invocation of the Name, may be considered as object inasmuch as it coincides with the Divine Response which it guarantees. *I answer the prayer of the pray-er when he prayeth.*[3] To meet this Response there must be an adequate subjective preparation, a maturity of understanding and virtue. Thus the Shaikh says:

Whoso acteth upon knowledge before its time hath come forfeiteth that knowledge. *And hasten not with the Qoran*

[1] See above, p. 93.
[2] See above, pp. 57–8.
[3] Qoran, II, 185.

until its revelation hath been perfected unto thee, and say: Lord, increase me in knowledge.[1,2]

The opening sentence clearly refers to a saying of the Prophet which has an untold practical importance in the spiritual path: 'Whoso acteth upon what he knoweth, God will cause him to inherit[3] knowledge of that which he knoweth not.' The Shaikh's aphorism is as much as to say: When the prophet speaks about acting upon knowledge he does not mean just theory but what a man knows deeply, what he has fully assimilated; and the Shaikh's quotation from the Qoran in this context amounts to an interpretation of the words *increase me in knowledge* as meaning 'increase me in depth of knowledge'.

But why does the Shaikh say, in another of his teachings:

To demand increase showeth ignorance in a disciple.[4]

The ignorance is of more than one kind. Firstly, it is ignorance of the truth expressed in the saying of the Prophet, failure to understand that he has no need to ask because he can have increase by acting upon what he knows. Secondly, it is the ignorance of supposing that things of the Spirit can be gauged like the things of this world, and that he himself can judge whether or not he is receiving increase. A disciple of one of the Shaikh's disciples once complained to his Master: 'I have regularly invoked the Supreme Name for more than ten years, but without any result.' His Master replied: 'If you could make in one moment all the spiritual progress you have gradually made in these ten years, it would cause a mortal rupture in your soul.' The aphorism which we are considering is no doubt directed against such complaints as this, but not, needless to say, against prayers for increase in accordance with the Qoranic injunction to ask for increase. It is entirely a question of the

[1] Qoran, XX, 114.
[2] *Ḥikmatu-hu*, 9.
[3] The use of the word 'inherit' is here particularly significant, for it shows that it is not a question of outward learning but of realizing what one carries in one's blood, as it were, for every human being is, by reason of his ancestry, a potential heir to the sanctity of primordial man.
[4] *Ḥikmatu-hu*, 50.

point of view. The very invocation of the Divine Name is, implicitly, a prayer for increase.

The Shaikh's warning that to act upon knowledge prematurely leads to loss of that knowledge recalls another of his warnings:

Knowledge without any support to lean on may cause remoteness.[1]

In both cases it is a question of superficial knowledge—knowledge with nothing to fall back on reminiscent of the seed in the Gospel parable[2] 'which fell on stony ground'; and it is because of the dangers inherent in such knowledge that esoteric truths are, in principle, kept secret or at least withheld until the 'ground be cultivated'.

The word here translated by 'support' is *i'timād* which literally means being supported by a prop or pillar (*'amūd*). The support referred to by the Shaikh is the Divine Presence in the microcosm, the most outward manifestation of this Presence being the virtues of the soul which are reflections of the Divine Qualities. The seeds of knowledge, if they have not enough initial depth of soil to root in, that is, if they have not at least the virtues, will never be able to make roots strong enough to support their growth up to the Archetypes of the virtues.

The gist of the last quoted saying is expressed also in another:

Whoso setteth out[3] for God reacheth Him not, but whoso leaneth upon Him for support is not unaware of Him.[4]

This brings us back to the aphorisms which exhort to Self-Knowledge, seeking to thrust the disciple more deeply into himself, for 'leaning upon God for support' is the first stage in finding the answer to the question 'Who am I?' The Shaikh also says with the same meaning[5]

Whoso seeketh God in other than himself directeth his path far wide of his mark.

[1] *Ḥikmatu-hu*, 39.
[2] St Matthew, *X*III.
[3] That is, as one setting out upon a journey.
[4] *Ḥikmatu-hu*, 40.
[5] *Ibid*, 25.

The seeker in question is one who 'setteth out for God', possibly despising the more humble attitude of leaning back for support.

One of the errors of him who 'setteth out for God' is that he allows his conception of the Divine Transcendence to leave no room for any awareness of the Divine Immanence. The Shaikh says:

The furthest of all men from their Lord are those who go most beyond measure in affirming His Incomparability.[1]

He also says:

It is not a question of affirming beyond all measure His Incomparability but of knowing Him by analogy.[2]

It is not a question of knowing God when the veil be lifted but of knowing Him in the veil itself.[3]

Comparisons that are based on the certainty of His Oneness are better than the abstractions of one who is veiled from His Oneness.[4]

Once in a setting of unsurpassable grandeur one of the Shaikh's disciples said to me, with a movement of his hand towards mountains towering with pine-forested slopes and summits white with snow, and blue sky with white clouds and half-hidden sunlight: 'God is like that'; and I understood in that moment with far more than mere mental understanding, that if it were not for the Divine Beauty everything that lay before my eyes would vanish in an instant. The same Master has also said:

[1] *Ḥikmatu-hu* 25.

[2] *Ibid*, 26. Muhyi 'd-Dīn Ibn ʿArabī quotes from the Qoran *Naught is like unto Him, and He is the Hearer, the Seer*, to show how in one verse (XLII, 11) it affirms both his Incomparability and the analogy between Him and His creatures.

[3] *Ibid*, 16.

[4] *Ibid*, 27.

'In the cave the Prophet taught Abu Bakr[1] the mysteries of the Divine Name. A spider's web prevented the infidels from entering. This web is metaphysical doctrine, which separates the profane world from Gnosis, and Gnosis from the profane world. The spider's web is the exteriorization of the Self.'

He went on to explain that the concentric circles represent transcendence, for they portray the hierarchy of the worlds one above the other; the Incomparability of the Self, Its Absolute Transcendence, is represented either by the outer circumference or by the centre, according to whether we are considering the aspect of All-Embracingness or that of Inwardness. The radii which connect the different circles one with another represent the Divine Immanence which enables us to make comparisons and to draw analogies. Each point of intersection of radius and circumference is a sanctuary of Divine Presence which makes it possible to say: 'God is like that' or even 'That is God'; and since every point on every circumference has virtually its radius which connects it with the centre, every point may be the place of the manifestation of a Secret. But those who 'affirm beyond all measure His Incomparability' are those who consider only the circles; and they are 'the furthest of all men from their Lord' because, in refusing to consider the radii, they are depriving themselves of all connection with God, and depriving this world of all symbolic meaning. In this sense the Shaikh says:

Lean not overmuch unto the knowledge of the Truth lest thou be veiled by it from the Secrets of Creation.[2]

The following aphorism, no less paradoxical in its outset, conveys ultimately much the same teaching, if we consider that the greatest of 'the Secrets of creation' is the Self:

[1] When the Prophet fled with Abu Bakr from Mecca to Medina, they were pursued by the Meccans who intended to kill them, and they were saved by a spider which spun its web over the mouth of the cave where they had taken refuge, as much as to say that it was pointless to continue the search in that direction, since no one had passed beyond that point.

[2] *Ibid.*, 38.

Neither abandon thy soul, nor oppose it, but go along with it and search it for what is in it.[1]

In these words the Shaikh opens up a whole vista of spiritual method which is, practically speaking, a most necessary complement to the better known asceticisms of self-denial. It often happens that when the first enthusiasm of the novice has worn off, he suffers a period of aridity in which he finds himself at times to be totally lacking in spiritual fervour. He needs to be reminded that his soul *chose*, of its own free will, to enter upon the spiritual path. If this choice was not dictated by a unanimity of psychic elements (for such unanimity marks the end of the path, not its beginning) there was none the less an overwhelming predominance in favour of the Truth, that predominance being what is called 'vocation', for the Divine summons comes from within as well as from without. Much resistance can be overcome by questioning the soul at every turn; for even in such practices as the spiritual retreat, from which some psychic elements shrink as from death, the soul can be forced to admit that it is in fact doing what it has chosen to do, and that it desires to do nothing else. This method is as a first stage upon the path which leads to the question 'Who am I?' The Shaikh refers to a later stage in the words:

Whoso hath known God in his soul returneth unto it and seeketh to gratify its desires.[2]

The words translated by 'his soul' could equally well be 'himself', with or without a capital, so that this aphorism could be taken to refer to a whole range of spiritual experience, from a first glimmering of Gnosis to the End of the path. Elsewhere the Shaikh has said, with reference to the many verses of the Qoran which condemn those who follow 'their passions', that such verses refer to all but the Gnostics who are allowed to 'follow their passions', since only the Absolute, the Infinite and the Eternal has power to move them to any such strength of feeling as might be called 'passion'.

[1] *Ḥikmatu-hu*, 12

[2] *Ibid*, 5.

CHAPTER XIV

SELECTIONS FROM HIS POETRY

I. THE INTELLECT[1]

The Sun's Light shineth in the Moon[2] of the dark.
I am of its branches, and It is my Root.
Our intelligences are made drunk with the wine of love,
As though we were mad, yet mad we are not.
Thou seest us amongst men, but we are not as thou seest,
For our Spirits shine clear above the highest heights.
Ours is an intelligence, a flawless jewel,
Exquisite in beauty; it perceiveth naught but God.
This is the bond[3] which bindeth, be it but a glimmering.[4]

Folk, ye are welcome, the elect of your Lord,
The works of His Art, made perfect for Himself.
You hath He privileged by lifting the veil
From the Light of His Face. What gratitude can give thanks
For the Infinite? Yet give what gratitude ye may
Unto Him who hath vouchsafed what transcendeth all price.

[1] The titles are mine. The first six extracts are taken from the Shaikh's longest poem, with which his *Dīwān* opens, pp. 3-12. These I have translated into the metre of Beowulf, with four heavy stresses, variously arranged, in each line; but to avoid forcing the translation I have taken many liberties with the rhythm, and have invariably sacrificed the alliteration—the Old English metre's outstanding characteristic—when it would not come easily. All the other extracts, except 'Laila', are complete poems in the original. In the short-lined poems, most of which were written for the express purpose of being chanted during the sacred dance, as they still are, I have kept as near to the original metre as possible, but without attempting any rhyme.

[2] p. 40.

[3] The word *'aql* means above all 'Intellect'; but *intellectus* coincides only with the purely transcendent aspect of *'aql*, whereas the Arabic word comprises in its meaning the whole range of the intelligence including even the reason, in virtue of what the reason was primordially and what it still remains virtually, that is, a conscious projection of the Intellect, whose light it distributes to the other faculties, knitting them together while remaining itself 'tethered' by the Intellect to its Divine Root. This brings us to the other basic meaning of the Arabic letters *'Ain-Qāf-Lām* which denote 'binding' as well as 'perception'. Thus the Shaikh says that the intelligence (*'aql*) which perceiveth (*ya'qil*) is the bond (*'iqāl*) which bindeth (*ya'qil*).

[4] Referring to the first glimmering of intellectual perception in the novice (See p. 136).

Exult then upon the Throne and upon the soil of earth,[1]
For ye, none but ye, are the slaves of God.
In you bodies that were bone-dust have life
For ye are of God's Spirit that entered into Adam,
Breath that Gabriel breathed into Mary.
Dance then in ecstasy and pride and joy,
And trail ye the robes of the glory that is your due.

2. THE IMPOSTOR

But thou, hast thou sensed aught of what they perceive?
If thou art as they, then authority is thine,
But if thou findest nothing in thyself of what is theirs,
Then claim justice from thy soul; heed this description:
Hast thou folded up the world out of sight with one look,
Witnessed the All-Merciful where Manifest He is?
Hast effaced mankind from thy ken with one glance,
And strayed beyond the bounds of all, beyond the heights
Of heaven and earth's deep? The whole universe
Hast encompassed with full pilgrimal visitation?
And hath that same universe made thee its shrine,
The holy axis of its reverential orbit?
Have the screens vanished from before thee in thine honour?
Hath the cloak been thrown off, the veil set aside?
And hath it been said unto thee: 'Draw nigh:
Here is Our Beauty: welcome, enjoy it
As thine, at thy most intimate ease'?
Hath the Summoner summoned thee, and hast moved to his command?
Hast doffed thy sandals, as one that is steeped
In the courtesies of the path? Hath the Infinite closed
Around thee on all sides? And when the moment came
For Union, didst to it lean with all thy bent?
Hast kept faithfully the Secret of God
After Its revelation, robing thyself in His Qualities?
All this would be some evidence of thy nearness.
Else—there are secrets which are not for the many.
If to this description thou answerest, then all hail!
If *not*, then art thou far from the Presence of the Lord.

[1] Since the Saint has Being on every plane throughout the whole hierarchy of existence.

Stand away from the lore of the Folk: thou art not of them;
Nor lay hands on the heritage of the orphan,[1] offence
Most grievous. Unto God it is hateful to put
Painted promises in the place of deeds.
What use is a tongue that in euphemies is fluent?
What good to o'ergild gashes and not heal them?
Doth aught but his cure avail the sick man?
Doth the exile take delight in an alien folk?
Rehéarse well thy speech; thou canst talk as they talk,
But 'tis the hornet's wax, not the honey-comb of the bee.

3. THE PATH

Will the seeker of God be content to be far?
Nay, for he needeth no less than Union.
The true seeker hath a sign on his face,
A light shineth gleaming upon his forehead.
Ever near is he, courteous, reverential,
Resolute, forbearing before censure, true friend
Honouring. His purpose all purposes transcendeth:
Naught can prevent him, the steep he seeth as level.
He hath no aim aside from his mark.
Longing for family diverteth him not, nor blame.
Fair his description, he needeth no other
But this, most excellent, that he seeketh the Truth.
Whoso is Its seeker, he maketh his quest
Sole object of his eyes. Then strippeth he his soul
Of all faults he can detect, and when stripped, robeth it
In their opposites. God's slave at each time and place,
His bounden debt of worship fulfilling,
He addeth thereunto of his own free will,
Until the Truth is his Hearing, Sight,
Tongue and Utterance, and Hands and Feet.
He dieth before his death to live in his Lord,
Since after this death is the supreme migration.
He calleth himself to account ere he be called,

[1] While taking this often repeated Qoranic injunction in a literal sense, the Sufis understand it to refer also, on the highest plane, to sobriety in Gnosis, the special heritage of the orphan Muḥammad as indicated in the verse *The eye wavered not nor did it transgress*.

He herein most fitted to act for the Truth.
The Truth's Being he seeth before his own,
And after it, and wheresoever he turn.
Alone God was, and with Him naught else.
He is now as He was, lastly as firstly,
Essentially One, with naught beside Himself,
Inwardly Hidden, Outwardly Manifest,
Without beginning, without end. Whate'er thou seest,
Seest thou His Being. Absolute Oneness
No 'but' hath and no 'except.' How should God's Essence
Be confined with a veil? No veil there but His Light.

4. THE MASTER

If a summoner call unto guidance, alluding
To his attainment of the Truth, and the Supreme Station,
Of remissness beware, and examine well his words.
Question him of Union; see if he reflect It.
If he say It be far, 'tis because he is far,
But if he say It be near, count him most worthy.
He will make plain to thee the path unto the Truth
Whereby thou mayest seek the Face of God.
He will take thee at once, even at thy first meeting,
And set thy foot on its way unto the Lord.
Keep in thy mind's eye the Name's letters
Through his grace thou wilt come to see them shine
Clear on the horizons, though they shine but in thy Heart,
And when the Name is thine, all forgetfulness will vanish.
Magnify then the Letters to as large as thou canst;
Trace them on all things, both high and low.
Through keeping the Name in thine eye, thou wilt rise
By Its Light to where the worlds vanish into nothingness.
But at the Shaikh's order, not at thine, do they vanish.
He is the Finger with which God pointeth.
Trust him then to take thee out of the cramp of prisons
To Freedom, to the First, Who all beginnings doth precede,
And thou seest the whole world nothing in His Essence,
Less than nothing in the Infinity of the Lord.
When the Infinite doth appear thereat thou vanishest,
For 'thou' hast never been, from first until last.
Thou seest not who thou art, for thou art, yet art not 'thou.'

Thou endurest, yet not as thyself; no strength is there but God's.
After thine extinction to Eternity thou wilt rise,
Endlessly in Eternity of Eternity art affirmed,
Crown of all Altitude; for is it not Face
To Face with the Truth that our riders dismount?

5. THE CUP

Sweet is the Folk's drink. I tell of its flavour,
And I mean not wine nor mean I honey,
But an Ancient Draught beyond my power to describe,
For words ever fail Beauty's describer.
Its cup[1] is like it, can also be drunk,
Sufficient unto itself,[2] and needing naught else.
I marvel at this cup that itself quencheth thirst,
And of itself goeth the round, from lover unto lover.
Of its qualities is magic that is graven round its rim:
To gaze on this seal is to be emptied of all strength.
Wondrous that I have not uttered its secret.
Other than me, drinking it, would neither fast nor pray.[3]
If the prayer-leader beheld its beauty's light
He would bow down to *it* rather than towards Mecca.
If the learned in mid lesson scented its perfume
They would cease teaching on the instant without delay.
If the pilgrim in full course between Ṣafā and Marwah
Sighted its splendour he would stop, nor go round
The Ancient House,[4] nor kiss the Black Stone.
Nay, the rim of this cup demandeth to be kissed
Where each one seeth, in his mirrored self,[5]
The meaning of his quest. How shall he be restrained

[1] The wine is Divinity, that is, Gnosis. In Ibn al-Fārid's *Khamriyyah* the cup is the full moon which, according to the commentary of 'Abd al-Ghanī An-Nābulusī signifies Universal Man, personified by the Prophet.

[2] The cup is the *Bā'* of the *Basmalah* whose 'greatness is none other than the greatness of the *Alif*' (p. 156)

[3] Only one who is truly an heir to the Prophets can retain sobriety in drunkenness.

[4] Even for the pre-Islamic Arabs the Ka'bah was 'the Ancient House,' as it is called in the Qoran.

[5] For the mystics of Islam the Prophet is the mirror in which they see themselves not as they appear to be at the moment but as they will be when all their latent possibilities have been realized.

Who thought himself vile and is become full of honour?
He must needs break all bounds in exultation and joy.
This is an ancient wine, most rare to drink;
It inciteth to no harm; fear no bemusedness.
In it is no heat, nor any cold,
Nor cloudeth it the wits, causing them to falter.
Subtle it is, elusive, beyond my powers to describe,
For words ever fail Beauty's describer.

6. THE PRESENT REALITY

The Summoner unto God's Nearness hath called to them:
Lo, I am with you,[1] for *wheresoever ye turn*
There shineth My Light. One in My Essence,
In all things I am seen. Hath ever aught been seen
But Me? The veil of creation I have made
As a screen for the Truth, and in creation there lie
Secrets which suddenly like springs gush forth.
Whoso is ignorant of My Essence beneath My Veil,
He asketh where I am. Say 'am' without 'where',
For in My Being is no gap, as from one 'where' to another.
Confer but the point of the Zain on the Rain,[2]
And behold it: the stain is an ornament, perfect
In virtue of the point. Come then unto Union
With the Eternal. Is there aught beside Him to oppose Him?
Nay, He alone was, is and shall be.
I then[3] am Absolute in Essence, Infinite.
My only 'where' is 'through Myself I am.'
Ignorance, to know[4] me either 'here' or 'there.'
The 'Above all "above"' is not bounded by any top;
The 'Beneath all "beneath"' hath no nethermost depth.
I am the Secret of the Essence, Treasure Inscrutable.

[1] Qoran, V, 12. The 'I' refers to God, whereas the Summoner is the Prophet, but in this context the distinction between 'wine' and 'cup' is effaced.

[2] The letter *Rā'* is called *Rain* in many dialects, which word means also 'dirt.' A dot above the *Rain* changes it into the letter *Zain*. (See p. 183, note 2).

[3] Since there is no room in the Infinite even for nothingness, I cannot be nothing; and since the Infinite has no parts, I am therefore the Whole.

[4] Probably referring to the Tradition: 'Verily there is knowledge which is ignorance and ignorance which is knowledge.'

No end to My Breadth, no end to My Length.
I in the Inward Hiddenness was Manifest
Ere It outwardly showed. I asked Myself
Of Myself, and a pure positive was the answer,
For can other than God appear in God's Truth?
He struck terror, then inclined; He o'erwhelmed, and then spake.[1]
I am Essentially One, Single, Unencroachable
By the least object. Leave I any crevice,
Any space vacant that to another might go?
For the Inside am I of the Essence in Itself
And the Outside of the Quality, Diffuse Concentration.[2]
'Thither' is there none whither I am not turning.
Doth other than Me exist, empty of My Attribute?
My Essence is the Essence of Being, now,
Always. My Infinity is not limited by the least
Grain of mustard. Where can the creature
Find room to intrude on the Truth's Infinite?
Where other than It, when All is Full?
Union and separation are thus in Principle the same,
And to behold creation is to behold the Truth,
If creation be interpreted as it truly is.
Interpret then all in the Light of *He is Near*,
And thou thyself of that Nearness shalt partake.
Deem not this localization. That were impossible,
For He cometh not to dwell in any place.
Extol the Essence of God above the touch
Of other than It. It is borne by none,
Beareth no burden; It is Hidden in Its Own
Outward Manifestation, wherein It doth appear
As Veil after Veil made to cover Its Glory.

[1] This line, which is really in parenthesis, sums up as it were in retrospect the spiritual alchemy which led to the 'pure positive' just mentioned. The reference is to the two Aspects of the Essence expressed in the Names *Aḥad* (One) and *Ṣamad* (He who utterly and eternally satisfies all aspirations) which from the point of view of the creature correspond to extinction (being terror-stricken and overwhelmed) and extinction of the extinction (being inclined to and spoken to—or rather, speaking to oneself, since there can no longer be any question of subject and object).

[2] The Truth of the Indivisibility of the Infinite can only be expressed through such antinomic terms as this, or 'expanse of contractedness,' 'unfolded synthesis,' 'differentiated sameness,' etc.

7. COUNSEL[1]

Accept none other for thy love but God.
All things apart from Him are pure illusion.
Here is my counsel, if thou canst counsel take.
The rememberers are ever absent in their Beloved,
For none have life save those who are near to Him.
Between such and the Truth there is no veil.
What are the blessings of Paradise to them?
Passion God's slaves hath melted; they have drunk,
And still drink, His eternal-treasured Wine,
The draught whereof hath robbed them of themselves.
Would thou couldst take one sip out of their cup!
'Twould help to bridge the gap twixt thee and me.
A good slave he who saith: 'I am at Thy service,'
Hearing God's Call which I address to him.
If God thou seekest, then companion me:
For thee, be very sure, there is no way else.

8. THE SUPREME STATION[2]

O thou who understandest not
My words, why speakest thou against me?
Thou art empty of the Spirit,
Nor knowest the Divinity.
Wert thou acquainted with my state,
Thou wouldst admit mine excellence,
Wouldst see me amongst human kind
As a sun shining on creation.

My Lord hath granted my prayer, fulfilled
My needs: He guided me, now hath robed me
In robes of His Beatitude,
Hath quenched my thirst from a rare cup
With draught more precious than the elixir,
And raised me to a high estate,
Loftier than the Pleiades.

If thou seekest me, O Saint,
Question thou the Lord of me,

[1] *Dīwān*, p. 35.
[2] pp. 25-6.

Look for me above all heights,
It may be thou wilt light upon me.
Exalted, rare, secret and strange
Are such as I, for I have found
The buried treasure that was mine:
All things lie hidden here within me.

But thou, what knowest thou of my states,
Who hast no knowledge of the elect?
Thou thinkest within me is a void.
Think as thou wilt: since the Beloved
Is mine, I look not to the world.
Whatever my detractors purpose
In their opposition to me,
My Heart is mine, remaineth mine,
My senses do I give to them.
Since all my days are now unclouded,
I count not woes as others count them.
Who knoweth God, were he to lose
The entire world, would need no solace.

The empty-souled, the opaque of Heart,
Hath eyes but for this fleeting life.
He rusheth blindly into error
To amass something in this world,
Nor looketh to the fated ends
Of all things, nor to his death's nearness,
Nor felloweth any perfect man,
But hath no outlet from transgression,
Firm-fixed in his contentiousness,
Forever warring against God.

May my Lord grant my prayer, that I,
Turned t'wards Him ever, be ever welcome.
Shield me always, and shield all
Muḥammad's people; and let Thy Beauty
Flow over in Beatitude,
As endlessly as worshippers,
As endlessly as Saints invoke It,
Upon the noblest of the Prophets,
All his Companions and his House,
Their heirs that guidance give and seek,
And every pious man and holy—
My greeting's light enfold all these!

9. THE HERDSMAN OF THE FOLK[1]

O thou that herdest the Folk, come sing us homewards,
And as we go, in God's Name, spare one look
For me; or shoot an arrow of thy voice:
'Twill strike some vigilant ears, and pierce my heart.
They that surround me know not what love is.
Seeing me so smitten, they would say: 'He is mad.'
If it be madness to love whom I do long for,
May God let languish with wasting sickness my frame.
If the denier would give ear to my speech,
He would not turn from my teaching, but would lean
Unto it, and become my follower.
Ask them, *the day when faces are all humbled*
Before the eternal Living,[2] if they were with me.
That day is even as that other day
Of *Am I not your Lord*:[3] I said 'Yea' then,
And have not ceased to say, 'Lord, at Thy service.'
God's Summoner I answered when he did call.
Will ye not answer the Summoner, my people?
If ye seek solace in love, such as ye see
Me blessed with, turn from all who slander it.
If thou wouldst know the rank of those who love,
Here is my answer, that will cure all doubts:
We and the men who fought at Badr[4] of old
Are equal: what is mine is theirs, and what theirs, mine.[5]

[1] p. 33. *Ḥadiya 'l-Qaum*. The word *ḥādī* (all the more significant for being suggestive of *hādī*, guide) means 'one who urges on camels by singing to them.' The herdsman here is the Prophet, his songs are the Qoran and the traditional formulae out of which the Sufic litanies are woven.

[2] Qoran, XX, 111. The reference is to the Day of Judgement of which it is said in v. 109: *On that day no intercession availeth save his whom the All-Merciful permitteth to speak, with whose words He is well pleased*. He means that those who turn from him now will wish that they had followed him, so that he might have interceded for them.

[3] *Remember when thy Lord took the seeds of the sons of Adam from their loins and made them bear witness against themselves, and said: 'Am I not your Lord?' They said: 'Yea, we testify.' This was lest ye should say on the Day of Resurrection: 'Of this we were unaware.'* (Qoran, VII, 172). He means that in his case the 'Yea' has been prolonged, and will be until the Resurrection, whereas for them it has been interrupted and forgotten.

[4] See p. 149, note 2.

[5] Referring to the words of the Prophet: 'How knowest thou that God hath not looked upon the men of Badr and said: "Do what ye will, for I have forgiven you".' (Muslim, *Faḍā'il aṣ-Ṣaḥābah*, 36).

10. THE WINE[1]

Friends, if the truth of my state ye have understood,
Here lies your path before you: follow in my footsteps,
For by Heaven, here are no doubts, no vague imaginings:
I know God, with a knowledge part secret, part proclaimed.
I drank the cup of love, and then possessed it,
And it hath become my possession for all time.
God reward him who lavished[2] his Secret upon me,
For bounty, true bounty, is to bestow the Secret.
I hid the Truth on a time, and screened It well,
And whoso keepeth God's Secret shall have his reward.
Then when the Giver vouchsafed that I might proclaim It,
He fitted me—how I know not—to purify[3] souls,
And girded upon me the sword of steadfastness,
And truth and piety, and a Wine He gave me,
Which all who drink must needs be always drinking,
Even as a drunk man seeketh to be more drunk.
Thus came I to pour It—nay, it is I that press It.
Doth any other pour It in this age?
Marvel not that I speak thus, for our Lord
Himself hath said that He singleth out for Grace
Whomso He will and giveth unsparingly.
This is God's Grace: He giveth It whom He will.[4]
Surpassing Praise and Glory and Thanks be His!

Lord, with the Spirit of the Beloved,[5] Thy Spirit,
With the Spirit of Holiness help me, *make easy my task.*[6]
Untie my tongue, Lord. *Let one share my burden*
From Thy true helpers, and confound me not
The Day of the Gathering.[7] Lord, whelm with Thy Presence
And greet with Peace, bless, magnify, extol,
The Beloved's Spirit, in the Abode of the Secret.

[1] p. 35.
[2] The Shaikh Al-Būzīdī.
[3] *Tajrīd*, literally 'abstraction,' 'disentanglement.' He is probably referring to what is alluded to on p. 54 in the words: 'Then the Shaikh would show the way out of this standpoint—it is impossible to express in words how he did so, etc.'
[4] Qoran, V, 54.
[5] The Prophet.
[6] This and the following quotations are from the prayer which Moses uttered on being told to go to Pharoah. (Qoran, XX, 25-35).
[7] The Day of Judgement.

II. LAILĀ[1]

Full near I came unto where dwelleth
Lailā, when I heard her call.
That voice, would I might ever hear it!
She favoured me, and drew me to her,
Took me in, into her precinct,
With discourse intimate addressed me.
She sat me by her, then came closer,
Raised the cloak that hid her from me,
Made me marvel to distraction,
Bewildered me with all her beauty.
She took me and amazèd me,
And hid me in her inmost self,
Until I thought that she was I,
And my life she took as ransome.
She changed me and transfigured me,
And marked me with her special sign,
Pressed me to her, put me from her,
Namèd me as she is named.
Having slain and crumbled me,
She steeped the fragments in her blood.
Then, after my death, she raised me:
My star shines in her firmament.
Where is my life, and where my body,
Where my wilful soul? From her
The truth of these shone out to me,
Secrets that had been hidden from me.
Mine eyes have never seen but her:
To naught else can they testify.
All meanings in her are comprised.
Glory be to her Creator!

Thou that beauty wouldst describe,
Here is something of her brightness.
Take it from me. It is my art.
Think it not idle vanity.
My Heart lied not when it divulged
The secret of my meeting her.
If nearness unto her effaceth,
I still subsist in her subsistence.

[1] p. 22. *Lailā*, a woman's name meaning 'night', here represents the Divine Essence.

12. THE SIGNATURE[1]

Thou who seekest to know my wisdom,
Unto God address thy questions,
For mankind knoweth me not.
Hidden are my states from them.
Seek me as thou drawest nigh
To Him, beyond the state of slavehood,
For in the created universe
No residue of me remaineth.
A manifesting of the Supreme
Presence Dominical am I,
Even as my state plainly declareth.
A river, I, of the o'erflowing
Mercy of the All-Merciful
In flood on earth for men to see.
Spirit was I before my slavehood,
Now home have come, am free once more.
Think it not me thou seest here,
Clad in human qualities,
For beyond these are archetypes,
The Eternal Raiment of the Spirit.
If thou couldst look to where I am
In the All-Holy Presence, thou
Wouldst see Me One, nor any other;
But Truth hath given me a cloak,
Nor can thy sight to me attain.
Thou seest me, yet thou seest me not,
Giving but a heedless glance.
Sharpen thy faith's eye, and look
With a look of purest vision.
Then if thy faith prove certainty
It may be thou wilt light upon me.
Thou wilt find me clothed in Secrets,
And Lights belonging to our Prophet.
Thou wilt find there heavenly Angels,
Eyes vigilant for my needs. Thou'lt find
That my Lord hath chosen me.
He shineth from me through what is in me,
Thou seest Him when thou seest me,
But thou sensest not the truth.

[1] pp. 17-19.

Guidance my Lord hath given me,
And vouchsafed me purest vision,
Taught me knowledge of myself,
Taught me to know the truth of the Spirit.
Thus if thou wouldst grasp my wisdom,
Companion me, and heed me well,
Listening to me, telling of me,
Raising ne'er thy voice above me.
Thou seest naught in the world but me.
Seek not then to look beyond me,
Nor account thyself secure:
Not hidden from me is thy state.
So if thou art truly mine,
A slave sincere unto his Lord,
Prove it, not with tongue alone,
For the tongue is wondrous false.
Thy soul to the spear point stretch out,
And die utterly the death.
Busy thyself with me, not thee,
Or take thy leave else, and depart.

I lay upon thee what my Master
Būzīdī, dead to all creation,
Laid upon me ere his body's death.
Leave thine all here, where now I am,
Rise up to God, slough off the worlds,
And leave no vestige of them on thee.
Alike are this world and the next;
Behold them but with full-grown vision:
The World-Creator and the worlds
Both manifest His Unity.
Look but truly face to face,
Thou wilt find naught to be afraid of,
For all is even now extinct
Except the Countenance of Lordship.
When thou knowest what we experience,
Then, if thou wilt, dispense with me—
Yet wilt thou not, by Heaven, for none
But empty souls can e'er forget me.

God well knoweth my estate.
May He shield me for the rest
Of life, and shield my brethren all,
From the trials of the heart,

And whoso entereth my house,
Whoso is present at our Sessions,
Whoso seeth one who saw me,
If he would have wished to see me.

Lord, make my tongue the instrument
Of Thy Blessings on the Prophet.
Turn me to walk in all his ways.
If I heed Thee, he commendeth,
If I do wrong, he intercedeth.

I have placed my signature
At the ending of these verses,
For so my brethren did request.
My body's lineage belongeth
Unto the tribe of 'Alawī.
My line of spiritual descent
Is through Būzīdī's gracious presence.
Have Mercy, Lord, on both these lines,
And Mercy on my posterity
In both, unto the world's end.

APPENDIX A

HIS WRITINGS

His writings fall into two groups, according to whether or not they were published in his life-time. Those which he did not publish, and which presumably he did not wish to publish, or intended to revise, are:

1. *Miftāhu 'sh-Shuhūd fī Maẓāhiri 'l-Wujūd.*

A hand-book of cosmology, and in particular of astronomy, modern as regards facts but traditional in that the complete dependence of physics on metaphysics is never lost sight of. Its many references are mostly to the Qoran, to Brūsawī's *Rūh al-Bayān*, and to Ghazālī. (See pp. 58f.)

2. *Tafsīru'l-Qur'ān.*

A Qoranic commentary in which each verse is given four interpretations, ranging from the literal to the purely spiritual. It only goes as far as verse 40 of the *Sūrat al-Baqarah.* The reason why it was discontinued is given on p. 58. It has not yet been published, and the only manuscript is at the Mostaganem Zāwiyah.

3. *Al-Mawāddu 'l-Ghaithiyyah an-Nāshi'u 'ani 'l-Ḣikami 'l-Ghauthiyyah.*

A commentary on the aphorisms of Shu'āib Abū Madyan. Sidi Muhammad al-Hāshimī tells me he thinks it was written about 1910, that is, shortly after the Shaikh Al-Būzīdī's death. Part of it was published in 1942.

Works published during his life-time:

4. *Al-Minahu 'l-Quddūsiyyah fi Sharhi 'l-Murshidi 'l-Mu'īni bi-Ṫarīqi 's-Ṡūfiyyah.*

(See p. 58, note 1 and pp. 176ff.)

5. *Al-Unmūdhaju 'l-Farīd.*

Written c. 1910. (See pp. 148-57).

6. *Al-Qaulu 'l-Maqbūl fī-mā tatawaṡṡalu ilaihi 'l-'Uqūl.*

A brief exposition of *Islām, Īmān* and *Ihsān*. Written in 1913.

7. *Lubābu 'l-'Ilm fī Sūrati Wa'n-Najm.*

A commentary of Chapter LIII of the Qoran. Written in 1915. (See pp. 173-5).

8. *Dauhatu 'l-Asrār fi Ma'na 's-Ṡalāti 'ala 'n-Nabiyyi 'l-Mukhtār.*

A short treatise on the invocation of Blessings upon the Prophet. Written in 1917. (See p. 169, note 1.)

9. *Dīwān.*

First published in 1921. (See pp. 214–28)

10. *Nūru 'l-Ithmid fi Sunnati Waḍ'i 'l-Yaḍi 'ala 'l-Yad.*

A short tract written to show that the Imam Mālik, like the other three Imams, held that the worshipper's hands should be placed on his breast, the right clasping the left, during the recitation of the *Fātiḥah* in the ritual prayer. As a result the 'Alawīs adopted this practice, which they still keep to, whereas nearly all other members of the Mālikī school place their hands by their sides during the *Fātiḥah*. This is the Shaikh's only piece of writing which is altogether confined to the domain of jurisprudence.

11. *Ar-Risālatu 'l-'Alawiyyah.*

An exposition, in 1,000 verses, of Islamic theology, ritual and mysticism, composed on the lines of Ibn 'Āshir's *Al-Murshid al-Mu'īn* but in much simpler language.

12. *Al-Qaulu 'l-Ma'rūf fi 'r-Raddi 'alā man ankara 't-Taṣawwuf.*

First published in 1920. (See pp. 88–102).

13. *Mabādi'u 't-Ta'yīd fi ba'ḍi mā yaḥtāju ilaihi 'l-Murīd.*

A very simple prose exposition of the minimum of instruction necessary for a novice in the 'Alawī Ṭarīqah, on the same lines as (11). Part I, comprising theology, and the rites of purification, was finished in 1926, but the whole was never completed.

14. *Tafsīru Sūrati Wa 'l-'Aṣr.*

A commentary on Chapter CIII of the Qoran. Whereas most commentators take the words *Verily man is in a state of ruin* to refer to the degeneracy of the pre-Islamic Arabs, Persians, and others, he takes them to refer to the state of bodily man on earth as compared with his purely spiritual state in Heaven after he was 'created' (*makhlūq*) but before he was 'formed' (*muṣawwar*).

15. *Allāh: al-Qaulu 'l-Mu'tamad fī Mashrū'iyyati 'dh-Dhikri bi 'l-Ismi 'l-Mufrad.*

Written about 1927 (See pp. 112-4).

16. *Risālatu 'n-Nāṣir Ma'rūf fi 'dh-Dhabbi 'an Majdi 't-Taṣawwuf.*

Written about 1927. (See pp. 109-11).

APPENDIX B

THE SPIRITUAL CHAIN

This tree of the 'Alawī's spiritual ancestry[1] has been taken in the main from Irshād al-Rāghibīn by Ḥasan ibn 'Abd al-'Azīz, a disciple of the Shaikh, and completed from a manuscript tree in possession of another disciple and from Muḥammad Ẓāfir al-Madanī's *Al-Anwār al-Qudsiyyah*, pp. 15, 42.

[1] See p. 74, note.

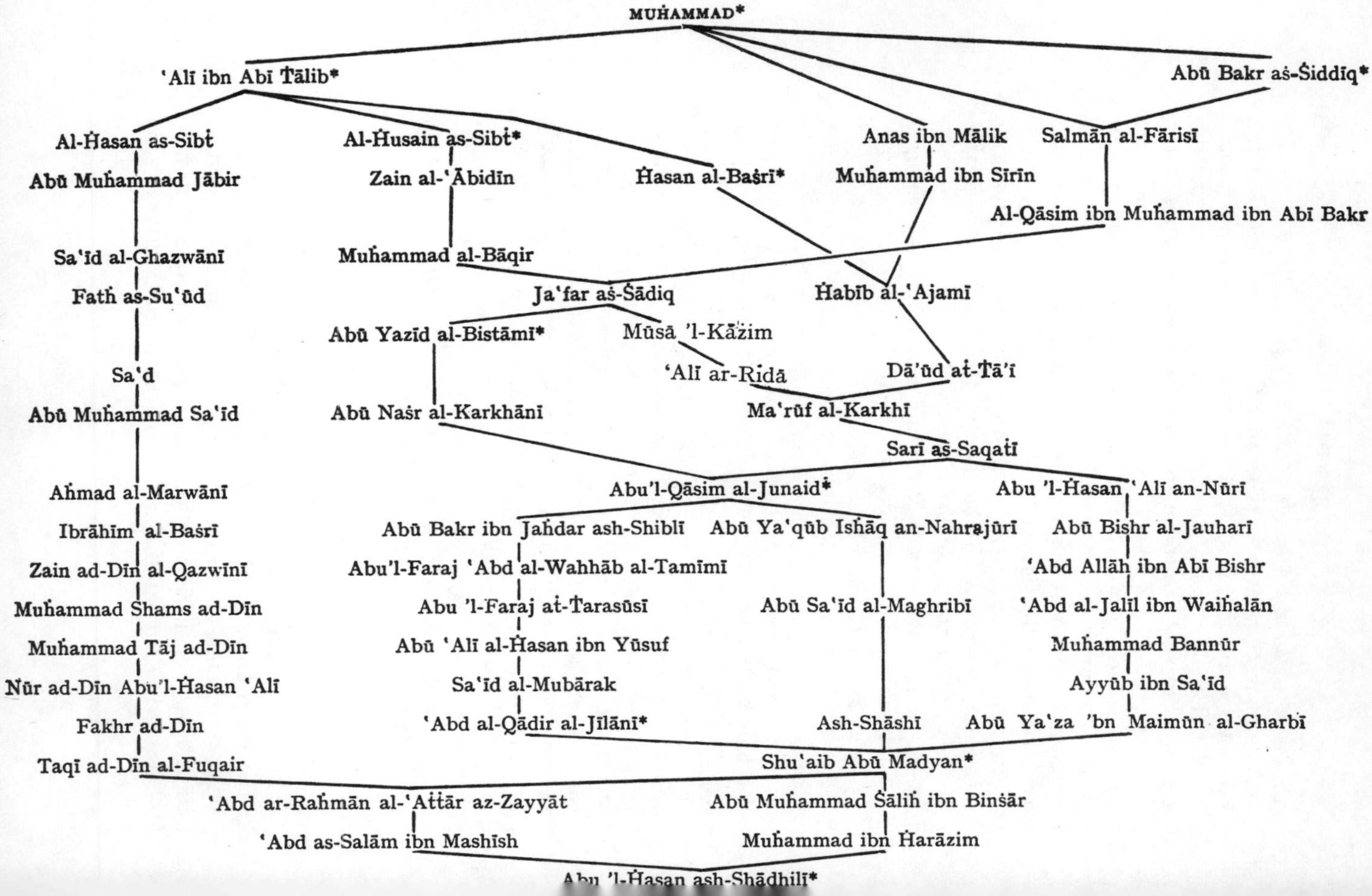
MUḤAMMAD*
'Alī ibn Abī Ṭālib*
Abū Bakr aṣ-Ṣiddīq*
Al-Ḥasan as-Sibṭ
Al-Ḥusain as-Sibṭ*
Anas ibn Mālik
Salmān al-Fārisī
Abū Muḥammad Jābir
Zain al-'Ābidīn
Ḥasan al-Baṣrī*
Muḥammad ibn Sīrīn
Al-Qāsim ibn Muḥammad ibn Abī Bakr
Sa'īd al-Ghazwānī
Muḥammad al-Bāqir
Fatḥ as-Su'ūd
Ja'far aṣ-Ṣādiq
Ḥabīb al-'Ajamī
Abū Yazīd al-Bisṭāmī*
Mūsā 'l-Kāẓim
Sa'd
'Alī ar-Riḍā
Dā'ūd aṭ-Ṭā'ī
Abū Muḥammad Sa'īd
Abū Naṣr al-Karkhānī
Ma'rūf al-Karkhī
Sarī as-Saqaṭī
Aḥmad al-Marwānī
Abu'l-Qāsim al-Junaid*
Abu 'l-Ḥasan 'Alī an-Nūrī
Ibrāhīm al-Baṣrī
Abū Bakr ibn Jaḥdar ash-Shiblī
Abū Ya'qūb Isḥāq an-Nahrajūrī
Abū Bishr al-Jauharī
Zain ad-Dīn al-Qazwīnī
Abu'l-Faraj 'Abd al-Wahhāb al-Tamīmī
'Abd Allāh ibn Abī Bishr
Muḥammad Shams ad-Dīn
Abu 'l-Faraj aṭ-Ṭarasūsī
Abū Sa'īd al-Maghribī
'Abd al-Jalīl ibn Waiḥalān
Muḥammad Tāj ad-Dīn
Abū 'Alī al-Ḥasan ibn Yūsuf
Muḥammad Bannūr
Nūr ad-Dīn Abu'l-Ḥasan 'Alī
Sa'īd al-Mubārak
Ayyūb ibn Sa'īd
Fakhr ad-Dīn
'Abd al-Qādir al-Jīlānī*
Ash-Shāshī
Abū Ya'za 'bn Maimūn al-Gharbī
Taqī ad-Dīn al-Fuqair
Shu'aib Abū Madyan*
'Abd ar-Raḥmān al-'Aṭṭār az-Zayyāt
Abū Muḥammad Ṣāliḥ ibn Binṣār
'Abd as-Salām ibn Mashīsh
Muḥammad ibn Ḥarāzim
Abu 'l-Ḥasan ash-Shādhilī*

Abu'l-'Abbās al-Mursī*

Aḥmad ibn Aṭā'Allāh al-Iskandarī*

Dā'ūd ibn Bākhilī

Muḥammad Wafā Baḥr aṣ-Ṣafā

'Alī ibn Wafā

Yaḥya 'l-Qādirī

Aḥmad al-Ḥaḍramī*

Aḥmad Zarrūq*

Ibrāhīm al-Faḥḥām

'Alī aṣ-Ṣanhājī ad-Dawwār

'Abd ar-Raḥmān al-Majdhūb

Yūsuf al-Fāsī

'Abd ar-Raḥmān al-Fāsī

Muḥammad ibn 'Abd Allāh

Qāsim al-Khaṣṣāṣī

Aḥmad ibn 'Abd Allāh

Al-'Arabī ibn 'Abd Allāh

'Alī al-Jamal*

Al-'Arabī ibn Aḥmad ad-Darqāwī*

Muḥammad ibn 'Abd al-Qādir — Abū Ya'za 'l-Muhājī

Muḥammad ibn Qaddūr al-Wakīlī*

Muḥammad ibn al-Ḥabīb al-Būzīdī*

Aḥmad ibn Muṣṭafa 'l-'Alawī*

**Persons mentioned in the text are starred.*

INDEX OF PERSONS,[1] BOOK TITLES (in italics) PLACES, etc.

[1] As regards the pronunciation of Arabic, *ḣ* is a tensely breathed *h* sound; *ḋ, ṡ, ṫ, ż* are pronounced somewhat heavily, far back in the mouth; *q* is a guttural *k* sound; *dh* is like *th* in *this*, *gh* like a French *r*, *kh* like *ch* in Scottish *loch*; ' stands for the letter *'ain* which might be described as a sharp catch in the throat. ' in the middle and at the end of a word stands for *hamzah* which marks a break of continuity in the breath. Since in English initial vowel sounds are regularly pronounced with a *hamzah*, the initial *hamzah* has not been transcribed here, eg., *Aḣmad*, not *'Aḣmad*. ' at the beginning of a word is an apostrophe indicating an elided vowel, e.g. *bismi 'Llāh* (the first vowel of the Divine Name Allāh is always elided except at the beginning of a sentence or when the Name stands alone).

The vowels *a, i, u* are like the vowel sounds of *sat, sit, soot*; *ā* is like that of bare, but back consonants next to it attract it to the vowel sound of *bār*; *ī* and *ū* are like the vowel sounds of *seen* and *soon*; *ai* is between those of *sign* and *sane*; *aw* is like that of *cow*.

INDEX OF ARABIC WORDS (except book titles and names of persons and places)